# Dislocating the Color Line

*Identity, Hybridity,
and Singularity in
African-American
Narrative*

# Mestizo Spaces

*Espaces Métissés*

V. Y. Mudimbe
EDITOR

Bogumil Jewsiewicki
ASSOCIATE EDITOR

# Dislocating the Color Line

*Identity, Hybridity, and Singularity in African-American Narrative*

**Samira Kawash**

STANFORD UNIVERSITY PRESS
STANFORD, CALIFORNIA

Stanford University Press,
Stanford, California

© 1997 by the Board of Trustees of the
Leland Stanford Junior University

Printed in the United States of America

CIP data appear at the end of the book

Stanford University Press publications are
distributed exclusively by Stanford University
Press within the United States, Canada, Mexico,
and Central America; they are distributed exclusively by Cambridge University Press
throughout the rest of the world.

# Preface

This is the story of the boundaries and borders of race in the United States —boundaries and borders that penetrate to the depths of the subject and reach through every level of society. The borders or boundaries of racial difference have been manifested in different ways throughout the nation's history. There is nevertheless a certain continuity in this history, the continuity of what I will call the "color line." By going back to the color line, by plunging into the space of the boundary, this book aims not to efface or go beyond race but to use the paradoxical persistence of the color line against itself. Dislocating the color line is thus neither a refutation nor a celebration of the idea of race or of racial difference but rather a critical pressure brought to bear on the interpretations, practices, and assumptions that correspond to and buttress representations of racial difference. The work of dislocating the color line lies in uncovering the uncertainty, the incoherency, and the discontinuity that the common sense of the color line serves to mask while at the same time elucidating the pressures that transform the contingent relations and formations of the color line into common sense.

I begin by taking stock of the color line as it continues to be represented in contemporary American life. In Chapter 1, I suggest a framework for thinking about the history of the color line with particular reference to a currently attractive alternative metaphor for difference, that of hybridity. Chapter 2 picks up where the real story of the color line begins, which is also of course where the story of race in America begins—with slavery.

Once slavery was firmly entrenched as the basis of economic production in the British colonies (around 1660), the color line became a central feature of its functioning. And in relation to slavery, this color line was always also a property line, the boundary between a whiteness that could own but would never become property and a blackness that was defined in terms of its status as (potential or actual) human property. As I will argue, the figure of escape in fugitive slave narratives challenged slavery's foundational division between subject and property, suggesting that true freedom might demand more than the rearranging of positions around the color line.

The end of slavery did not bring the end of social division along racial lines, of course. Rather, what emerged after slavery was another principle of division along the color line, now in terms of segregation and the law of "separate but equal." "Separate but equal" promised a certain symmetrical justice. But, as I will suggest in Chapter 3 through a reading of Charles Chesnutt's *The Marrow of Tradition*, the putative justice of the color line could only ever be a mask for racial violence. The color line conceived of as a social practice of racial segregation presumed an absolute distinction between white and black. But in reality there were those whose ambivalent appearance lodged them firmly in between. Thus, in Chapter 4, I discuss the destabilizing effects of the breakdown of racial knowledge and certainty represented in "passing" novels by James Weldon Johnson and Nella Larsen.

When the racial knowledge seemingly guaranteed by the color line becomes tenuous, it becomes increasingly apparent that while the color line may be a condition for violence, it is also a condition for the security and certainty of identity, a way of ordering and organizing the social world. But this doubled function suggests that order and violence are not necessarily distinct. In Chapter 5, I take inspiration from Zora Neale Hurston to seek out an alternative to the rigid identities of the color line. What emerges is a risky practice of singularity that recognizes the securities of identity and community to be illusory and takes a chance on the unknowable and the uncertain.

This book too is, perhaps, something of a risky practice. The contingencies of interest, opportunity, possibility, and attraction that have resulted in this book have also involved a certain impropriety on my part, namely, my own crossing of the color line. But if W. E. B. Du Bois is right, if the problem of the twentieth century is still the problem of the color line, then confronting the color line itself is a task and a responsibility from which no one is exempt. Michael Awkward's words suggest the balance on which such a crossing might be weighed: "boundary transgression—interpretive movement across putatively fixed biological, cultural, or ideological lines in order to explore, in a word, difference—has come to require either extreme theoretical naïveté or perhaps unprecedented scholarly daring" (*Negotiating Difference*, p. 4). The boundary lines Awkward names, as well as the risks and opportunities of boundary transgressions, are the central concerns of this book. As I will argue, the question of the boundary is absolutely crucial to an understanding of the power and pervasiveness of racism. In this book I can only hope that some readers will find that the possible risks of "theoretical naïveté" may be outweighed by the rewards of "scholarly daring."

I would like to thank those who provided various forms of support, guidance, feedback, and gentle admonition as this project traveled along the path from germ to dissertation to book: Cathy Davidson, Tom Ferraro, Don Gibson, Toril Moi, Michael Moon, V. Y. Mudimbe, Jan Radway, Barbara Herrnstein Smith, and Ken Surin. I have profited greatly from their generous advice; whatever errors of fact or naïveté remain are wholly my own. Generous and ongoing financial support from the Graduate School of Duke University, in the form of a James B. Duke Fellowship and a dissertation award, made it possible for me to dedicate myself wholly to this project while it was in the dissertation stage. I am also thankful for eleventh-hour research assistance from Lisa Lynch, Alice Kawash, and Ghaida Firestone. My final, and endless, debt of gratitude is to Roger Cooper. He has been my most generous reader and my toughest critic. The pleasure of writing this book has come in large measure from the pleasure of sharing it with him.

S. K.

# Contents

# Dislocating the Color Line

*Identity, Hybridity,
and Singularity in
African-American
Narrative*

# 1. Conditions

## *Hybridity and the Color Line*

To speak of the color line today is apparently to refer to a particular historical era in U.S. history, the era of Jim Crow and legal segregation. In the late nineteenth and the first half of the twentieth centuries, the color line was a palpable, physical boundary of separation. With a fine enough lens, one could map out the separate zones of blackness and whiteness within the nation's borders: black in the back of the bus, white in front; black schools and white schools; black towns, parks, restaurants, and neighborhoods, each with its (usually much nicer) white counterpart. Although *Plessy v Ferguson* (1896), the court decision affirming the legality of segregationist practices, insisted that there was no inherent harm in separation, in the context of America's racialized history such a geography of division could hardly be neutral.

### *The Persistence of the Color Line*

As was implicitly recognized in *Brown v Board of Education* (1954), some 60 years after *Plessy* removed the last barriers to legalized segregation, the codification of the color line assured white privilege in the form of unobstructed access to the resources and pleasures of public space, while providing harsh sanctions against those on the other side of the line who risked reaching for something more. In addition to the explicitly spatial politics of formal and informal racial segregation, however, the color line also named and continues to name the more personal distinction of race itself. Expressions for racial transgression, such as "passing," "crossing over," or "marrying across the line," suggest that the individual racial identity of black or white remains demarcated by a symbolic color line that is conceived in geographical terms echoing the spatial divisions instituted by segregation.

"But the color line is ancient history!" someone protests. "Sure, some people are racists, but times have changed, segregation is a thing of the past, American laws are color-blind, everyone has an equal opportunity." The color line seems, today, uniquely the purview of extremists such as white supremacists who shamelessly call for a purified America or Afrocentrists who call for political, economic, and social separation and autonomy for African-Americans. So it seems.

The popular consensus view that the color line is ancient history is shared in the broadest sense, if not in the particulars, by many cultural critics thinking and writing about race and ethnicity in contemporary American life. In particular, antiessentialist work on diversity, hybridity, and multiculturalism has explicitly refuted the reality of the color line by carefully documenting and demonstrating the gap between, on the one hand, the idea of an essential blackness eternally divided from an essential whiteness and, on the other, the constitution of the national (and global) community as made up of hybridity, creolization, or syncretism. In the place of the essentialized identities that formed the categories of understanding in the past (identities based on national, ethnic, or racial borders that were presumed to separate pure cultures or groups) critics now look at the ways in which the pure is always already contaminated. Thus, one hears of hybrid identities, diaspora identities, borderland identities — all terms intended to designate such historical conditions as interaction, interdependency, cultural transformation, and movement. It follows then that every appeal to some originary, authentic, pure identity (conceived of most often in biological terms as "blood") can only be an appeal to a *mythical* purity. Recent attempts to account for the history of racial identity have rigorously repudiated the inherent racism of biological models of absolute racial difference, turning instead to the complexities of culture. Contemporary cultural criticism emphasizes the multiple ways in which the fixity, autonomy, stability, and separation of the racial categories of black and white are undermined, subverted, and destabilized.

In 1994 Tricia Rose and Andrew Ross invited several of the most well-known, active, and influential thinkers on race in the cultures of the United

States to respond to a series of questions on race and racism in hopes of shedding some critical light on the paradoxical circumstance that "highly public race talk no longer appeals to the concept of a politically homogeneous black community, and yet monolithic representations continue to fuel pathology-based attacks on African-Americans."[1] Their challenge to respondents begins from precisely this question of the persistence of oppositional difference in spite of the increasing complexity and heterogeneity of U.S. cultures: "Despite the extensive intermingling of U.S. cultural groups, group identities continue to be narrowly racialized to the point where the dominant public *image* of an America divided into two nations—black and white—bears little relation to the *actual experience* of social and cultural life in this country for all groups."[2] Although this question is posed in terms of an empirical gap between the experience and representation of the population in general, I would suggest that the question is equally addressed to an increasingly disturbing dissonance in the experience of the critic. The question suggests that we as critics are confronted with a troubling discord between what we know as good antiessentialists, that culture is fundamentally heterogeneous, and what we see represented and reflected in everyday life, namely, that the color line is as intransigent as ever.

Yet as several of the respondents to Rose and Ross's query are careful to note, there is no experience outside the "dominant public image" of the color line. David Roediger cautions "against regarding the 'two nations—black and white' lens as simply a kind of anachronism or false consciousness to be exposed and easily discarded. The lens is, to be sure, an ideological one. As such it not only distorts but accounts for lived experience."[3] Similarly, Steven Gregory insists that the public image of racism as binarized in black-versus-white terms provides the discursive context within which all racial identities and experiences are constructed and managed.[4] Thus, there can be no simple distinction between "image" and "actual experience." The principle of "two nations—black and white" is as much an organizing principle of experience and expression as it is of dominant public images. The popular discourse about race as typically expressed by individuals and as reflected in and refracted through the media relies not on the opposition between heterogeneity and essentialism but on that between the absolute division of the color line and the liberal ideal of race blindness. This circumstance creates something of a bind for the antiessentialist critic who wishes to abandon the essentializing logic of the color line. If the cultural and political force of the color line is not merely so much false consciousness, to be educated away through rigorous demonstrations of the fallacy of cultural or biological purity, how are we to counter its damaging effects?

In this context, a critical return to the color line might seem anachronistic, especially in light of the general trend in current cultural criticism, which is largely engaged in explorations of difference, hybridity, and heterogeneity as a counter to the reductive, normative, or essentializing representations of authentic and autonomous racial and cultural identities.[5] *Hybridity* in particular has become an increasingly powerful term for marking "the fractal, opaque, fragmented structure of what originally appeared as a cohesive whole."[6] Hybridity appears to escape from the essentialist logic that characterized previous understandings of cultural identity and difference, and this accounts for much of its appeal. In this light, one might wonder whether the rush to embrace hybridity has been fueled as much by a desire to flee essentialism as by the necessity to reconsider what we mean when we speak of cultural difference. By opening again the question of the color line, I do not intend to recuperate an overshadowed essentialism. But I do think that *essentialism* has become such a fraught term that it is difficult to avoid a reflexive gesture of dismissal when the question of essentialism arises. I do not mean to overlook or minimize the enormous labors by feminists, queer theorists, and antiracists to open our eyes to the insidious operations of essentialism in representational, political, and social practices. But within the critical community at times it seems that invoking something like hybridity serves as an inoculation against the dreaded essentialism. One stakes one's claim in hybridity and points one's finger at "those bad essentialists," secure in the knowledge that having discovered hybridity in and for oneself, essentialism has been effectively banished.[7]

Teresa de Lauretis's concern about the distance the term *essentialism* has traveled, from "convenient label to buzzword . . . time and again repeated with its reductive ring, its self-righteous tone of superiority, its contempt for 'them,' — those guilty of it," applies equally well to antiracist theory as to the feminist theory to which she refers.[8] So perhaps it might not be a bad idea to linger a little longer in the dim light of essentialism, not to return to the reductive and oppressive certainties of essentialized social identities, but rather to recognize that in the effort to surpass apparently erroneous ideas of purity or essence that seem to be part of the logic of the color line one might be tempted too quickly to ignore or forget the constitutive power of the color line itself as it produces and organizes knowledge, power, and subjectivity.

In a recent book examining the dual genealogy of the ideas of race and culture, Robert Young raises some provocative questions about the ambivalence of the idea of hybridity. Young locates the historical antecedents for the use of the term *hybridity* in Victorian racial science. The question of hybridity was at the center of the most contentious debate in race theory of the nineteenth century: whether the different races were in fact different species (polygenesis) or had developed along different paths but were of the same species (monogenesis). The resolution of this question hinged on the fertility of an individual who was a cross between two races. In plant and animal science, a hybrid was understood to be the product of a cross between two distinct species. The most common example is that of the mule, the result of a cross between a horse and a donkey. The sterility of the mule is the definitional basis for distinguishing horse and donkey as distinct species. Similarly, racial theorists argued that if a hybrid of black and white parents were sterile, then that would prove that the black race and the white race were not merely different varieties of human but different species altogether. Not surprisingly, this hypothesis was accompanied by (spurious) data proving the sterility of the racial hybrid.[9] The term *mulatto* as an appellation for an individual of mixed race is, in light of this history, revealed to be deeply implicated in the theoretical efforts to prove scientifically a permanent and absolute racial division. The word *mulatto* derives, after all, from a reference to the sterile hybridity of the mule. Just as the mule proved the horse and donkey were distinct species, so the mulatto proved that white and black were forever separate and distinct.

Thus, the question of hybridity and its relation to racial identity and difference is not a new one, and its history is inseparable from the history of the development of the idea of race. This genealogy cannot be cordoned off from contemporary thinking about hybridity. Young insists that we ought to consider the idea of hybridity as always double-voiced. Even when the critical emphasis is placed on its radical promise of absolute heterogeneity, disruption, and discontinuity, hybridity continues to be haunted by an idea of fusion or mixture that implicitly assumes "the prior existence of pure, fixed, and separate antecedents."[10]

Young's historicizing account of hybridity has important implications for contemporary cultural analysis and interpretation. In trying to supplant the idea of racial or cultural identities with a more complex notion of hybridity, it is easy to forget that the very notion of hybridity is already predicated on conditions named by the essentializing division it seeks to counter, that is, the color line. It bears repeating that such essentializing cultural divisions as the color line *both* distort *and* account for lived experience; there is no realm of experience or subjectivity outside or beyond the effects of the color line. So while we may know, as Anthony Appiah has put it, that "the truth is that there are no races: there is nothing in the world that can do all we ask 'race' to do for us,"[11] nevertheless, the color line continues to appear as a fundamental way of organizing understanding and experience in the world. In this way, the color line signals the limit of the here and now, the conceptual, political, and geographical boundary beyond which lies the utopian promise of a community of hybridity or heterogeneity. But utopia is not a place that you can go; we are always only in the here and now. That is, "we" are "here" insofar as we are subjects of and subjectified by the color line. We cannot be otherwise.

What Michael Omi and Howard Winant have called racial formations—the production and operation of systems of racial distinction and meaning over time—constitute the subject as always a racialized subject, a subject located in and in relation to systems of racial meaning.[12] Such a subject cannot be separated from such systems of racial meaning and identification because the latter are part of what makes up the subject. Thus, insofar as it appears simply to name the putatively obvious difference between black and white, the color line is essentializing, naming a reductive, natural, supposedly commonsensical opposition. But the color line must also be taken to name the complexity behind common sense, what Judith Butler refers to as those "fully embedded organizing principles of material practices and institutional arrangements, those matrices of power and discourse that produce me as a viable 'subject.' "[13] Thus, the color line is not simply a limit to thought or action that can be recognized and traversed. The stubborn persistence of the color line in representation and experience is not a problem of false consciousness or anachronistic thinking; rather, it indicates the power and continuity of the cognitive, discursive, and institutional workings of the color line as simultaneously the limit and constitutive condition for cultural and social life.

One need not look far to conclude that, as Du Bois predicted nearly 100 years ago, the problem of the twentieth century has indeed been the problem of the color line.[14] It is true that the multiplication of racializing discourses since the 1960s and the successive waves of immigration from places other than Europe have compounded and complicated the work of racial distinction and racist discrimination.[15] But, somehow, in spite of the fact that empirically (from the perspective of multiple ethnic groups or census categories) it makes little sense to think of the United States as a nation divided into black and white, this racialized opposition persists in both explicit and subtle ways. Indeed, in the past decade, questions of binarizing boundaries have increasingly become the medium of politics. While the color line does not explicitly appear to be the issue in each of these instances, I would argue that the appeal of the politics of boundary in the United States to white privilege and white exclusivity indicates a more subtle and complex retrenchment of the color line, poised for the new century.

Nativist politics in the United States, echoing the resurgence of nationalism based on ethnic purity and exclusion, seek to isolate and protect the national community from interlopers and outsiders. The so-called reform of the welfare system is predicated on revising conditions of entitlement to correspond with the social boundaries of legitimate belonging. One important and virtually unopposed "reform" has been to deny benefits to all immigrants, both legal and illegal. In debates over welfare, distinctions are continually drawn between the deserving poor and the undeserving poor. Beneath the surface, such distinctions are immediately recognizable as originating in the geography of the color line, identifying those deserving as the industrially obsolete, predominantly white working class outside the cities and those undeserving as the urban, predominantly African-American and Latino un- and underemployed. The color line thus reworks American nationalism in relation to the enemy within, the sexually and economically pathological criminal, drug addict, or welfare mother of the inner city, who is sapping the nation's strength in the form of the massive burden on the welfare system.

The gutting of federal powers in favor of state and local governance further polarizes opportunity and life chances in favor of the white suburban middle class. Thomas and Mary Edsall's 1991 diagnosis of the effects of the "suburbanization" of national politics proved prophetic of the transformations being enacted throughout the 1990s: "With a majority of the electorate equipped to address its own needs through local government, not only will urban blacks become increasingly isolated by city-county boundaries, but support of the federal government, a primary driving force behind black advancement, is likely to diminish."[16] At the same time, the dismantling of affirmative action in the name of equal rights is working to restore an unquestionable and invisible white prerogative. The framing of affirmative action as an economic threat to whites—the charge of "reverse discrimination"—implies that all jobs, schools, and the like are a white prerogative, and preference given to anything but whiteness illegitimately deprives whiteness of its privilege. But as Cheryl Harris points out, the backpedaling on affirmative action is symptomatic of "the Court's chronic refusal to dismantle the institutional protection of benefits for whites that have been based on white supremacy and maintained at the expense of Blacks."[17]

In this context, the lure of cyberspace in American political rhetoric lies not merely in its Platonic promise of transcending the body but in its capacity simultaneously to exclude a whole class of bodies, remaking the American map as a virtual space that excludes those implicitly un-American bodies that inhabit such locales as the urban ghetto. Perhaps most ominously, the fact that the blatantly racist, reactionary thesis of inherent, genetic black inferiority advanced by Charles Murray and Richard Herrnstein in *The Bell Curve* (1994) would receive widespread national attention in the form of debates, conferences, TV specials, news reports, magazine features, and so on indicates that the fundamental premise of the color line, that of an uncrossable chasm of incommensurability between black and white, in which white is normal and American and black is deviant, pathological, and a threat to the national body, remains firmly at the core of U.S. racial common sense.

Thus, it is imperative to resist viewing the color line as a relic from a distant past of social, economic, and legal segregation; Jim Crow; lynch law; and so on. The color line is with us today, sometimes more subtle, but no less destructive, than in the days of Jim Crow. Therefore, rather than refuting the essentialism of the color line by demonstrating the failures of racial categories to account for lived experience, I want to take the color line seriously, on its own terms. How has it persisted over time? What sorts of reconfigurations has it undergone? Under what conditions does its seemingly natural logic, the apparent self-evidence of separation between black and white, come under stress? In what ways might the color line itself be viewed as a form of violence, and what is its relation to racial violence?

## Geographies of the Color Line

The idea of the color line metaphorizes racial distinction as spatial division. Historically, the idea of race has a long-standing relation to the idea of geography. As David Goldberg notes, "just as spatial distinctions like 'West' and 'East' are racialized in their conception and application, so racial categories have been variously spatialized more or less since their inception into continental divides, national localities, and geographic regions."[18] Even as metropolitan populations become increasingly diverse, the supposed morphological distinctions that mark the races continue to bespeak geographical origins, however distant: where you are from, where your parents are from, where your ancestors are from. One small but telling example of the mutual implications of race and geography is given by the recent semantic shift from "black" to "African-American," evidencing a certain substitutability between the language of race and the language of geography.

In Enlightenment racial thought, geography was often taken as the cause of racial differentiation. Environmentalists of the seventeenth and eighteenth centuries understood differences in climate and environment to be the source of the apparent physical distinctions between the races. To the extent that it was understood to be related to environmental influences, racial character was seen as potentially mutable and the perceived inferiority of certain races but a less developed stage on the path of human progress. But there was also, especially in the writings of Johann Gottfried von Herder, an emphasis on the role of the land itself and the intimate connection of the people to the land. For Herder, the coincidence of land and language created a people, racially conceived, whose geographical and cultural boundedness would naturally correspond to the political boundaries of a nation. Hence, for example, the Anglo and the Gaul found their natural differences of character, culture, and language reflected in the channel separating England and France. This Enlightenment conception of racial difference as the product of geography and environment was not displaced by the nineteenth-century ethnological turn to an essentialized biology of the races; rather, it was deepened and stripped of its contingency, such that the inferiority of the so-called darker races began to be explicitly understood as inherent and permanent.

Throughout the modern era, running as a constant current underneath the epistemological shifts from environmentalism to ethnology to a sociology of cultures, the delimitations of racial difference have been understood to correspond to a global map. According to this cartographic logic, just as we can observe the fact of separate continents, zones, and climates, so too can we observe the fact of separate human populations, the so-called races, that are the natural counterparts to each of these regions. Indeed, in the modern disciplinary arrangement of knowledge, the systematic production of a global map of land and peoples bears a particular institutional form, that of the science of geography. Geography as a positive science, what Edward Soja has called "Modern Geography," claims only to describe, catalog, and name the natural, physical formations that make up our world.[19] In effect, the history of positive racial science has been Modern Geography applied to human diversity: the races are the natural, physical formations that make up the social world.

In the positivist view of the human races, the color line plays a purely descriptive role. Along the color line, racial difference is spatialized as a natural division and understood in the terms given by Modern Geography. Race, like the places geography takes as its object, "is reduced to physical objects and forms, and naturalized back to a first nature so as to become susceptible to prevailing scientific explanation in the form of orderly, reproducible description and the discovery of empirical regularities."[20] From this perspective, the human division of races is of the same order as the continental division of a mountain range or the expanse of ocean separating one locale from another: simply a natural fact out there in the world, to be described in the most neutral and objective terms possible.[21] The result is that the color line itself is removed from the realm of critical analysis. Like a mountain or an ocean, the color line is just there, and the reason for the persistence of the color line is tautologically determined by its very existence. In effect, the color line persists because it is real; the color line is real because it persists. Put another way, seemingly natural racial differences are equated with supposedly natural racial divisions. If the races appear to be different, it must be because they are naturally divided, be it by culture, language, geography, or blood.

The contemporary tendency to see racial distinction as innocent spatiality is especially evident in the widespread rhetorical appeal of so-called color-blind institutions and rules. In Supreme Court Justice Clarence Thomas's recent defense of de facto segregation in his concurring opinion in *Missouri v Jenkins* (1995), for example, he insists that there is nothing inherently discriminatory in separateness and that those who argue that integration is necessary for equality are implying that there is in fact something inferior about blackness. The foundation for such a line of reasoning was laid in *Brown v Board of Education* (1954), which found the harm of school segregation not in the specific inequities of resource and opportunity but in a much more subjective discussion of the meaning of segregation: "the policy of separating the races is usually interpreted as denoting the inferiority of the Negro group. A sense of inferiority affects the motivation of a child to learn. Segregation with the sanction of law, therefore, has a tendency to retard the educational and mental development of Negro children." [22] The implication of this argument is that some kinds of separation would not imply inferiority and that if the stigma of inferiority were lifted then segregation in itself would not be a harm.

Such reasoning returns with a vengeance in Thomas's opposition to state support for Kansas City's plan for magnet schools to lure white suburban students into the predominantly black urban public schools. By refuting the fragile premise that blacks cannot succeed without the presence of whites, Thomas is able to insist that racial imbalances in and of themselves are not unconstitutional. It is only when there is evidence of *intentional* government action to create or maintain such imbalances that harm has been done. Thus, where "social and demographic phenomena" are the "real source of racial imbalance or of poor educational performance in a school district," it is "beyond the authority and beyond the practical ability of the federal courts to try to counteract these social changes." [23] From Thomas's perspective, the disparities between Kansas City schools and their suburban counterparts is politically innocent because it is not the product of government action but rather the result of the combination of "neutral policies" of local school assignment coupled with "individual private choices concerning work or residence." [24] The latter are not intentional agents of harm, that is, they do not aim to produce feelings of inferiority among African-Americans. Thus, if these neutral forces result in de facto segregation, such a result must also be neutral.

But the dynamics of both de jure and de facto segregation are more complex than Thomas would recognize. Many would argue that the question of harm is not one of intent but of result. Harm is not then a matter of feelings but of material hardships and diminished opportunities. As Gary Orfield points out, educational research carried out in the 1960s and 1970s supports the materialist interpretation of harm:

> The basic damage inflicted by segregated education comes not from racial concentration but from the concentration of children from poor families. The studies show that the economic and social background of the majority of the children affects the educational achievement of a school more than any other single school factor. . . . The central educational problem is that not only are many children in racially—and linguistically—identifiable segregated schools

but that their classmates are from poor families. With their limited resources, these schools must cope with large numbers of children from families that are disorganized, in grave financial difficulty, and constantly moving.[25]

A magnet school program such as that attempted in Kansas City is not simply an effort to infuse a prophylactic dose of whiteness into black schools. Rather, it is a strategic response to the increasing material disparity that distinguishes urban from suburban space. The transition from an industrial to a service economy has decimated the economic foundations of the largely nonwhite urban population. While those able to take advantage of the gradual lowering of racial barriers in education and employment have enjoyed upward mobility, "capital flight and fiscal crisis have further impoverished low-skilled and undereducated African-Americans, leading to the much-publicized dilemma of the 'under-class,' or 'ghetto poor.' " [26] In contrast, the suburbs are populated by those with the means and opportunity to flee a city abandoned by both federal and state governments, a city where the grim and merciless realities of the police state are rapidly displacing the reformist promise of the now bankrupt welfare state. The increasing domination of national politics by an isolationist suburban middle class suggests that we are experiencing a geographic splintering in which "the suburbs allow white middle-class voters to meet their own communities' needs by taxing themselves for direct services (e.g., schools, libraries, police) while denying resources to the increasingly poor and non-white cities." [27] In this context, urban schools are perceived as holding-pens for the next generation of welfare mothers and drug dealers, and regarded as a hopeless effort to stem the tide of an urban pathology implicitly coded as black. The aim of magnet schools in this context is not to bring white students into urban schools because "blacks cannot succeed without the benefit of the company of whites," as Thomas characterizes the program. Rather, it is an attempt to intervene in the increasingly divisive geography of resources, privilege, and access.

As is becoming increasingly clear in the contemporary standoff between urban and suburban polities, racial politics are spatial politics: race is a fundamental element of social space. The color line persists as the organizing principle of racial space, that is, the maintenance of an absolute boundary between black and white and, more especially, the exclusionary line demarcating and bounding whiteness and assuring the continued value of "whiteness as property." [28] Although the color line originates as a spatial metaphor for the persistence of racial division and tension in U.S. culture, this metaphor is always more than a metaphor, operating to enable and justify the social and spatial distribution of power, wealth, access, and privilege. The Modern Geography of the color line takes the fundamental division of race as its uninterrogated ground and simply aims to describe or, in more interventionist modes, to justify the distribution of positions. But there is nothing natural about the distinctions of race; such distinctions are both produced and given meaning within a social context. Hence, rather than viewing the spatial organization of social life as simply natural or neutral, "we must be insistently aware of how space can be made to hide consequences from us, how relations of power and discipline are inscribed into the apparently innocent spatiality of social life, how human geographies become filled with politics and ideology."[29] Understanding this geography means attending simultaneously to both its aspects: the color line as metaphor for the perceived political, social, or cultural division between "two nations—black and white" and the color line as a nonmetaphorical divide marking the discriminatory distribution of access and resources throughout society in such diverse areas as housing, jobs, and schools. The overlap of metaphor and materiality points to the complexity of the color line, both as it is inscribed on particular bodies and as it organizes, codifies, regulates, and impacts on various forms of social interaction.

It is imperative to resist any reductive or simplistic view of the color line as some sort of error, either on the one hand to be legislated away or on the other to be diffracted and diffused into the true heterogeneity of lived experience. The color line is absolutely real, both as a source of power and as a condition of material effects. The problem in grasping this reality lies in its complexity: the reality of the color line is split and doubled between the color line as historical product and the color line as ontological ground. From a historical perspective, it is clear that the color line is not absolute, nor does it operate in idealist fashion from above, outside the influence or control of social agents. Its modalities, forces, and locations shift with time and circumstance, and it is produced and reproduced at several levels. At the macrosocial level, as it emerges between social groups, the color line can be seen to be the product of complex relations of power, conquest, and exploitation.[30] At the microsocial or individual level, the color line is produced and reproduced through various social technologies of embodiment, identification, and representation.[31] Thus, one might say, the color line is entirely a social construction. Nevertheless, the power of the color line derives from its appearance as timeless, immutable, and utterly natural. In moments of conflict, the color line emerges as absolute, like a natural law voiced from outside culture or history. This points to a central paradox of the color line: it essentializes racial difference even as such difference can be shown to have no essence. If we are to take this paradox seriously, as something more than an impasse, then it is clear that the play of racial identity and hybridity must be considered in some way that avoids the over-burdened critical opposition of essentialism and anti-essentialism.

## The Color Line at Work: 'Imitation of Life'

In this section, I want to begin addressing the question of essentialism by examining carefully the work of the color line in a particularly dramatic scene from Douglas Sirk's 1959 film version of Fanny Hurst's *Imitation of Life*. The film focuses on rising actress Lora Meredith and traces her career as a performer. As Judith Butler has suggested, *Imitation of Life* also traces the emergence of Lora's femininity as gender performativity. Gesture in this film, Butler argues, operates as the constitutive moment of gender. Gesture is not expressive but functions performatively to constitute femininity as a certain frozen stylization of the body. Hence, the appearance of life (or reality) is dependent on its own imitation: "Clearly not present to herself, [Lora] is no self-identical subject or primary presence; rather, she performs the incessant repetition of the gesture through which the effect of presence is secured." [32] Butler focuses on the production of a dazzling white femininity that sustains itself by continually marking its distinction from the ever present blackness of Lora's maid, Annie. But what of the consti-tution of blackness that makes the black woman available as an alternative and contrasting version of the feminine? While the relation between Lora and Annie is determined in advance by the structurally racialized positions of white mistress and black maid, Annie's daughter, Sarah Jane, troubles this order, and it is through Sarah Jane that one discovers the workings of the color line as it clears a space of whiteness in which Lora's white femi-ninity becomes possible.

Unlike her mother, Sarah Jane can pass for white. It is this bodily am-bivalence, the gap between her social place and the legibility of her body, that wrenches open a rift in the usually stable order of division marked by the color line. Sarah Jane barely disguises her contempt for her mother's servility and hungers for more than the limited possibilities open to the black daughter of a black maid. In an effort to escape the limitations that will inevitably follow from her racial identity, she begins passing. One night she sneaks out of the house to see her new white boyfriend, Frankie. They meet in a deserted street; he seems distant and aloof. Suddenly he turns on her. "Just tell me if it's true" he asks menacingly. Sarah Jane looks alarmed and puzzled. "Tell me if it's true your mother's a nigger!" Sarah Jane looks horrified: "What difference does it make? You love me." Frankie shouts out, "Are you black?" Finally Sarah Jane shouts back: "No! I'm as white as you are!" To which Frankie responds, "You're lying!" and slaps her across the face. Repeatedly shouting "liar," he beats her down to the ground.

Frankie's violence seems triggered by the unbearable fear that he himself might be polluted by Sarah Jane's blackness. The specter of miscegenation hovers over this scene, and the ringing retort of Frankie's slap echoes into the future, insisting that there can be no legitimate union between Sarah Jane and Frankie once Frankie knows the truth. But we should note that the force of sanction on the future marked by the slap (no miscegenational union) derives from the way in which the slap seems merely to confirm the truth of the past. That is, Sarah Jane really is black, Sarah Jane really has deceived Frankie, and the slap marks the judgment and the sanction against such a transgression. Frankie's violence then appears to be fully justified by the racial order that demands that blackness remain in its place. At the same time, Sarah Jane's fall into blackness has exposed her to this violence by removing the protective shroud of white femininity. Despite the patriarchal codes of gallantry that ought to guide Frankie's behavior toward his girl, the mark of blackness instantly transforms Sarah Jane into less-than-woman. The camera reinforces this transformation, leaving Sarah Jane abject, muddied, struggling to get up in the road as Frankie disdainfully struts away without a look back.

This scene highlights an ongoing tension between image and interpretation. The camera shows Sarah Jane's fall, her visual transformation under the mark of blackness. Yet the narrative interprets this transformation as the exposure of the truth of a blackness she already possesses. The ensuing gap points to some ambiguity about just what has occurred in this exchange. Indeed, it is ambiguity itself that motivates the scene, as the film works to resolve the uncertainties surrounding Sarah Jane's body and her place in relation to the boundary between black and white. Elsewhere in the film, the color line is absolute and unquestioned; Annie knows and accepts her place as black, while Lora unthinkingly assumes the privilege of her own whiteness. It is only in relation to Sarah Jane's illegible body and her desire, which refuses to be bound by the strictures of color, that the color line itself comes under stress.

The ambivalence of Sarah Jane's body reinforces the displacement of ontological grounding that Butler locates in relation to Lora's femininity and repeats this effect in terms of blackness and whiteness. In the scene just prior to her confrontation with Frankie, Sarah Jane mortifies Lora and her mother by serving Lora's friends in an exaggerated imitation of a southern black servant. Entering the room with a flourish, a plate of hors d'oeuvres balanced atop her head, Sarah Jane announces in a mocking drawl: "Fixed y'all a mess a' crawdads, Miz Lora, for you and your friends." Lora looks stunned, asking her where she learned such a clever trick. Sarah Jane replies, "Oh, no trick to totin', Miz Lora. I larned it from my mammy, an' she larned it from ole massa 'fore she belonged to you." The camera reinforces the view of this scene as an elaborately staged performance by shooting through a grille in the room so that Sarah Jane is enclosed in a circular frame, rhyming the ever present camera that has documented Lora's own performances. When confronted, Sarah Jane responds sarcastically, "My mother's so anxious for me to be colored, I was going to show you I could be." Thus, her blackness, too, becomes part of a performance.

Unable to accept her mother's wishes that she attend a colored teachers college, Sarah Jane runs away to become a burlesque singer and dancer. While we are given very few scenes of Lora performing on stage (further reinforcing the idea that Lora herself is the performance), the film gives us two long sequences of Sarah Jane performing in nightclub acts of questionable taste. The camera lingers over her body, her legs and arms, as she gestures suggestively. As a performer, Sarah Jane has become a dark shadow to Lora's dazzling whiteness. But where Lora stages herself as an object for the gaze while remaining sexually aloof in her frozen whiteness, Sarah Jane becomes the true object of desire, the body the camera can't get enough of. The camera documents Sarah Jane's performance, not only of the sensuality Lora has repressed, but equally of a whiteness to which Lora stakes a continuing claim. In these burlesque performances, the camera fetishizes Sarah Jane's ambivalent body, revealing the extent to which her exotic blackness is the source of desire, even as that blackness is visually disavowed.

Reading the racialized fetishization of Sarah Jane's body back into the scene of the slap, it appears that Sarah Jane's passing becomes most threatening at the moment when the self-sufficiency of white masculinity finds itself destabilized by desire and uncertainty. The possibility of Sarah Jane's not-whiteness threatens the certainty and security of Frankie's own whiteness. Hence, it is not merely the "fact" of her blackness but her claim on whiteness—"I'm as white as you are"—that causes him to strike out. Her claim challenges the ontological guarantee of whiteness that Frankie takes for granted, suggesting that if whiteness can or must be claimed, then Frankie's whiteness is no more real then her own. Likewise, Sarah Jane's ambiguity threatens Frankie with the unknowability of his own desire. Frankie's "tell me if it's true" seeks to resolve this ambivalence, not only in relation to Sarah Jane's passing, but also in relation to his own transgressive desire. In the violence of his response, Frankie simultaneously repudiates his desire for blackness and shores up his own whiteness—a whiteness whose fragility is exposed by the very vehemence of his repudiation.

From one perspective, the violence of Frankie's slap appears simply to enforce the natural law of the color line. This is what Walter Benjamin, in his 1921 "Critique of Violence," calls "law-preserving violence," the violence whereby the law is enforced and thereby conserved. Benjamin opposes this preserving violence to "lawmaking violence," the violence that founds the rule of law and is absolutely outside the realm of law.[33] But if we question the natural status of the color line, then it is not clear that the slap falls so easily on one side of this distinction. While the slap appears to restore the racial order of the future momentarily disturbed by Sarah Jane's lie, it may also be seen as reverberating into the past in order to produce the very truth that it appears simply to confirm. That is, the slap simultaneously punishes Sarah Jane's transgression of the color line and iteratively produces the very distinction that the color line names. The distinction of the color line is not simply before but is also in the violence of the slap that enforces it. It is here that the performativity of the law's distinction between black and white intervenes to trouble the boundary between founding and enforcing the color line. As Jacques Derrida remarks with respect to Benjamin's attempt to distinguish founding from conservation, "position is already iterability, a call for self-conserving repetition. Conservation in its turn refounds, so that it can conserve what it claims to found."[34] The slap both reveals Sarah Jane's "true blackness" and makes Sarah Jane "black"; the slap simultaneously conserves and founds the color line dividing Frankie and Sarah Jane. The violence of the slap is simultaneously the racializing violence that insists on Sarah Jane's blackness and the supremacist violence that enforces the separation and superiority of whiteness.

While the natural law of the color line commonsensically orders racial identities throughout the rest of the film, at the moment of the slap it is revealed that such a law must be imposed continually and violently in order to maintain its apparent naturalness. In this sense, the slap reveals a gap in the natural order of races, knowledges, and identities that distributes position and power in both the world of the film and the world outside. Something has erupted into this order, a something that is marked by Sarah Jane's passing but becomes recognizable only in the slap that returns her to her place. The eruption of the violence of racial discipline on and *as* Sarah Jane's body simultaneously reveals and ensures the conditions of racial order. Thus, the narrative and historical production of differential identities—the black woman as servant, the white woman as movie star— is exposed in its contingency at the moment when the slap reveals the violence with which this hierarchy has been produced and sustained.

Viewed in relation to the narrative and historical production of racialized identities, the time of the slap is doubled between a narrative time of logical causality and an irruptive time of iterated and originary violence. On the one hand, the slap is firmly embedded in the narrative of race that structures the film. As an element of the narrative, the slap demands that blackness is fixed in nature and punishes any attempt to transgress that fixity. The narrative itself is necessarily constructed around the presumption of the existence of fixed and irrevocable racial identities because it is only in relation to such a conception of race that passing is possible in the first place. This means that, within the time of the narrative, the slap is the application of the rule of law. Sarah Jane's blackness is a fact, and in passing she has broken the law. The slap is, in that sense, just. But this narrative time has been interrupted, momentarily suspended, by the brief glimpse offered of the workings of a violence that is both founding and conserving, the violence of the law of racial division that iteratively constitutes the racially marked subject. Thus, while the slap initially appears as the working of racial justice (in this context, the justice of white supremacy), the slap simultaneously reveals the conditions necessary to establish such a regime, that is, the originary violence at the heart of any such justice. Racial violence in this scene is revealed as always double: the violence that creates the body as racially marked and the violence that disciplines the racially marked body. Both of these forms of violence happen, not only under the protective cover of law, but as the workings of the law itself.

## Beyond Essentialism?

The scene of the slap in *Imitation of Life* might be taken as one instance of what Gayatri Spivak has called the "irreducible moment of essentialism" in any account of identity or difference.[35] It is at this moment that the workings of history are rendered effectively irrelevant in the violent restoration of the racial order that claims its origin in timeless nature. Thus, it is important to recognize that my reading of Frankie's slap as the force of the color line *does* essentialize race. Such a reading insists that when racial difference appears, as in this scene, as the final irreducible element, then it is appearing only as essence, emptied out of any content, history, or culture. As it is enforced, the law of the color line, the law determining racial identity, is an essentializing law, and racial identity as determined by the law is at its core an essentialist identity. In the essentializing moment of the law's operation, the essence of racial identity—the absolute, irreducible being of race independent of any property or attribute—appears as both source and effect of the law's functioning. It is because, within this law, the restoration of racial order operates as a form of justice (merely carrying out the rule) that the violence of its operation continues to be viewed as an aberrant and lamentable relic of an out-of-date racism that merits little attention beyond the "tsk-tsk" of liberal social commentary. That is, from the traditional liberal perspective, such violence is always separable from race.

While such incidents as a black woman being refused entrance to an uptown clothing boutique or a black restaurant patron being mistaken for the doorman exemplify the casual insults of everyday racism, such incidents also operate like the slap to restore and reaffirm the color line. The doubled aspect of the color line, as both a historical location of domination and struggle and as a seemingly external, absolute command, suggests that the question of essentialism with regard to race must always be suspended in an uneasy tension: on the one hand, there can be no essential black identity, but, on the other hand, blackness is always determined as an essence insofar as its very existence is dependent on its being essentially (although not necessarily in any particular property) different from whiteness, and it is precisely this essential difference that is continually founded and conserved by the color line. Thus, the essentializing moment of the color line cannot simply be dismissed as error. The critical task, then, is to confront the essentialism of the color line without resorting to yet another version of essentialism that would function as a naturalizing explanation for the way things are. The color line continually both produces and maintains social order and hierarchy. Therefore, it must be addressed doubly, as both the origin of an absolutely real division and as the product of an utterly false and impossible distinction.

Contemporary claims for the value of multiculturalism as a pedagogical program often seem to suggest that by recognizing and valuing cultural diversity we will move "beyond race" or "beyond racism." In effect, such claims propose that after we recognize the fallacy of racial essentialism and racism, we are prepared to emerge into the true light of diversity. The critical turn from identity to heterogeneity or hybridity often repeats such a narrative of the movement beyond error to truth. Mireille Rosello's account of "amnesic creolity" illustrates this narrative quite effectively.[36] Identity, Rosello suggests, is always the product of forgetting or repressing the inherent hybridity or creolity that constitutes it. The politics of hybridity then calls for the remembering of the truth that was always already there, for the recovering from the amnesiac sleep of identity. It is almost as if the error or illusion of our misplaced faith in identity can now be replaced with a new creed of hybridity: I once was lost but now am found, was blind but now I see. But is not this teleological narrative of redemption curiously similar to modernity's promise of history as the gradual emergence of humanity into the dazzling light of the truth? The narrative of the beyond—beyond identity, beyond race, beyond racism—is in many ways a revision of the Enlightenment narrative of the universal subject which gradually sheds all particularity and contingency to emerge into the light of its true being, with the signal difference that this being has now been recast as essentially hybrid rather than essentially singular. But hybridity is a challenge, not only to the question of human "being," but to the status of knowledge itself, the question of how and if we can *know* identity or hybridity. To rest with the conclusion that identity is really always hybridity deflects the real challenge of hybridity itself, a challenge posed to the very conditions of modern epistemology and subjectivity.

It has become something of a commonplace to note that the Enlightenment faith in the emancipatory promise of positive knowledge that has formed the epistemological foundation of modernity has lost its luster. Yet we are nonetheless subjects of that very knowledge and subject to the knowledges thus produced. Thus, the deconstruction of the categories of objectivity, the autonomous subject, and so on is not an escape from their operations. So long as we continue to think in terms of the beyond, to see race as a category mistake and racism as an unfortunate lapse, we fail to recognize the constitutive power of the knowledges that produce and perpetuate race and racism. We may know that race is a fiction (that "there is nothing in the world that can do all we ask 'race' to do for us"), just as we know that the autonomous subject cannot exist (that what we call "the subject" is not a point of essential coherence but is rather a nexus of complex, shifting, and fully contingent articulations). This knowledge, however, does not launch us into a new orbit of experience. Rather, this knowledge names and marks the historical, epistemological, and philosophical limit of modernity, a limit at which we continually find ourselves. If racial difference is simultaneously a mode of subjectification and a representation of the subject, then race and racism cannot provide a simple "beyond" because the concepts and relations named by *race* and *the subject* are limit concepts that both signal and structure our understanding of community and the subject. It is impossible to effect an unambiguous, absolute move beyond the "false" representation of the color line to a "true" representation of heterogeneity, hybridity, creolity, or cultural diversity. Thus, a hybridity that would be something other than a revision of the universal subject of modernity must also somehow be beyond race, but *its* beyond would be a beyond other than that of simply crossing over from error to truth.

But if race is both the condition and the limit of the subject, then we seem to arrive at an impasse for thought and action. If we ourselves, our sense of self and identity, are a product of the very knowledges and ideologies and powers we seek to surpass, how can we do anything but reiterate and reinforce their dynamics? It is the conundrum posed by this question that I intend to address throughout this book, by considering the boundary itself, not simply as that which must be crossed over or crossed out, but as simultaneously limit and possibility. If the color line is such a boundary, then perhaps its beyond does arrive in the form of hybridity—but this will not be a hybridity that takes the place of, surpasses, or negates the identities legislated by the color line.

Hybridity, as Young has argued, is always double-voiced, tending in one direction back toward the essentializing distinctions of discrete identities and in the other away, toward a rupture of absolute heterogeneity. If hybridity is mixture, it is also the in-between, an in-between that cannot appear as a positive alternative but whose eruption denaturalizes the natural stuff on either side. Hence, the recognition that there can be no pure identities and that identity is always hybridity does not do away with identity or go beyond identity. Hybridity cannot substitute for identity: the relation of hybridity to (racial) identity is not one of negation or of a narrative beyond that would allow what amounts to a surpassing of error. Rather, identity is shot through with hybridity, a force utterly heterogeneous and unrecuperable. Hybridity necessarily remains unknowable, unrepresentable. This does not mean that it does not happen but rather that its happening can never be known in advance. Hybridity is always, then, a surprise. Hybridity in its most complex sense is in fact an impossibility; it is not something that one can *be*. Rather, it appears as the limit, the rupture, the constitutive outside of identity. In this limit relation to identity, hybridity is not narrativizable, not subject to representation or positivist description. Heterogeneity or hybridity is the difference that interrupts the relation of same and different, a *different* different that does not relate to the order of the same. Hybridity does not conform to any law or follow any rule. Hybridity is rather what penetrates the certainties of narrative and the mimetic premise of representation, what sets knowledge scrambling to shore up its fragile assurances of certainty.

If hybridity offers another version of the beyond, then we may imagine its force thus: where the boundary has served as the mark of exclusion, of an irreconcilable and absolute difference across which position and privilege are determined, then its effects are not challenged by effacing the boundary ("beyond race, beyond racism"—on the further side of, outside the limits of). Instead, they are challenged from the zone of the boundary itself, as the eruptive possibility of its own (nontranscending) beyond, a beyond that recognizes the boundary as both its own limit condition and its own condition of possibility. Thus, not by trying to efface or escape the limits of race but by plunging into the zone of the boundary—the zone of the color line—can we perhaps begin to imagine the possibilities of an *elsewhere*.

# 2. Freedom and Fugitivity

## *The Subject of Slave Narrative*

The slave narrative is a story of crossing over many lines: from slavery to freedom, from subjection to subjectivity, from property to proprietor. The slave's geographical journey of escape, from the slave territories of the South to the free soil of the North or Canada, also records a transformation, from chattel personal to person, from one possessing no rights or will to one who demands the recognition and the rights of a human subject. While the freedom of various sectors of the nonslave population of the nineteenth century might be severely constrained, the absolute deprivation of any form of freedom was what defined the slave's existence. The nation had been founded on the repudiation of "enslavement" to the mother country; in the emerging body of slave narrative, the meditations on metaphorical bondage and political freedom that sparked American revolutionary rhetoric were stripped of their metaphoricity, intensified and given a new corporeality. Jean-Jacques Rousseau's famous revolutionary dictum, that "man is born free, and everywhere he is in chains," was literalized on the body of the slave; as Frederick Douglass charged in 1848, "it is more than a figure of speech to say that we are all in chains." But this did not mean that freedom became purely a corporeal question. *Chains* is, and is more than, a figure of speech; freedom for the slaves would demand something beyond the literal and physical removal of those chains. The slave's journey to freedom would necessarily become a meditation on the possibility of freedom itself. The fugitive slave in flight, the slave who had successfully escaped, or the freed slave, was property transformed into free subject. These three terms, *property*, *subject*, and *freedom*, are the hinges on which the narrative transformation is enacted: the slave becomes a free subject when he or she is no longer the property of another.

But what is this freedom gained as the negation of being property? The freedoms that are granted and guaranteed by the state are freedoms granted to, belonging to, a subject. On the other side of slavery, the three terms (freedom, property, and subject) come together in another way: freedom is the property of the subject. But if freedom is realized as a shift in the position of property and subject, then property and subject must fix radical limitations on the possibility of freedom. Here it is necessary to pose a challenge to the thinking of freedom as it is conventionally understood, as substantive freedoms, rights, and protections: what if, as Jean-Luc Nancy suggests, " 'freedoms' do not grasp the stakes of 'freedom' "?[1] What would it mean to "deliver ourselves from the thought of 'freedom' as a property of the subjective constitution of being, and as the property of an individual 'subject' "?[2] For the slave, these questions are more than the armchair speculations of the philosopher. What are the stakes of freedom? Is there any way of thinking freedom other than in terms of the freedoms belonging to the citizen, freedoms granted by the state to the subject of the state? What might be gained by thinking about freedom in another way? What might be lost? The rhetorical promise of freedom failed to deliver again and again for those Americans whose entry into the nation was not as subjects of the state, but as entirely subjected to another. The slave narrative poses the question of freedom and the subject; and its often ambivalent response suggests that the failures of freedom for African-Americans throughout the history of the nation may be not only the result of a failed application of freedom but of a conception of freedom itself that can only ever be partial and incomplete.

## Context and Conditions of the Slave Narrative

If one must choose a date to mark the beginning of an era, perhaps 1833 is no worse than any other: 1833 is the year the American Anti-Slavery Society was founded, a move that was to have profound implications for the future of slavery in America and, equally important for my purposes, for the future of the slave narrative. The moment was ripe for the emergence of an organized, adamant oppositional voice. By 1829, all the slaves in the Northern states had been freed through various programs of gradual emancipation. In December 1831, three months after the infamous Nat Turner slave insurrection in Virginia, that state's legislature debated whether the slaves were to be freed and, if so, whether by abolition or gradual emancipation. The legislature concluded, not only to reject any form of emancipation, but to increase the stringency of laws governing the behavior of both free blacks and slaves in the state.[3] This was the last recorded antislavery debate south of the Mason-Dixon Line and marks a significant shift in proslavery rhetoric from an apology for slavery as a necessary evil to a defense of slavery as a positive good.

Before the 1830s, justifications of slavery were generally unnecessary because there was no immediate attack threatening its continuation. Until the 1830s, there existed an implicit national consensus regarding the position of slavery within the nation.[4] In general, in the years following the Revolution, Americans neither questioned the constitutional legitimacy of slavery in the states where it existed nor believed that the federal government had the power to abolish, regulate, or in any way interfere with slavery in those states. Antislavery sentiment and action before 1830 was moderate, gradual, and oriented toward action at the local and state levels. In contrast, the American Anti-Slavery Society worked on a national scale to organize around the demand for the immediate abolition of slavery in the United States, by federal action if necessary.[5]

The American Anti-Slavery Society and its successors provided a forum for escaped slaves to recount their histories and a venue for the publication and circulation of their narratives. The explosion of the popular press in the 1820s had created the means to bring the question of slavery into public discourse, even in places where citizens might never encounter slavery in the flesh. The first antislavery journal began publication in 1820; ten years later, William Lloyd Garrison founded what was perhaps the most influential abolitionist journal, *The Liberator*. By the end of 1836, there were over one million subscribers to a total of eleven antislavery journals.[6]

Escaped slaves such as Frederick Douglass, Josiah Henson, and William Wells Brown gained fame and some degree of fortune as lecturers at abolitionist meetings and as authors of extremely popular narratives published both in England and the United States. Some of these narratives were bestsellers: Douglass's narrative sold over 11,000 copies in the first three years after its appearance and went through nine English editions, as well as Dutch and French translations.[7] William Wells Brown sold 10,000 copies of his narrative in the United States from 1847 to 1849 and 11,000 copies in England in 1849 alone.[8] Others were less commercially successful; but the sheer volume of book-length narratives (about 100) published in an approximately 30-year period demonstrates the centrality of the genre, both to the abolitionist project and to the development of nineteenth-century literary forms.

Although today the importance of slave narrative seems virtually self-evident, the critical centrality of the slave narrative in accounts of American literature or the African-American tradition is in fact a fairly recent phenomenon.[9] The contemporary recovery of slave narrative has a history, one that is important to reconstruct in order to contextualize the current critical appreciation and approach to the genre. As an example of the increasing importance of slave narrative in the curriculum, a 1990 Modern Language Association survey of teachers of nineteenth-century American literature concluded that Frederick Douglass and Harriet Jacobs were two of five authors most frequently added to course syllabi in the past decade.[10] How did these narratives move from the relative obscurity of the literary margins to such a position of centrality? One obvious reason is the growing interest on the part of nonspecialists in African-American literature and the incorporation of African-American literary texts into American literature courses.

But slave narrative in particular (of which Douglass and Jacobs are exemplars) has its own critical history. For example, in 1918 historian Ulrich Phillips concluded that "books of this class are generally of dubious value."[11] In Marion Starling's dissertation on the slave narrative as literature, written in 1948, slave narratives were acknowledged to be worthy of study, but as a preliterary form, of primary interest to the social historian and the literary scholar not so much in themselves as "in their generic relationship to the popular slave novels of the 1850s."[12] Some 40 years later, in contrast, Henry Louis Gates Jr. and Charles T. Davis, writing as the editors of *The Slave's Narrative*, the most significant contemporary anthology of criticism on the slave narrative, understand slave narrative to be "the very generic foundation which most subsequent Afro-American fictional and non-fictional narrative forms extended, refigured, and troped," in short, "the basis on which an entire narrative tradition has been constructed."[13] Of course, much has changed in the decades separating these evaluations. Phillips's insistence on the inauthenticity, and hence worthlessness, of the narratives as historical evidence has been countered by the changing understanding of evidence in the field of history, which has been necessitated in part by a desire to discover stories other than those official, documented ones. In literary studies, aesthetic evaluations such as Starling's have been somewhat displaced by historical, political, and cultural concerns. Leaving these broad disciplinary movements aside, however, I want to focus on two changes that relate directly to the contemporary revaluation of slave narrative: transformations in African-American racial consciousness in the wake of the Civil Rights movement and the growing interest of African-American literary studies in the relation between literacy and power.

Revisionist slave historiography, growing in prominence and force by the early 1970s, gave added visibility to the project begun around the turn of the century to write the history of slavery from the slave's point of view. It found in slave narrative a crucial body of testimony to the individual and collective experience of slavery.[14] At about the same time, the personal narratives of black revolutionaries of the 1960s such as Malcolm X, Eldridge Cleaver, and Angela Davis began to appear. Searching for a precedent for these writers' "apocalyptic tone and revolutionary message," critics rediscovered Frederick Douglass's 1845 *Narrative*, "a work that seemed to accord much better [than Booker Washington's *Up from Slavery*] with the experience and rhetoric of the most popular black autobiographers of the 1960s. Douglass soon became the most celebrated black autobiographer before Malcolm."[15] The depictions of the struggle against oppression, the desire for freedom, the experiences of suffering and triumph, and the promise of transformation characteristic of slave narrative resonated powerfully with the sentiments of the period. The struggle against slavery could be invoked as a powerful historical precedent for the struggle for civil rights. The late 1960s and early 1970s saw the republication of several important slave narrative anthologies, dominated, it should be remarked, by male narratives, which were much more likely to support a heroic and revolutionary tone than their female counterparts.[16] Thus, the renewed interest in slave narrative was inseparable from the contemporary political struggle for rights and recognition.

As suggested by the interplay between the rhetoric of the 1960s revolutionaries and the rhetoric of the slave narrative, it is more generally the case that throughout the century, African-American literary study has been inseparable from the political, social, and economic struggles for the full liberation of black people in America. Literature has been viewed as one path to freedom, insofar as "a number of Afro-American writers and critics saw black mastery of the tropes of literary expression as a means of gaining the race's liberation from the debilitating tenets of white hegemony."[17] One aspect of this connection between politics and expression has been to emphasize the responsibility of black artists to counter racist representations of African-American life with their own accurate and positive representations. A second aspect has been to emphasize the role of literacy itself in the struggles for black freedom. The link between literacy and freedom is nowhere better exemplified than in certain of the slave narratives, most significantly Frederick Douglass's. Hence, within the traditional and still dominant African-American critical framework joining writing to freedom, the literary value of slave narrative is most often perceived to lie in its power to "find a voice" or "write the self" of the previously silent and invisible slave.

Like the genre of autobiography with which it shares certain features, slave narrative is interpreted as enacting a creation of a self, constituting, as James Olney puts it, "a bringing to consciousness of the nature of one's own existence, transforming the mere fact of existence into a realized quality and a possible meaning."[18] But further, as several commentators have pointed out, this project carries a special political charge in the case of slave narrative because slaves were excluded from the human community on the grounds of allegedly inferior capacities of reason and in particular of language. Writing the self was not only constructing a subject of representation but also insisting on the essential (and denied) humanity of that subject. In this context, the literary claims for the importance of slave narrative are always also a particular sort of political claim: slave narrative is viewed as a political act that intervenes in the dominant discourse of race by countering the claim that the slave as subject is less rational or less human than the (white) nonslave. Writing about the eclipse of Phillis Wheatley by Frederick Douglass as a representative figure of black genius in abolitionist circles around the middle of the nineteenth century, Gates remarks, "it is clear enough, I think, why a black author was needed in the discourse of abolition. Since the Enlightenment, the index of any race's 'humanity' was its possession of reason, which was to be known through its representation in writing, particularly writing in its more exalted or 'literary' forms."[19] Although before about 1830 black intelligence as embodied in Phillis Wheatley "was called upon as evidence that the African's 'place in nature,' in the 'great chain of being,' was with human beings rather than with apes," in subsequent years "the idea that 'the arts' could secure for the African an elevated place on the great chain of being [came] to be reified. . . . [Thereafter,] authors of the slave narratives would use literacy to attempt to secure their literal freedom." [20]

This is a powerful argument and one that accords extremely well with historical evidence documenting the debates about the status of the slave in terms of reason and language. But the implications of this historical argument have been extended far beyond the context linking literacy with literal freedom that Gates so carefully delineates. Eric Sundquist, for example, suggests that "Douglass demonstrates that literacy is linked to the power to enslave and, alternatively, to the power to create one's own subjectivity and redeem one's community." [21] This is a power that implicitly exceeds the particularities of historical circumstance, bordering on the divine powers of creation and redemption.

Houston Baker's interpretation of the significance of slave narrative makes even more explicit the slippage between historical or political freedom and an extrahistorical—I would say metaphysical—freedom of the subject. Baker has argued that for the enslaved the problem of self-representation was not the problem of being American, but of *being* itself. For Baker, the writing of the self represented by the autobiographical slave narrative is coterminous with the coming into (human) being of the slave: "He first had to seize the word. His being had to erupt from nothingness. Only by grasping the word could he engage in the speech acts that would ultimately define his selfhood. Further, the slave's task was primarily one of creating a human and liberated self rather than of projecting one that reflected a peculiar landscape and tradition." [22] Thus, Baker implies that the de novo creation of a "human and liberated self" is the aim and object of the literary act given form in the slave narrative. Baker takes to an extreme an interpretive posture shared across a wide range of slave narrative criticism. For Baker, as for many other contemporary readers, the politics of slave narrative far exceeds its particular function in the historical discourse of abolition. In what I will call the "subjectifying reading," the slave narrative not only chronicles the freeing of the slave and calls for an end to slavery for others; it also wrenches open a gap in the racial order that has denied the subjectivity of the slave and performatively instantiates the transformation of slave into subject.

If such a subjectifying reading has indeed come to be the standard for slave narrative interpretation (and frequently evaluation), then it seems crucial to ask what sort of subject it is that has been understood to be the political (and in Baker's reading, at least, metaphysical) achievement of slave narrative. And further, we might also ask whether the creation or invention of such a subject would fully exhaust the ways in which slave narrative might be understood as a critical intervention into the discourse of racial difference and hierarchy. I do not think these questions have been adequately addressed thus far, in part because it seems to me that the conjunction of literary value and political value has tended to reinforce a closed circuit of evaluation and interpretation. The descriptive relation between literacy, freedom, and subjectivity evidenced in some narratives becomes the normative standard of evaluation for all narratives. In turn, this evaluative standard is misrecognized as merely descriptive. For example, Donald Wesling claims that "most of the slave narratives magnificently turn on this topos of self-instruction in reading and writing, with literacy the first step to the slave's understanding his situation, the first gesture of flight. Thus the slaves are able to think their freedom before they achieve it physically; and their narratives, after the fact of flight, are the proof of achieved self-realization." [23] In this reading, literacy is the prerequisite to freedom, freedom necessarily follows from literacy, and the freedom in question is the freedom of the self-realized subject.

I would go so far as to say that in contemporary slave narrative criticism, the priority and necessity of these connections and transformations are considered axiomatic. It is not accidental that the slave narrative universally regarded as the best, Frederick Douglass's *Narrative of the Life of Frederick Douglass, an American Slave*, is also the narrative most centrally concerned with the relation of literacy to subjectivity, freedom, and (self-)mastery. One of the things that makes Douglass's narrative so excellent, from the contemporary critical perspective, is the fact that it so precisely does just what a slave narrative ought to do. My point is not to deny the extraordinary complexity of Douglass's narrative or to devalue the creative, original, and forceful readings that narrative has provoked and inspired; rather, I want to suggest that Douglass's brilliance has perhaps cast a shadow over other equally interesting elements of slave narrative.[24] Many critics focus on elucidating those aspects of slave narrative that most closely correspond to what is understood to be Douglass's project, the project of the writing of the self into being. As I intend to demonstrate both in relation to Douglass's narrative and in relation to others that are quite dissimilar, such a reading strategy is limiting and risks effacing the slave narrative's most powerful critiques of the modern liberal ideals that define, determine, and delimit the meaning of "freedom" and "the subject."

The life narrated in the individual slave narrative is not only the life of the narrator but also the life of a collective defined as those sharing the identity of slave. As Gates puts it, "the black slave's narrative came to be a communal utterance, a collective tale, rather than merely an individual's autobiography. Each slave author, in writing about his or her personal life's experiences, simultaneously wrote on behalf of the millions of silent slaves still held captive throughout the South." [25] But when this reading is removed from its nineteenth-century political and polemical context, in which those who could speak were understood as speaking for their figurative brothers and sisters still in bondage, the commonality binding the individual's voice to the experience of the collective tends to become essentialized.

When the voice of the individual slave narrator is taken to speak for slavery in general, slavery itself becomes an abstraction, a universalized idea that may find expression in any number of particular incarnations. Slavery and race become, in this reading, interchangeable, mirroring the nineteenth-century discourse of race that identified slavishness as the essential quality of the "Negro race." The slave narrator speaks for others enslaved, but also for and in the place of the race. Davis and Gates, for example, argue that against the *false* essence that Europeans assigned to black people in order to naturalize and neutralize their domination, early black writers "record[ed] an *authentic* black voice . . . [that was] the millennial instrument of transformation through which the African would become the European, the slave become the ex-slave, the brute animal become the human being." [26] Thus, while speaking for the enslaved is a particular, limited political act directed toward the abolition of slavery, speaking for the race implicitly evokes the essence of the race in order to create the race anew.

What is interesting to me in Gates's and Baker's readings is the extent to which the political force of the slave narrative is perceived to derive from a paradoxically double-edged essentialism. On the one hand, the slave narrator "becomes a man" (in Douglass's apt phrase) through the act of writing, thus revealing the essential humanity of the slave. The political efficacy of this essential humanity, of course, is that it is universal, shared by black and white. But, on the other hand, at the same time the slave narrator expresses the "face of the race," which, in its very existence, belies the claim that universal humanity applies to all. This apparent contradiction indicates a possible opening for what Gayatri Spivak has called "strategic essentialism." [27] I specify Spivak's use of the phrase here because, unlike more casual invocations of strategic essentialism that sometimes become indistinguishable from traditional humanist or positivist essentialisms, Spivak is careful to articulate how strategic essentialism can *only* be strategic insofar as it undermines the very terms that it invokes. The strategic use that Spivak describes is not the positing of an essential subaltern identity that would explicitly stand in opposition to a dominant identity but rather the strategic recourse to an idea of the subaltern subject *that is irreducibly and unavoidably essentializing* precisely in order to critique the humanist (and essentialist) notion of the subject that constitutively excludes the subaltern. [28]

The idea of the humanist subject that Spivak locates as the object of subaltern critique is, I think, the same idea of the subject that is mobilized by readers of slave narrative as the implicit standard of the slave narrator's self-realization. This is the modern, liberal subject understood as individually autonomous, sovereign, and rational. The slave as slave by definition cannot be such a subject; the slave is a thing, not a person. In contrast, the objective of writing, in the traditional interpretation of slave narrative, is to be recognized as a subject, that is, as rational (master of the word) and as sovereign (master of oneself, as Douglass puts it). Such recognition is, within the framework of the American liberal polity, the necessary (but not sufficient) condition of political and social equality. Douglass claims to be such a subject at the conclusion of his narrative. But Spivak's suggestion that the subaltern's recourse to the modern liberal notion of the subject might in fact undermine the very universality or hegemony of such a subject suggests that there might be some ambivalence in Douglass's account of the freedom realized by the "slave become man."

In making the claim to subjectivity, the slave is claiming a humanity that has defined itself—its freedom, its self-possession, its independence—in relation to the negations of those attributes embodied in the slave. In the context of republican America, this is the only kind of subject that one can be; claims for political and ethical recognition must be made from the position of the politically free, ethically responsible subject. Thus (as I will argue in greater detail in relation to Frederick Douglass), the slave become man necessarily takes up a position as a subject whose humanity has always already been defined in relation to the excluded slave. If we approach the subjectifying aspect of slave narrative in this way, then the humanist subject itself—especially its relation to property and to freedom—comes

under critical scrutiny, even as it appears that it is precisely the emergence
and recognition of such a subject that is at stake in slave narrative. By pur-
suing the tension between the political necessity of being recognized as a
subject and the implicit critiques of the claims of such a subject to universality, it becomes possible to interrogate the presuppositions inherent in
both "subject" and "race" and to inquire into their mutually implicated
constitution. This will be my intention in considering the relation between
race, slavery, and the subject in that exemplary slave narrative, the *Narrative of the Life of Frederick Douglass, an American Slave, Written by Himself.*

## Reading Douglass

One might assemble an impressive array of Douglass criticism written in
the last decade that focuses on subjectivity and consciousness.[29] For these
critics, the force of Douglass's *Narrative* lies, not simply in its literary ex-
cellence, but in its almost mystical power to transform object into subject,
to bring a man into existence. As read in Douglass's *Narrative*, what Baker
calls the slave's "quest for being" is a story of transcendence: subjectivity
emerges out of, or in resistance to, a system that would deny the humanity
of the slave by treating him as a mere thing.[30] For Douglass, the deprived,
the enslaved, is *made* a brute; his subsequent coming-to-consciousness reveals his true humanity. In the most famous line of his narrative, Douglass
writes "you have seen how a man was made a slave; you shall see how a slave
was made a man." This turning between slave and man transforms these
terms from essential conditions to historical products, undermining the
power of the recourse to the nature of the slave on which slavery depends
for its legitimacy. As Henry Louis Gates Jr. suggests, Douglass exposes the
constructed character of the apparently natural binary oppositions that are
supposed to correlate with the absolute, essential differences between slave
and man; his narrative is the performance of a process of transformation
whereby "slave has become master, creature has become man, object has
become subject."[31]

However, while Douglass wrenches these terms from their fixed places,
he leaves untouched the basic structuring opposition: *slave* and *man*, *object*
and *subject* continue to stand as absolutely opposite and mutually exclusive
terms. To move from object to subject, from slave to man, in this system,
where the positive term has meaning only because it persists in relation to
the negative, is not to radically transform in any way the basic structure of

opposition. This marks the limit of Douglass's narrative of slave-become-man. And to the extent that readers have celebrated Douglass's achievement without questioning the relation between the man he has become and the slave he was, they too have consented to Douglass's foundational opposition of slave and man. Such a reading can take no account of either the contingency of this way of demarcating and dividing up the world and consciousness, nor of the possibility of textual elements that resist the reduction to mutually exclusive and collectively totalizing elements. But if we consider the contingencies and limits of *both* slave and man, a new set of questions becomes possible: How does this binary itself become instantiated, and what elements must necessarily be left out of the account? What is gained by the perpetuation of this division, and what is the cost? How might we think about the constitutive "outside" that must be suppressed or repudiated in order to guarantee the appearance of plentitude and naturalness by which this system of oppositions sustains itself?

Although there are several scenes of transformation in the *Narrative*, the most significant is Douglass's self-characterized conversion from slave to man in his resistance to and physical struggle with the cruel overseer, Mr. Covey. In the course of this reversal, however, slavery is effectively naturalized as the constitutive condition of manhood. In the account of this conversion, we can see that the nineteenth-century ideas of subjectivity, race, and history that inform Douglass's narrative are not so distant from those assumed by readers today. If Douglass's narrative invokes, as William Andrews puts it, an "apocalyptic tone and revolutionary message," the promised revolution is conceived wholly within the terms of a republican polity of sovereign, independent men.[32] Douglass maintains a deeply ambivalent relation to the narratives of freedom, sovereignty, and history that implicitly structure his own narrative. Becoming a man for Douglass is becoming his *own* master; becoming a historical man is staking a claim for his race to join in the history of man, the progress of civilization that has marked some races as barbaric, others as superior. Thus, while Douglass struggles against those representations of the subject and the slave that have relegated the slave to the side of the nonhuman and the nonhistorical, he is constrained to do so from within the very discursive terms that have produced such an exclusion. Against the *metaphorical* invocation of slavery in opposition to which freedom is determined in the political theories of such signal liberal thinkers as Jean-Jacques Rousseau or G. W. F. Hegel, Douglass insists on the *material* reality of slavery that subtends other men's freedom. But at the same time, Douglass remains firmly within the liberal tradition of thinking exemplified by Rousseau and Hegel, in which the relations of mastery and possession that define the relation between master and slave also define the relation of the sovereign subject to itself.

In the climactic resolution of the story of how "a slave was made a man," Douglass insists that he ceased being a slave at the moment he resolved to resist the physical domination of Mr. Covey, who was known for "breaking" difficult slaves such as Douglass. Halfway through his tenure with Covey, Douglass turns on him, refusing to accept passively the beating Covey intends: "Mr. Covey seemed now to think he had me, and could do what he pleased; but at this moment—from whence came the spirit I don't know— I resolved to fight; and, suiting my action to the resolution, I seized Covey hard by the throat. . . . This battle with Mr. Covey was the turning-point in my career as a slave. It rekindled the few expiring embers of freedom, and revived within me a sense of my own manhood" (pp. 112–13).

This confrontation marks a turning point in Douglass's career. Once he has made it known that "the white man who expected to succeed in whipping, must also succeed in killing" him, he can say with confidence that he is no longer a slave, despite appearances to the contrary. In the four years that pass before Douglass gains his freedom, he is never again whipped. In Douglass's formulation, "however long I might remain a slave in form, the day had passed forever when I could be a slave in fact." This distinction between form and fact separates the physical, material aspect of Douglass's enslavement from the enslavement of his mind and will. For this reason, Douglass's freedom is disjunctive with his material escape from slavery. His true freedom is represented as the freedom of his will, manifested as his refusal to recognize the mastery of the master. Having become a man "in fact," the form will naturally follow.

Douglass's recounting of his fight with Covey seems almost a reenactment of the drama of self-consciousness played out in the figures of Lord and Bondsman (also often translated as "Master" and "Slave") in Hegel's *Phenomenology of Spirit* (1807). Paul Gilroy has suggested that Douglass's account might be read "as an alternative to Hegel: a supplement if not exactly a trans-coding of his account of the struggle between lord and bondsman." [33] Gilroy notes that while Hegel's allegory of modernity ensures the power of the master through the submission of the slave, "Douglass's version is quite different. For him, the slave actively prefers the possibility of death to the continuing condition of inhumanity on which plantation slavery depends." [34] Thus, Douglass writes against the grain of Hegel by emphasizing the lived experience of Hegel's allegory of power as enacted in the face-to-face struggle between master and slave. But I think it is also important to note that, at the same time, Douglass writes with the grain of Hegel's attempt to chart the emergence and development of a unified, self-sufficient subject. Reading Douglass *with* rather than against Hegel reveals the extent to which Douglass's potentially violent revolutionary rhetoric remains within the terms of a fairly traditional philosophical idealism. For Douglass, freedom from slavery as a material circumstance is meaningless without the possibility of the freedom of will that would make him a sovereign subject.

Both for Douglass and for Hegel, what is at stake for the slave in the struggle for recognition is history itself. But Douglass's history from the point of view of the enslaved is quite different from Hegel's "History," which proceeds by erasing the material and historical relations of slavery by transforming the slave into a metaphor. Effacing the historical fact of the master's absolute domination over the slave, Hegel inverts their relation by suggesting that it is the master who is forever dependent on the slave, while the slave is eventually freed from his dependence on the master: "servitude in its consummation will really turn into the opposite of what it immediately is; as a consciousness forced back into itself, it will withdraw into itself and be transformed into a truly independent consciousness" (§ 193). Hegel implies that history is on the side of this abstract slave who gradually achieves independence by working on, and thus transforming, the world. But if Hegel ignores real slaves (very much in evidence during his lifetime) while making the abstract "slave" the subject of history, Douglass insists that real slaves are in fact *excluded* from history. Nevertheless, the *reason* for this historical exclusion turns out to be quite consistent with Hegelian principles. Douglass's slave, as slave, is ahistorical because he lacks consciousness. Douglass writes: "I have found that, to make a contented slave, it is necessary to make a thoughtless one. It is necessary to darken his moral and mental vision, and, as far as possible, to annihilate the power of reason. He must be able to detect no inconsistencies in slavery; he must be made to feel that slavery is right; and he can be brought to that only when he ceases to be a man" (p. 135).

The success of slavery lies in its power to strip a man of thought and reason and reduce his intellect to "a sort of beast-like stupor, between sleep and wake" (p. 105). The slave as slave is content with slavery and desires nothing. But the slave-become-man desires freedom: it is precisely this desire that separates the slave from the slave-become-man. If, as Hegel puts it, "self-consciousness is *Desire* in general" (§ 167), then it is this desire that launches the slave-become-man into history. In literalizing Hegel's allegory of the slave, Douglass writes the Hegelian story against itself; where Hegel begins his inquiry into the development of world spirit by definitionally excluding Africa from world history, Douglass places the African slave at the point of origin for the emergence of man into history.[35] In launching the slave into history, Douglass explicitly counters the notion, found not only in Hegel but more generally in eighteenth- and nineteenth-century European thought, that the African is outside human history, part of the conditions of nature. In effect, Douglass's slave-become-man stands in for a narrative of the race: black-become-human, launched into universal, human history. As Gates concludes, "not only has an *idea* made subject of object, but creature has assumed self and *the assumption of self has created a race*."[36] Thus, Douglass simultaneously echoes the Hegelian narrative of consciousness in his own narrative of becoming a man and at the same time turns its political investment in the maintenance of European dominance on its ear. But a question arises here: what is the cost of this implicit myth of origins that positions Douglass, and the kind of subject Douglass comes to represent, as the condition, sign, and source of the race's claim to humanity?

Thus far I have treated as interchangeable "slave-become-man" and "slave-become-human." Of course, in Douglass's narrative these two are synonymous. For this reason, feminist critics such as Deborah McDowell take to task both Douglass and many of Douglass's contemporary critics for their elision of the black woman's body: "Douglass's 'freedom'—narrative and physical alike—depends on narrating black women's bondage."[37] Throughout the *Narrative*, black women appear as voyeuristic objects of pity and horror. In the last pages of the book, the reader is surprised to discover that Douglass has acquired along the way an intended wife; the first mention of Anna is in the same paragraph that announces their marriage. We learn nothing more of her in the narrative beyond the fact that she was a free woman, and she quickly fades from view. That her only existence is in the moment of their marriage—which is the first thing Douglass does when he arrives on the free soil of New York—itself suggests that her significance in the narrative is solely as a sign of Douglass's freedom. Houston Baker points to the inscribed marriage certificate as evidence that "the black man has *repossessed* himself in a manner that enables him to enter the kind of relationship disrupted, or foreclosed, by the economics of slavery."[38] In this reading, the difference between slave and free man is that a free man's wife cannot be taken away from him: marriage marks the self-possession of the man through and in terms of the possession of a wife. Carla Kaplan has pointed out that marriage is of particular significance for the subject that Douglass has become: "It is marriage, after all, that engenders contractarian individuality. It establishes male possessive individuality through the exchange of women who mediate social relations not by being possessors of property but by being property. The entry into individuality available to Douglass necessitates a woman's exclusion from it." [39]

In marriage, Douglass's capacity to possess himself—the rational self-possession taken as a sign of the political and ethical subject—is signaled by his possession of another. Thus, he has shifted from being possessed as a slave to possessing another in marriage. Marriage is not slavery, of course, and the implicit rhetorical equation of the possession of a wife with the possession of a slave is fraught with problems on both sides. As Karen Sánchez-Eppler argues in her compelling analysis of the continuities and interrelations between nineteenth-century feminist and abolitionist discourse, "though the metaphoric linking of women and slaves uses their shared position as bodies to be bought, owned, and designated as a grounds of resistance, it nevertheless obliterates the particularity of black and female experience, making their distinct exploitations appear as one." [40] But while joining feminist concerns with abolitionist concerns risks effacing the important differences between the situations of women and slaves, it also emphasizes the centrality of *possession*, and the capacity to possess, in determining who is free and independent. The fact that Douglass's freedom is marked by his entry into a marriage contract indicates that freedom means something more than simply the absence of slavery—it means contract, property, and (self-)possession.

It is not unusual or surprising that Douglass's understanding of freedom should be consistent with the conceptions of freedom emerging from American revolutionary and postrevolutionary thought. Douglass casts his faith with the rhetorical promise of the freedom of the sovereign individual in a republic of equals, but although liberal political philosophy proclaimed such a freedom to be universal in practice it operated through exclusion and opposition. For example, in debates about the meaning of freedom and the rights of the citizen in nineteenth-century America, the concept of American citizenship was frequently opposed to the highly visible material condition of slavery. The rhetorical invocation of slavery to oppose any diminution of liberties was not simply an ill-conceived metaphor. Judith Shklar suggests that American freedom and citizenship took on particular meanings precisely because they emerged in relation to a palpable example of their negation in slavery. Before the Fourteenth Amendment to the Constitution of the United States provided a juridical standard for determining citizenship, various poles of opinion on the matter agreed on only one thing: "No slave was a citizen. . . . Black chattel slavery stood at the opposite social pole from full citizenship and so defined it." [41] The exclusion of slaves from citizenship was not simply a matter of status but was understood more profoundly in terms of the nature of the slave. David Roediger explicitly links revolutionary republicanism with the rise of white racism, arguing that the seemingly contradictory persistence of slavery in republican America was explained by racializing the slave, attributing the persistence of enslavement to the essential slavishness of black people and therefore "stigmatiz[ing them] as the *antithesis* of republican citizens." [42] Thus, while Douglass is insisting that he as a black man is fit for citizenship, he is constrained to do so through an appeal to conceptions of the citizen that developed in relation to the explicit exclusion of blacks as slaves, not simply unfree, but essentially unfit for freedom.

The political efficacy of Douglass's claim to freedom is complicated not only by the question of whether, in the political context of postrevolutionary America, the freedom to which he appeals can be universal or whether it demands exclusion; his claim to freedom is further complicated by the question of how that freedom is itself to be conceptualized. Slavery bears a more complex relation to the liberal idea of freedom than simply an external measure of un-freedom. This much is revealed in Rousseau's political writings, from which much revolutionary rhetoric took its cues. Just prior to the Revolution, for example, John Adams insisted that "the very definition of a freeman is one who is bound by no law to which he has not consented," [43] echoing virtually word for word Rousseau's argument that man is free in the modern democratic state because his freedom is limited only by the laws that he himself has made. This is what Rousseau calls "moral liberty," the obedience to the law one has prescribed for oneself. [44] But the centrality of metaphors of slavery in Rousseau's working through of the theory of moral liberty suggests that the historical reality of slavery bears more than an accidental relationship to liberal thought. Slavery was not, as political thinkers of the seventeenth and eighteenth centuries including Rousseau insisted, a historically aberrant violation of the principles of

human equality and liberty that were rhetorically animating political transformations in Europe and later in the United States. Rather, slavery was
the very condition, both theoretically and materially, for the possibility of
thinking about or creating institutions to further that human equality and
liberty in whose name it was decried.

A closer look at the relation between slavery and liberty in Rousseau's
thought will illustrate my point. In "On the Social Contract," Rousseau begins with the question of slavery, insisting that because there is no right of
slavery, there can be no right of the collective (metaphorical) enslavement
of a people; just as an individual cannot alienate his liberty by becoming
a slave, so a people cannot alienate their collective liberty by submitting
to the rule of a king or dictator. Thus, Rousseau argues, a legitimate state
cannot be based on the submission of the people to the rule of the sovereign; the legitimate state is opposed to slavery. But in this opposition Rousseau implicitly suggests that slavery, as the submission of one to the will
of another, is the most foundational form of sociality prior to the intervention of the social contract that would create a *legitimate* authority.[45] When
the state is not constituted in the sovereign will of the people, as is the case
under an arbitrary or tyrannical government (and also in a corrupt democratic state), the people are "in chains," slaves to the will, backed by force,
of an illegitimate sovereign power alien to them. Under such conditions,
the sovereign's freedom to act or appropriate is limited only by force. In
contrast, the "moral liberty" of the citizenry of the state constituted by
the social contract is figured as self-mastery: not absolute freedom as the
freedom from all constraints but rather a self-limiting freedom, a preferable alternative to the "slavery" suffered under the tyrannical or arbitrary
government. The freedom of the citizen-subject is thus not unlimited freedom as the opposite of slavery but the internalization of limits on freedom
through the transformation from the external mastery of slavery to the
self-mastery of freedom. Freedom in the modern state, as Rousseau and as
American descendants of Rousseau such as Adams conceived it, is slavery
dislocated from a *between* (master and slave) to a *within* (self-mastery). And
this is precisely the way in which Douglass characterizes his own condition:
"I will give Mr. Freeland the credit for being the best master I ever had, 'till
*I became my own master*" (p. 121, emphasis added). For this reason, Douglass's conception of freedom remains firmly within the liberal tradition, in
which slavery persists as the foundational social relationship such that the
physical and historical relation of slave to master is neither destroyed nor

abandoned; rather, it has reinstalled itself as the basis for the rational free subject.

As master of himself (and, in marriage, of his wife), Douglass claims freedom as property right. But as the system of slavery reveals, in nineteenth-century America property right is inherently racialized: the right to hold property is distributed based on racial distinction, which determines whether one can be enslaved or whether one is shielded from slavery by the protective cover of whiteness. Whiteness itself, Cheryl Harris argues, is a property, insofar as it is the prerequisite for and basis of other property rights.[46] Thus, Douglass's claim of freedom in terms of property right suppresses both the racialization of property under slavery and the complex material and theoretical interdependence of slavery and liberally conceived freedom. This is not to say that Douglass is misguided or deluded; such a masterful freedom is the only politically meaningful freedom to which he might make a claim. But the necessary ambivalence in such a claim suggests that for Douglass, and for the other enslaved for whom he speaks, freedom poses itself as not simply a solution but also as a problem.

Douglass gains his freedom. Nevertheless, from a certain perspective his freedom appears partial and inadequate. Is this failure of freedom simply an administrative matter, a shortfall in the granting of rights and freedoms? Or is the liberal conception of freedom as self-mastery itself deficient? One way of approaching the question of freedom from outside the liberal framework implicitly upheld by Douglass might be to consider the literal, material mechanisms of freedom, in particular escape and purchase. Interestingly, these aspects of freedom are precisely the ones suppressed by Douglass in his first narrative account of his passage from slavery to freedom, an account that foregrounds the ideal rather than the material aspects of this passage (although as I will discuss later, he does take up these topics in subsequent versions of his life story). I will suggest that it is in the mechanisms of escape and purchase as they are narrated in slave narrative that we may locate, if not an alternative vision of freedom, then at least a counter to the humanist freedom of a subject whose self-evidence is purchased through the appropriation of the slave body as not-subject. In escape and purchase, the peculiar status of the slave as human property is foregrounded. Working through the contradictions of "human property" as they emerge in slave narratives will provide an alternative approach to the questions of the subject and freedom raised in Douglass's narrative.

## Race, Property, and the Status of the Slave

It is a popular notion that European racism accounts for the enslavement of African people and that a belief in the African's natural inferiority was necessary before the European could imagine the African as slave. But the divisions of race do not exist independently of the social forms and circumstances through which they become meaningful. The modern conception of racial difference as inherent and heritable emerged from a context in which, through a process Winthrop Jordan terms an "unthinking decision," some had already been deemed suitable for enslavement. Like race, slavery too came to be understood as inherent and heritable; it was these characteristics that distinguished slavery from other forms of bond labor. Explicit connections between slavery and race took time to emerge; from the date of the arrival of the first Africans in Virginia in 1619 until 1660, when slavery began to be fully institutionalized and regulated by statute in the colonies, the various conceptions of difference between Africans and others were slowly transformed into an implicit assumption that the African was, by nature and by definition, a slave.

While it may have been inevitable that the European perception of distinct, naturally formed races would also imply a hierarchy of races, prejudice alone did not cause slavery. As Jordan insists, "slavery and 'prejudice' may have been equally cause and effect, continuously reacting upon each other . . . [resulting in] a mutually interactive growth of slavery and unfavorable assessment, with no cause for either which did not cause the other as well."[47] Throughout the eighteenth century, there was little organized opposition to race slavery and therefore little reason to reflect on the causes or justifications for such an institution. By the time racial theorists began positing scientific proofs of the inherent inferiority of the "Negro race" in the early nineteenth century, slavery's foundational distinction between those who could be enslaved and those who could not was fully entrenched as a totally natural, unquestionable distinction. In the racial distinction between black and white, the idea of race was inseparable from the idea of slavery, and the debasement of Africans and African-Americans was a function, not simply of racial prejudice, but also of the institution of slavery as a system of property relations and definitions. White could never be slave, while black was essentially slave. Under slavery, the color line was always also a property line.

This is not to deny that there were any free black people where slavery existed or that some black people owned slaves. However, as slavery became further entrenched in national life, such exceptions to the rule that black meant slave became less and less tolerable. Unlike the presumption of freedom that applied to whites, both custom and law dictated that one identifiable as black was presumed slave until proved otherwise. As Kenneth Stampp notes,

> all Negroes were brought to America in bondage, and legislatures soon adopted the principle of *partus sequitur ventrem* — the child inherits the condition of the mother. Therefore, the English common-law presumption in favor of freedom did not apply to Negroes; in all the slave states (except Delaware) the presumption was that people with black skins were slaves unless they could prove that they were free. Any strange Negro found in a southern community without "freedom papers" was arrested as a fugitive.[48]

While such a presumption of slave status did not apply in nonslave states, the force of various fugitive slave codes effected virtually the same result. The "fugitive slave clause" incorporated into the original U.S. Constitution allowed the slaveholder to reclaim a slave who had escaped to another state.[49] The safety of fugitive slaves in free states was further eroded by the Fugitive Slave Act of 1850, which made the aiding or abetting of runaway slaves a federal crime. Fugitive slaves could and did settle in free states, but their safety was never completely assured. The slaveholder or his proxy slave catchers might find them, "friends" might betray them for principle or profit, kidnappers might take them south and sell them again into slavery. The profits to be had in the dealing of captured runaways ensured that even free black people were never entirely safe. A black body was a body that could be entered into the slave marketplace and sold; because no slave could testify in his or her own behalf, there was no way for the one thus enslaved to demonstrate his or her legally free status. While no one ever could be sure just how often legally free persons were impressed or sold into slavery, both legal and social presumptions equated being visibly colored with being a slave.

The popular narrative of Solomon Northup, subtitled "A Citizen of New York, kidnapped in Washington City in 1841 and rescued in 1853 from a cotton plantation near the Red River in Louisiana," revealed graphically the dangers to the free black population created by an increasingly profitable internal slave trade.[50] Northup, a freeborn man living in New York State, was lured to Washington under the pretext of potential employment in a circus. His friendly benefactors drugged him, stole his free papers, and sold him in the Washington slave market. His attempts to protest were greeted with threats and cruelty. It was twelve years before he had an opportunity to send a letter to friends in New York who might intervene. Most significant in Northup's story was a white lawyer, Henry Northup, who as a relative of the master of Solomon Northup's father was Solomon's kinsman after a fashion. Henry Northup was enjoined to pursue Solomon's legal case because the latter had neither opportunity (being closely watched by a very harsh master) nor standing. Thus, while Northup's narrative made a case for abolition, it also vividly illustrated the program laid out by the *New England Anti-Slavery Almanac for 1841*: "Things for the Abolitionist to do, 1. Speak for the Slave. . . . 2. Write for the Slave. . . . They can't take care of themselves."[51] Although such statements suggest the abolitionists viewed themselves as the benevolent strong caring for the suffering weak, it is clear from Northup's tale that it was not any weakness on the part of such victims as Northup but rather the collusion of the legal system and economic opportunity, that demanded the intervention of white friends under such circumstances.

If the freedom of free black people is never absolute or unassailable in the context of race slavery, then that freedom maintains a kind of contingency not shared with the freedom applied to whites in general. Black is presumed to be slave, property of another, while white is presumed to be person, holder of property in the self. Under these circumstances, to what extent could slaves be recognized as persons? The foundational legal distinction between person and property became hopelessly muddled in the body of the slave. That slaves were distinct from other forms of property seemed evident, even to those most convinced of the slave's subhumanity. Nevertheless, their legal status as person was tenuous at best. The body of laws governing the relation between slaves and their owners that began to emerge in the early decades of the nineteenth century chronicles an effort to contain and control the contradictions between the necessity for treating the slave as property and the slave's frequent manifestations of an autonomous will or person-ality.

The increasing codification of slavery in the nineteenth century was coeval with the emergence of organized and adamant voices of opposition, suggesting that part of the function of slave law was to impose certain protections over the person of the slave, thereby ameliorating the worst abuses in order to sustain the defensibility of the institution as a whole. Complex

slave codes developed in the various states sought both to reconcile person with property and to ensure the owner's right to the slave's labor and
product, while at the same time imposing certain obligations on the owners
for the care and welfare of the slave.[52] But there was a certain illogic inherent in these efforts. As property, the slave is wholly subject to the will
of the owner. If the owner's right to dispose of his property is to remain
unimpinged by the state, at some point the person-hood of the slave must
come into conflict with the slave's legal status as property or thing. This
conflict is at the heart of slavery, and slavery's response was ultimately
unequivocal: the legitimacy and the efficacy of slavery demanded that the
absolute separation between person and property be sustained, a separation that could only be effected by denying the personality of the slave.

The most extreme legal expression of this inexorable logic is the famous
judgment of North Carolina judge Thomas Ruffin in *State v Mann* (1829),
a case involving the charge against a master for committing battery on his
slave. Charges of committing battery on a slave and even murder could be
brought against slaveholders or other whites. However, because only white
men could bring such charges and because almost any degree of cruelty
was defensible as "correction," the efficacy of such laws in actually prevent-
ing violence or abuse was probably close to nil. Ruffin's judgment made
explicit this inherent contradiction between slavery and the legal protection of the slave. In ruling on whether the master had committed battery or
justifiable punishment, Ruffin concluded that if the law was to protect and
uphold the system of slavery it must not impinge on the absolute power of
the master over the slave. His decision is worth quoting at length:

> With slavery . . . the end is the profit of the master, his security and public
> safety; the subject [i.e., the slave], one doomed in his own person, and his pos-
> terity, to live without knowledge, and without the capacity to make anything his
> own, and to toil that another may reap the fruits. . . . Such services can only
> be expected from one who has no will of his own; who surrenders his will in
> implicit obedience to that of another. *Such obedience is the consequence only of
> uncontrolled authority over the body.* There is nothing else which can operate to
> produce the effect. *The power of the master must be absolute to render the submis-
> sion of the slave perfect.*[53]

In *State v Mann*, the common sense of slavery demands account. Slavery
in its day-to-day operations functions according to what Hortense Spillers
has called an "American syntax," which works to concatenate, and thereby

equate, the slave with other sorts of things. In antebellum catalogs of property, "we are stunned by the simultaneity of disparate items in a grammatical series: 'Slave' appears in the same context with beasts of burden, *all* and *any* animal(s), various livestock, and a virtually endless profusion of domestic content from the culinary item to the book."[54] The problem that Ruffin must resolve is that while slaves might be understood as property, they often refuse to act like property. The danger to slavery of such signs of rebellion is not necessarily all-out revolt (the infrequency of events such as Nat Turner's rebellion suggests the success with which U.S. slavery was able to forestall such organized attempts at revolution); rather, such personal rebellion challenges the institution of slavery to recognize its own contradiction. To recognize the free will of the slave would require a recognition of the rights of the slave—and slavery demands the slave have none. Ruffin contemplates how to purge the slave of his or her will, how to render the slave perfectly will-less. But in facing this problem, Ruffin is implicitly acknowledging that the slave indeed possesses a will, a personality, of his or her own. To efface this will, it is necessary to efface the person of the slave. This effacement is effected in Ruffin's decision by the substitution of the slave body for the slave. The uncontrolled authority of the master over the slave's body will produce the appearance that the slave has no will. Ruffin signals the degree of violence—unlimited—necessary to assure the transformation of the person of the slave into property. Such a transformation is first characterized as an effect of the master's unlimited power; the possibility that this effect might be totally superficial or illusory is quickly suppressed in Ruffin's conclusion, that the submission of the slave under these circumstances will be perfect. The trajectory of Ruffin's reasoning reveals the fragility of the syntax of slavery and the conjunction of force and denial necessary to sustain it.

## Property and the Fugitive

The record of the everyday practice of slavery preserved in slave narratives gives eloquent testimony to the importance of slavery's denial of the person-hood of the slave. While the slave-as-slave might be viewed as a thing, the slave-as-person poses intolerable contradictions to a system that recognizes the personality only of those who are legally accorded property in their own person. The success and stability of slavery depended on its power to suppress the tension between person and property embodied in the slave.[55] The fault lines of this tension are revealed with special poignancy in a series of events in Douglass's life that followed as a result of the publication of the *Narrative*. In order to secure his safety, Douglass was forced to consent to his own purchase. Although this transaction and the controversy that ensued are virtually ignored by his major biographers, I will suggest that this commercial transaction exposes the material relations of purchase and escape that Douglass necessarily suppresses in his narrative.[56]

For Douglass, the "self-evidence" of the autobiographical *Narrative* was also self-exposure; the public and published disclosure of his identity put him in danger of recapture by his legal owner. To ensure his safety, Douglass departed for England at the same time his *Narrative* appeared. The danger was not simply hypothetical. His legal owner, Hugh Auld, had vowed to reduce Douglass to slavery once again, as soon as he should return to America. Auld asked $750 for Douglass's freedom. So that Douglass might return unmolested to his wife and family in the United States, his friends raised the money and secured his free papers.

Marion Starling documents the widespread dismay expressed in newspaper editorials throughout New England when news of this transaction became known. "A romantic storm broke loose among the New England abolitionists! Douglass had 'disappointed' them, 'let them down,' 'stumbled,' 'violated one of the fundamental principles of the abolition movement,' by succumbing to that transaction with a slaveholder, recognizing a fellow creature's 'right of property' in him!" (p. 42). The thrust of white objection was that Douglass had legitimated the entire slave system by purchasing his own freedom. The righteously indignant seemed little concerned that the other options for Douglass were permanent exile in England or return to slavery. The presumptuousness of these objections is extraordinary; white abolitionists seemed certain Douglass would not mind living as a symbol for the cause. One such activist opined, "Douglass, while here, may have been in danger, but we think not in much fear. He is a courageous man, and would have been glad of an attempt at recapture, as another arrow in his quiver against the 'abominable institution' from which he had escaped."[57]

The abolitionists' objections reveal the material impossibility of the fugitive where slavery reigns: the system of property demands that one maintain an unambiguous relation to its law of division, wholly on one side or the other. While the fugitive's tale of suffering and escape serves as a crucial rhetorical challenge to slavery's efforts at self-legitimation, the constant threat to the fugitive's *body* makes such a position extremely precarious. Attention to the disposition of the fugitive's body, rather than simply the fugitive's narrative, suggests that the power embedded in the material relations of slavery cannot be underestimated. Slavery can bring enormous force to bear in order to restore the fugitive to his or her proper place, as property. The slave is a commodity-thing, the property of the slave-owner; this is how Ronald Judy defines the term *nigger*. The fugitive, then, is what Judy calls a "bad nigger," "an oxymoron: rebellious property. In rebellion, the bad nigger exhibits an autonomous will, which a nigger as commodity-thing is not allowed to exhibit." [58] As rebellious property, that is, as a commodity-thing that behaves willfully, the fugitive upsets the foundational divide between subject and thing.

For the abolitionists, Douglass's necessary capitulation to Auld's demand for payment is distressing because he has yielded to the tyrants. But from the perspective of the materiality of the fugitive, this act suggests more: by revealing the extent to which the rebellion of the "bad nigger" is unsustainable, Douglass's self-purchase marks the power of the logic of property — the seemingly natural division between subjects who own and things that are owned. The subject's apparent priority and autonomy depends on sustaining and shoring up the division between subject and thing. In order to sustain this division, the necessary price of remaining a fugitive is either capture (and return to slavery) or death; one cannot be recognized, or granted any rights or protections, outside of the system of slavery constituted by property rights. One is owned, or one owns. Douglass becomes a proper subject by taking up a legitimate position in relation to property; that is, by becoming a *propertied* subject — a subject in full possession of himself.

Of course, if we turn to the thinking of the subject in the Western tradition of liberal political philosophy, it appears that the propertied subject is the only kind of subject there is. That is, self-possession is the prerequisite for subjectivity. As C. B. Macpherson has argued, the priority of self-possession to the determination of the rights and obligations of the individual has been a central tenet of modern liberal-democratic theory. [59] And self-possession in turn provides the grounds for every other kind of property. This is the conclusion that John Locke draws in working out the development of the conception of natural right and natural law that informs the American version of "self-evident truths." [60] Locke writes that although God has given the earth to mankind in common, the individual's possession of his own body ensures the right to private or personal property. Because "no Body has any Right" to man's own person, "the Labor of his Body, and the Work of his Hands, we may say, are properly his." Hence, property: "Whatsoever then he removes out of the State that Nature hath provided, and left it in, he hath mixed his Labor with, and joined to it something that is his own, and thereby makes it his Property."[61] Locke's analysis might better be understood as justification than as description; if in principle the subject is the natural source of property, in practice the existence and enforcement of the property rights of certain individuals is what effectively makes them subjects at all.

While the idea of the propertied subject put forth in Locke and those who followed claims universality, its selective application ensures that the ideal of the universal will be mobilized to support the power of some and ensure the exploitation of others. Colette Guillaumin suggests that the interrelation of property and the subject sets the stage for the "racialization" that proceeds from slavery: "whether one was deprived of one's rights or able to exercise them fully depended on one's place in the system of economic relationships. This place was seen in terms of possession of one's self. It was only later that the ability or inability to exercise one's rights came to be explicitly ascribed to 'nature.' "[62] That is, the legal status of the slave, as one who does not own the self and therefore has no rights, slowly becomes ascribed to the nature of the slave, such that blackness itself becomes a sign of the absence of self-possession. Ascribing to the slave a nature that is not exactly equivalent to "human nature" diffuses what Priscilla Wald has called "an important representational threat: human beings to whom *natural* property rights do not extend."[63] The nature of the slave—as one unable to possess property in the self—is thus the ideological glue necessary to paper over the "conventionality of the natural rights through which citizenship and . . . cultural subjectivity is constructed," granted to some and refused to others.[64] Thus, the condition of the slave is no longer ascribed to the enforced state of dependence but rather to the very nature of the slave.

The dependence of the subject on the maintenance of property right in order to sustain the subject's apparent autonomy and self-possession becomes especially evident in Hegel's working through of the links between the ontology of the sovereign, self-possessed subject and the economic relations of property in his *Philosophy of Right*. Property for Hegel is the foundation of sociality; *Philosophy of Right* opens with a discussion of property, from which all other ethical principles derive. What, then, is the role of property in the communal and ethical life of the subject? It is only by appropriating the external world to oneself, Hegel argues, that one transcends one's finite particularity and thus approaches true freedom. In appropriating something outside myself to myself (that is to say, in claiming property), I create an external embodiment of my will.[65] In property, my will has been projected outside my particularity. Having defined property as the externalization of the will, Hegel's argument takes an interesting turn: because my will is embodied in my property, it is in my property that another will recognizes me as a proper subject. Thus, it is only through a relation to property that the subject becomes a subject for another subject. However, there is no property that precedes the subject; property is not external to the subject as that which the subject may appropriate. Rather, because it results from the externalization of the will, this property is the *product* of the subject. That is, the subject appears to be absolutely foundational, the originary and sovereign ground of all else, including property. But note that property in Hegel's formula is also the *source* of subjectivity insofar as it is only through recognition by another subject that the subject becomes subject in the first place. The subject itself cannot be its own grounds of sufficiency; the subject demands both another subject to recognize it and property in which to be recognized. Property and the subject are mutually constitutive and mutually reinforcing. The sovereign subject, it seems, is not so sovereign after all.

If the fugitive is neither property nor subject, then the closed circuit of property and subject is momentarily interrupted or suspended in the disruptive figure of the fugitive. This is why Judy's "bad nigger" is so bad: "The real threat of the bad nigger is in exhibiting the groundlessness of the sovereign individual. Being a nigger appearing as a human, the bad nigger indicates the identification of human with thing, that the human can only be among things, cannot be beyond or abstracted from things."[66] If simply by existing the fugitive threatens to expose the groundlessness of the basic premise of slavery, then perhaps this is the reason for the abolitionists' infatuation with Douglass *as fugitive*: as fugitive (but not as slave-become-man), Douglass counters the apparently exhaustive logic of master and slave. The fugitive exposes the groundlessness of the originating distinction between person and property. The fugitive is neither, but the price of occupying this (non)place between master and slave is silence, invisibility, and placelessness. For the abolitionists, the symbolic value of Douglass is as a *man*, that is, a sovereign subject, who is at the same time another's slave. In this way, Douglass is intended to expose the falsity of the premise that the slave is less than human. Yet these two terms are by definition mutually exclusive. Douglass cannot be both a man and a slave; the two terms can only be held together under the sign of "fugitive" and the immanent threat of violence it entails.

In this light, it is significant that the narrativization of the physical escape from slavery itself is missing from Douglass's narrative. Robert Stepto praises Douglass's narrative for this omission, citing Douglass's criticism of writers who sensationalized escape: "Douglass's tale is spectacularly free from suspicion because he never divulges a detail of his escape to New York. . . . This marvelously rhetorical omission or silence both sophisticates and authenticates his posture as a participant-observer narrator." [67] But Douglass's formulation of both the temptation and the necessary resistance to representing escape suggests that more is at work than simply an effort to be true to his narrative. Douglass informs the reader that he has chosen not to give the details of his escape both to protect those who assisted him and to leave the route open for those who might follow. This necessary omission is costly, both for author and reader: "It would afford me great pleasure indeed, as well as materially add to the interest of my narrative, were I at liberty to gratify a curiosity. . . . But I must deprive myself of this pleasure, and the curious of the gratification which such a statement would afford" (p. 137). There is danger in being a fugitive; but for Douglass, there is also danger in representing fugitivity itself. Douglass rails for two pages against the practice of revealing slaves' means of escape. To represent the fugitive in flight, to reveal the ways and means of escape, is to return him or her to the master: "those open declarations are a positive evil to the slaves remaining. . . . They stimulate [the master] to greater watchfulness, and enhance his power to capture his slave" (p. 138).

The cost of representing the fugitive is recapture, punishment, possibly death. By forgoing the pleasures of this representation, Douglass transfers the slaves' terror to the master: "I would keep the merciless slaveholder profoundly ignorant of the means of flight adopted by the slave. I would leave him to imagine himself surrounded by myriads of invisible tormentors, ever ready to snatch from his infernal grasp his trembling prey. Let him be left to feel his way in the dark . . . and let him feel . . . he is running the frightful risk of having his hot brains dashed out by an invisible agency" (p. 138). If escape is not represented, then escape cannot be seen. Douglass's very refusal renders escape itself invisible and therefore threatening. The security of the slaveholder, and hence the stability of slavery, is undermined by the possibility, not simply of escape, but of an unrepresentable fugitivity that, in its invisibility, leaves the slaveholder ignorant and paranoid.

The invisibility necessary to make a successful escape is repeated in Douglass's description of his own escape. His escape slips through the syntactic gap between two clauses: "On the third day of September, 1838, I left my chains, and succeeded in reaching New York without the slightest interruption of any kind" (p. 143). It is not until the third autobiography, *Life and Times* (1881), that Douglass divulges the details of his escape in order "to satisfy this very natural curiosity." Even there, he equivocates: "But even since the abolition of slavery, I have sometimes thought it well enough to baffle curiosity by saying that while slavery existed there were good reasons for not telling the manner of my escape, and since slavery had ceased to exist there was no reason for telling it." [68] While Douglass seems to suggest that the means of escape have simply become irrelevant, it also appears that according to this formula there are no circumstances under which there exists a reason to represent escape. Such a reticence belies his understating of the significance of the event of escape itself. Would it be too much to speculate that Douglass maintains a certain taboo on the description of escape in a recognition of the power and danger embodied in the fugitive?

In various ways throughout the nineteenth century, slaveholders, abolitionists, and slave historians sought to tame the dangerous fugitive. In his examination of the history of slave historiography, William Van Deburg argues that until Herbert Aptheker's groundbreaking history of slave resistance and revolt was published in 1943, the fugitive was seen as deviant or marginal to slavery in general: "At one point in the evolution of slave stereotypes it was generally conceded that fugitives were atypical slaves. . . . Following the general outline of the planters' perspective, historians hypothesized that while an individual might rebel, such behavior was aberrant and classified as deluded, fanatic, or even childlike." [69] Eugene Genovese estimates that as many as 1,000 slaves escaped to freedom each year in the last decades of slavery. One can only imagine the energies of self-delusion expended on the part of slaveholders to continue to view such acts of refusal as aberrant. But the stakes in continuing to view fugitives as atypical were high; the price of enlightenment would be the collapse of the entire system of justificatory beliefs that helped perpetuate slavery and more generally white supremacy. Put simply, the fugitive challenged the presumptions of black inferiority shared by Southern slaveholders and Northern abolitionists by contradicting their belief that black slaves were in fact well suited to servitude and obedience and that slaves were content with their enslavement.

When one goes beyond the numbers of outright escape, the high incidence of other forms of rebellion makes it abundantly clear that there was nothing aberrant or even unusual about seeking some space of freedom, no matter how small. Fugitive slave narratives gave first-person testimony to the slave's resistance to her or his condition. Anyone who read or listened to these narratives must have been struck by the repeated acts of courage whereby both those who escaped and those who remained asserted their self-claimed right to determine the condition of their own lives. Drawing on the historical record, Genovese documents a variety of practices of slave resistance short of outright revolt: "Those slaves whose disaffection turned into violence and hatred—those who resisted the regime physically—included slaves who made stealing almost a way of life, killed their overseers and masters, fought back against patrollers, burned down plantation buildings, and ran away either to freedom or to the woods for a short while" (p. 597). The record of bravery, strength, and fortitude seems undeniable. Yet, even despite the popularity of fugitive slave narratives and of fugitive slaves themselves as public figures in the North and Britain, the fugitive slave's act of resistance to slavery continued to be represented as exceptional rather than as representative of the desires of all slaves. What abolitionists played up as representative in the fugitive slave's account was the portrayal of slavery itself, which was made to serve the abolitionists' attempts to convince the public that slavery was cruel and immoral.

For abolitionists, the fugitive served more as a symbol of the evils of the slaveholders than as testimony to the human dignity of the enslaved. In these symbolic terms, the fugitive became an extremely popular and ubiquitous figure in popular culture of the day. Marion Starling notes that

> The figure of the fugitive slave, panting in a swamp, with the slave holder brandishing a whip and surrounded by bloodhounds close upon his heels, became so popular as a symbol that dinner plates were made with the scene for a center motif; the handles of silverware were embossed with the story; the ladies of one Massachusetts town embroidered a bed quilt for Garrison of squares covered with drawings and inscriptions "illustrating the cause"; and the fad even extended to the embellishment of transparent window blinds. (p. 29)

However, these images were intended to emphasize, not the heroism and rebellion of the slave, but the ruthlessness of the slave catcher and the helplessness and fear of the fleeing slave. A contemporary newspaper account describes one such image:

> The main picture represents the pursuit and murder of a fugitive from slavery; the hunters with their rifles and broad hats, the blood hound on the scent, the poor trembling MAN hiding behind a rock, make up one group; and in another are seen the planters wiping their artillery, and the hounds retiring satiated with game, while in a stream appears the wounded and dying victim.[70]

The scene dramatizes the absolute power of the master and the absolute helplessness of the slave. It is consistent with the paternal benevolence of the white Northern abolitionists, which only barely concealed their own convictions regarding the natural inferiority of the descendants of slaves in America.[71]

However, the energies of fugitivity far exceed the confines white America would seek to place around the slave or the "Negro." The fugitive undermined the logic that held slavery to be benign and mutually beneficial. After all, if slavery was good for the slave, why were slaves so desperate to escape? At the same time, the fugitive posed a problem for the logic of race itself, which was solidifying even as slavery was becoming more and more unacceptable. Racialist theories insisted on an absolute, immutable difference between the masterful Anglo-Saxon race and the slavish Negro race. The courage, strength, and self-possession of the escaping slave represented a powerful counter instance to such a science. Moreover, the fugitive's refusal to acknowledge the property right of the master risked calling the entire system of property relations into question. No wonder the dominant culture sought to refigure the dangerous fugitive into a moral symbol of the wrongs and evils of slavery.

The escaping slave not only fled cruelty and oppression; she or he also deprived her or his master of a significant asset. Slave property represented a large portion of the total wealth of the slave states. The reported average value of "personal estate" for slave farms in 1860 (primarily slave property) was $19,828.[72] This was of course one of the principal barriers to peacefully ending the institution of slavery; to free the four million slaves held in the South on the eve of the Civil War would have been tantamount, from the slaveholder's perspective, to a loss of some $3 billion in assets.[73] Some masters were willing to allow slaves to purchase their freedom, but few slaves were able to earn the several hundred dollars necessary in their spare "free time."[74] In the decades before 1860, the average price of slaves never fell below $200, and sometimes rose as high as $800. The price of a prime field hand could be considerably higher.[75]

Both the significant monetary value of the slave and the division of the law of property were at play in the popular expression among slaves for escape, "stealing oneself." *Stealing* here exhibits a strange transitivity. Leaving in secret, without the master's knowledge or permission, the fugitive steals away, an action without syntactical object. But as property, this removal is simultaneously theft: the fugitive steals himself, subject and object of an action that aims at the removal of this very duality. Both the agent and the object of this theft inhabit the same body; and in this the enslaved risked capture, severe punishment, even death. In the real, corporeal danger of flight, the enslaved risks the body to regain the body, to rejoin person and property into one subject.

In stealing him- or herself, the fugitive has violated the law of property, has become an outlaw. But because it is the law of property that has granted to some property in their person and relegated others to the status of property simple, the fugitive's attempt to restore person to property is paradoxically a *violation* of the law (stealing) that requires for its success the *sanction* of the law (recognition of the fugitive as subject, that is, as one having property in himself). Thus, the fugitive cannot simply transform slavery under the law into freedom under the law. It is only by remaining outside the law that the fugitive escapes the status of (human) property; in flight, the fugitive is no longer property for another, but neither does he or she become property in him- or herself. That one might exist as neither subject nor property belies the foundational status of the "natural right" of property.

But the one who exists as fugitive never exists as subject; as outlaw, the fugitive is not subject to the law nor recognized as subject by the law. To represent the fugitive outside the law is also, then, to expose the law to its own outside. What is the relation between the subject and this outside? Judith Butler suggests that "the subject is constituted through an exclusion and differentiation, perhaps a repression, that is subsequently concealed, covered over, by the effect of autonomy. In this sense, autonomy is the logical consequence of a disavowed dependency." [76] Thus, it is not only the subject's dependence on property that disrupts its own autonomy (as I suggested in relation to Hegel's *Philosophy of Right*). If the law of property marks the boundaries of the excluded space of the fugitive, it also determines this space of the fugitive as being constituted by the disavowed operation of exclusion that establishes the apparent autonomy of the subject. That is, it is the law of property that guarantees the self-possession of the subject and hence the subject's "natural right" to the possession of objects. Object and subject are established in their complementary difference by this law. The emergence of fugitivity outside the opposition of subject and thing reveals a more originary dependence whereby the very possibility of subject and object is established through the disavowed exclusion of another other, marked by the fleeting figure of the fugitive.

Although I have been using the arguments of philosophers such as Locke and Hegel to examine the logic whereby the subject appears to be naturally autonomous and self-possessed, I do not want to leave the impression that it is the "Idea" (of property or the subject) itself, in some abstract universal sense, that accounts for the history of violence and domination institutionalized in slavery. Rather, the framework of slavery in which the relation between property and the subject becomes socially meaningful demands that we recognize that this subject is always a historically and materially situated subject, emerging out of and in terms given by the social relations it appears to precede. The cultural context of slavery is "already there as the disarticulated process of that subject's production, one that is concealed by the frame that would situate a ready-made subject in an external web of cultural relations." [77] The appearance of the fugitive, however precarious, breaks open this frame, exposing slavery and its attendant racialization to their own outside, even as the policing mechanisms of slavery bring pressure to bear on the fugitive to return to the proper position of property. Outside of slavery, neither self-possessed nor simply property, the fugitive cannot be recognized as a political subject and therefore can never be free so long as he or she remains fugitive. But the existence of the fugitive as something else, a kind of singularity, reveals that the freedom of the politically recognized subject is a freedom conditioned and determined to be in accordance with the being of such a subject. If this subject is not simply given (by "God" or by "Nature") but is a socially achieved effect, then the freedom of this subject cannot be the only possible freedom. And insofar as the figure of the fugitive points to a space beyond or outside this subject, it is in fugitivity that we may find the glimmerings of another thought of freedom.

## Henry Bibb's Escape

As I have argued, Douglass suppresses the disruptive force of escape in his *Narrative* and instead mounts a head-on assault on the fixity of the categories of master and slave. But the success of his tactic comes at the cost of reinscribing the principles of property and the proper (in his own self-mastery) that make master and slave appear to be natural and inevitable in the first place. The thematization of escape in a narrative such as the *Narrative of the Life and Adventures of Henry Bibb, an American Slave, Written by Himself* (1849) takes a different approach to the relation between slavery, freedom, and subjectivity by collapsing the distinction Douglass works so hard to erect and sustain between the form of slavery (in terms of his body) and the fact of slavery (in terms of his mind or his will).[78] The refusal in Bibb's narrative of any distinction between form and fact sidesteps the questions of authentic subjectivity raised by Douglass. Bibb's emphasis on escape *as* escape shifts the focus to the material relations of force and value at the heart of slavery.

In Bibb's narrative, the slave's power derives not from realizing his own humanity or throwing off ignorance and slavishness but from a consummation of the institutional logic of slavery. Bibb does not resist being defined as property in order to assert his own personhood, as does Douglass. Instead, he sinks into his property-ness: he becomes the property that slavery says he is. As property, he is able to manipulate his circumstances, and eventually escape, by manipulating his *value*. Bibb escapes slavery in part because he realizes (that is, he both understands and enacts) the power of the slave as it derives from the slave's property-ness. Freedom for Bibb lies, not in transcending the body, but in resolutely inhabiting and exploiting the very physicality of slavery. For Douglass, the wrongness of slavery derives from its denial of the essence of man in the slave. For Bibb, there are no essences, only circumstances—and it is through a manipulation of circumstances that freedom may be attained.

The narrative of Henry Bibb is the story of one who is "notorious for running away, even from . . . boyhood" (p. 118). He describes his childhood as an apprenticeship for escape: "Among other good trades I learned the art of running away to perfection. I made a regular business of it, and never gave it up, until I had broken the bands of slavery, and landed myself safely in Canada" (p. 65). His first flight is inspired by the failure of conjuring remedies such as secret powders to relieve him of his master's cruelty. Unable to attain relief through magic, "I was then convinced that running away was the most effectual way by which a slave could escape cruel punishment" (p. 71). The foregrounding of physical escape from the beginning in Bibb's narrative marks the distance from Douglass's narrative, in which

freedom depends on nonphysical forces, most importantly the supernatural (a magic root provided by the slave named Sandy that seems to protect
him from an expected whipping) and the metaphysical (becoming a man
in the struggle with Covey). Because Douglass suppresses the episode of
escape, it appears that the physical aspect of freedom is almost incidental.
In contrast, Bibb understands freedom only in terms of his body.

Throughout, the narrative is punctuated by comical images, sly asides
by the narrator, and a constantly mocking tone toward the slave owners.
Much of the humor, as well as the narrative motion, derives from Bibb's relation to slavery, which is not to confront it directly or to struggle against
it but to sink into it by fully realizing himself as property. Bibb works the
system, negotiating what Houston Baker calls the "economics of slavery"
with style and eventual success. But the terms of this negotiation pose a significant counter instance to the commercial negotiations Baker locates in
certain narratives, which provide the conditions for the "ironic transformation of property by property into humanity." [79] Baker argues, for example,
that Olaudah Equiano gains his freedom because he recognizes and takes
advantage of the significance of property: "He realizes, in effect, that only
the acquisition of property will enable him to alter his designated status *as
property*." [80] Equiano's plan for freedom is based on a mastery of the very
economy that has designated him as property; while he continues to be
designated as property, he acts as mercantile capitalist, engaging in various
trades and schemes to raise money to buy himself. His designation as property in this reading is purely nominal; he is in fact able to realize himself as
a propertied self prior to and in order to free himself from this designation.
Bibb, in contrast, does not manipulate property from the position of a propertied subject. Instead, he manipulates property by *being* property. Rather
than struggling against the law to insist on his humanness, Bibb satisfies
the law's premise that the slave has no human essence, that the slave is only
and purely property. This law that defines the slave as property aims to assure and enforce order; but Bibb exposes the futility of this aim by using
the terms of the law to provoke the very disorder the law struggles to prevent. The law separating person (master) from property (slave) is intended
to assure the stability and order of slavery and the absolute subservience of
slave to master; but, for Bibb, assenting to the principle of the law results
in the total contravention of its intent—escape rather than servitude.

Bibb's chronicle is marked by a persistent tension between two narrative
lines. The macronarrative is the conventional linear account of a growing

desire for freedom followed eventually by an escape to Canada. This narrative line is structured around the absolute opposition of the terms *slave* and *free*. Like Douglass's, it is a story of transformation, *from* slave *to* free. Slavery, then, is the narrative precondition of freedom, and freedom is the teleological outcome of the development from slavery. But this macronarrative is displaced by a recurrent, irrepressible micronarrative, a circular repetition of perpetual escape that evades the absolute opposition of the poles of slave and free. This perpetual escape does not move in a singular developmental line. Escaping evades slavery without leaving it behind, creates a free space without ever realizing freedom. For this reason, "Canada" and "freedom" are less objectives than totemic presences in the text, repeatedly invoked but seldom directly relevant to the action at hand. Bibb acts in the name of "Canada," that is, the goal of true freedom, but the action of escape is driven by its own internal logic. Thus, escape is momentarily wrenched out of the teleology of freedom that drives the overall structure of slave narrative. Where escape in Douglass is subordinated to becoming a man or becoming a free man, escape in Bibb stands alone, as an end in and of itself.

Bibb's propensity to run away at every possible opportunity, even when there was no hope of escape, was shared by many in similar circumstances who found the day-to-day degradations of enslavement unbearable. Eugene Genovese goes so far as to postulate a "type," the habitual runaway: "This type appeared everywhere and made a practice of leaving for periodic vacations in the woods and then returning to take his punishment, apparently regarding the one as well worth the price of the other" (p. 650). In Bibb's own day, slaveholders did not view these habitual runaways quite so benignly. Southern physician Samuel A. Cartwright, reviewing the large number of cases of slave runaways, concluded that the cause was somatic: a condition peculiar to the "Negro" race, which he called "drapetomania," characterized by an irresistible compulsion to run away from home.[81] Drapetomania was a curious condition, in which the symptom (running away) was completely equivalent to the disease and which would be entirely relieved, one surmises, by the decidedly nonmedical cure of emancipation. Moreover, one can only marvel at Cartwright's assumption that a normal slave should enjoy her or his enslavement (although of course this was an assumption widely shared in the antebellum South). Nevertheless, the need to invent a pathology to account for the running away of slaves points to how widespread and disruptive such running away must have been. In Bibb's case, his notoriety as an incurable runaway serves him well. Although he is powerless to prevent the cruelties and caprices of the slaveholders and does not have the resources to secure his freedom, he is able to manipulate the slaveholders with the only thing he has against them: his own body.

An early episode sets up a pattern repeated several times in the narrative, in which the freedom of the slaveholders to dispose of their property is compromised by Bibb's manipulation of his body. At the age of twenty, Bibb marries a woman named Malinda, a slave who lives a few miles distant. A few months after Bibb's marriage, Bibb's master sells his farm with the intent to move to Missouri. Rather than take Bibb with him and risk his running away to rejoin his wife, the master resolves to sell Bibb to his brother who lives in the vicinity of Malinda's master. Bibb does not much like his new situation: "[The new master] proved to be oppressive, and so unreasonable in punishing his victims, that I soon found that I should have to run away in self-defense. But he soon began to take the hint, and sold me to Wm. Gatewood, the owner of Malinda" (p. 80). The new master protects his investment by selling Bibb — precisely the effect Bibb aimed to produce by threatening to run away. It is not by resisting being defined as property but rather by taking full advantage of the fact that his only source of power is his propertied value that Bibb avoids being involuntarily separated from his family.

Bibb determines a few months later to make a break for Canada and freedom and after a tortuous journey arrives safely in Perrysburgh, Ohio. Hoping to rescue his wife but running low on funds, he tries to raise money by subscription. Two of the friends who offer to help him turn out to be traitors who inform his master of his location. He finds himself returning to Kentucky, not as a fugitive but as a captured slave. Along the way, he discovers he is to be sold to pay the expenses of his capture and reward. Although he is inwardly dismayed, he determines to make the best of it: "I knew then the only alternative left for me to extricate myself was to use deception, which is the most effective defense a slave can use. I pretended to be satisfied for the purpose of getting an opportunity of giving them the slip" (p. 95). His seeming cooperation persuades his captors to neither chain nor handcuff him because his value in the slave market would be reduced if it were known he had tried to run away. Bibb watches constantly for an opportunity for escape and finally gets his chance when his guard gets sick and has to go to the public horse stable to relieve himself: "At this time a thousand thoughts were flashing through my mind with regard to the propriety of trying the springs of my heels, which nature had so well adapted for taking the body out of danger, even in the most extraordinary emergencies. . . . I nerved myself with all the moral courage I could command and bolted for the door. . . . Dan was left in the stable to make ready for the race, or jump out into the street half dressed, and thereby disgrace himself before the public eye" (p. 97).

A high-speed chase through the streets of Louisville ensues; Bibb's only thought is to save himself from being recaptured. The will to escape is more than a desire or a wish; with Bibb, it has all the force of an instinctual drive: "My heart was gladdened to know there was another chance for my escape. No bird ever let out of a cage felt more like flying, than I felt like running" (p. 99). The analogy is instructive: *bird* is to *fly* as *Bibb* is to *run*. The flight of the bird let out of a cage is not only the flight of freedom after being trapped. More profoundly, the flight of the bird is an expression of its "bird-ness," and part of the cruelty of caging a bird is that the bird is thus prevented from flight itself. When Bibb compares his urge to run with the bird's urge to fly, running becomes more than a contingent response to a dangerous situation. In this moment, "Bibb-ness" is expressed as running itself.

Such episodes suggest that Bibb's narrative is less about Bibb-the-subject than it is about Bibb-as-escape. Taking into account the literary and political conditions for the contemporary interest in slave narrative as autobiography that I discussed in the first part of this chapter, one might conclude that it is this narrative failure to represent the proper subject of autobiography that explains why Bibb's narrative has been repeatedly dismissed as primitive or inauthentic. Most frequently, it has been charged that Bibb as author does not control or determine his own narrative; as James Olney puts is, "though actually written by Bibb, the narrative, for style and tone, might as well have been the product of the pen of [white editor] Lucius Matlack."[82] Robert Stepto views this failure in specifically political terms: "Bibb's tale proves that he has acquired a voice, but his narrative shows that his voice does not yet control the imaginative forms which his personal history assumes in print."[83] In both cases, it appears that the critical standard for evaluation assumes the priority of the autonomous, authentic subject, implicitly the classical subject of autobiography.

Such critics as Olney and Stepto judge Bibb's narrative inferior (aesthetically and politically) because Bibb's voice is never truly realized. But might we not reinterpret Bibb's seeming authorial failure as a successful and strategic *refusal* of the centrality of the self-contained, authentic subject deemed essential to the slave narratorial project? That is, the absence of subjective depth or authenticity in Bibb's text is a narrative failure only insofar as one has presupposed that the only legitimate object of the slave narrative is to demonstrate the humanity of the slave or to give the slave an authentic and self-possessed voice from within the terms of the liberal American polity. But as I have suggested, this political project is inherently limited by its presupposition of the natural status of the subject; this subject is necessarily a subject of slavery or a subject of freedom, mastered by another or mastered by the self. Bibb's narrative challenges the priority or necessity of such a subject, and of the political and economic relations it presupposes, by refusing to equate freedom with becoming a subject. Instead, Bibb's narrative gestures toward the outside of the subject not as a place or as an alternative subject-position, but as the state of escape itself.

It is escape, not truth, voice, or authenticity, that drives Bibb's narrative from beginning to end. Bibb's self is effectively abandoned to escape; there is no effort to establish or preserve any consistent sense of self beyond escape. Bibb constantly reinvents himself in order to improve his chances. Hence, it is not surprising that his most important weapon in the ongoing battle for freedom is dissimulation. He attributes his skill in running away to a talent for deception, "the only weapon of self defense that I could use successfully" (p. 66). For example, one of Bibb's strategies for escaping was to carry a bridle with him. "If anyone should see me in the woods, as they have, and asked 'what are you doing here sir? you are a runaway?' — I said, 'no, sir, I am looking for our old mare.' . . . For such excuses I was let pass" (p. 66). Bibb is especially skilled at fooling his captors and jailers into believing he is docile and cooperative, pretending "to be satisfied for the purpose of getting an opportunity of giving them the slip" (p. 95). Charles Nichols compares a slave narrator such as Bibb to the picaro character of classical Spanish literature: "Like a trapped animal, the picaro is alert to every possible avenue of escape. . . . He survives by stratagems; a trickster, he adopts protean roles — stage presences." [84] Bibb is a blank form, prepared to assume any shape in order to slip through the net of his captors. He does not dissimulate to hide the truth; rather, the only truth of Bibb is that which he becomes in dissimulation.

In Bibb's final escape, dissimulation comes together with the manipulation of his body-as-value in a brilliant scheme of collusion between owner

and property. After a series of escapades and attempted escapes that result in his changing hands several times, Bibb is finally sold to a group of
"Southern sportsmen" who purchase him "at a reduced price for specu-
lation" (p. 136), that is, they intend not to keep him as slave but to sell
him again quickly at a gain. These purchasers have no interest in mastery,
only in profit. To improve their own prospects in this regard, they make
a deal with Bibb: if he can persuade someone to buy him, they will give
him a portion of the proceeds and give him directions to escape to Canada.
Bibb's own interests now coincide with those of his owners; both seek to
increase his apparent value as a slave in order to increase their own gain.
By acceding to his value as property and allowing himself to be sold rather
than attempting to escape from these speculators, Bibb has the chance to
get *both* money and freedom. His buyers advise him how to behave so as
to secure the best deal: "They advised me to act very stupid in language
and thought, but in business I must be spry; and that I must persuade
men to buy me, and promise them that I would be smart" (p. 139). Thus,
by manipulating his body and his demeanor, Bibb becomes whatever he
needs to be to improve his chances. Opportunity comes when a Cherokee
Indian chief indicates interest in Bibb. Perceiving that this master offers
the most promising opportunity for escape, Bibb persuades him to make
the purchase. The speculators are good to their word and hand over "a part
of the money, and directions how to get from there to Canada" (p. 140).

What are we to make of the collusion of black slave and white profiteer
in attempting to cheat the Indian at the conclusion of this story? This is the
final escape in Bibb's narrative; he realizes his dream of getting to Canada
and can at last call himself a free man. In every other escape attempt, Bibb's
eventual capture protected the slaveholder's investment. It is only when
the Indian chief is dispossessed of his legal property that Bibb becomes a
free subject. Thus, it appears that it is the dispossession specifically of the
Indian that makes the position of self-possessed subject available to Bibb.
Bibb's final escape marks the differential power of property right: Bibb becomes a subject not by dispossessing the white man, whose property claim
appears as absolute and inviolable, but by dispossessing the Indian whose
property right proves to be historically contingent on the white man's whim
backed up by virtually unlimited force.

Thus, the circumstances of Bibb's final escape reinforce the differential application of "natural right" along racial lines. But at the same time,
by successfully arriving in Canada, Bibb has made some claim to his own

subjective sovereignty. Obviously, in relation to the legal system, Bibb's self-possession is continually at risk. But the very claim to self-possession suggests that he has, however precariously, crossed over the line from property to subject. The emergence of an Indian as Bibb's final master and Bibb's ultimate claim of self-possession complicate the current tendency to consider both black and native populations as simply dispossessed in relation to propertied whiteness in nineteenth-century America.[85] The shifting positions of white, Indian, and slave in relation to property at the end of Bibb's narrative suggest some possibility for slippage in the mapping of race onto subjectivity as determined in relation to (self-) ownership. But at the same time, the conclusion of the narrative reinscribes the centrality of property itself to the determination of subjectivity. In the context of slavery, this is a necessary and indeed desirable conclusion; after all, it is only within the prior terms of the law that freedom can be subjectively meaningful, no matter how circumscribed. The teleological structure of Bibb's narrative at the macrolevel supports the impression that this is the only possible freedom; but I have tried to suggest in foregrounding the theme of escape that this freedom, the freedom of the propertied subject, necessarily forecloses those elements that would interrupt the equation of subject with (self-)possession and object with property.

## Fugitivity and the Enclosed Outside: Henry Brown's Box

Bibb's narrative, I have argued, is less about the ultimate freedom with which it concludes than it is about the intermediate condition of escape. The displacement of end (freedom) by means (escape) is even more evident in two extremely popular slave narratives published in the two decades before the Civil War. The narratives of Henry "Box" Brown (1849, 1852) and William and Ellen Craft (1860) are concerned almost exclusively with telling the story of a thrilling escape from slavery. Douglass, one surmises, would not have approved. In both these cases, the public interest was piqued by sensational and surprising means of escape: Brown nailed up in a box and mailed to freedom, the Crafts in the disguise of an invalid white man (light-skinned Ellen passing as both white and male) and his servant. These fugitive slaves were popular celebrities. In their public appearances, Henry Brown and William and Ellen Craft both recounted and reenacted the circumstances of their escape. William and Ellen Craft often appeared at abolitionist meetings in the disguises they had assumed for their escape. In fact, the Crafts were hardly recognizable to their fans without their disguises; the frontispiece of their published narrative shows Ellen in her "white master" garb. The powerful identification of the Crafts with their means of escape continues today: in Davis and Gates's *The Slave's Narrative*, the portrait of Ellen disguised as a man is identified as being a likeness of *William* Craft. Similarly, Brown's public appearance was intimately bound up with the box that made him famous. Starling recounts one episode that occurred while Brown was touring England: "A box was made at Bradford to the specifications given in Brown's narrative, Brown was nailed inside it exactly as he had been in Richmond, and he was carried from Bradford to Leeds, a trip of two and three-quarters hours, preceded by a band of music and banners!" (p. 241). It is not Brown the man who appears in this parade but rather Brown disappeared inside the box. In the parade, Brown effectively *is* the box. Brown's appearance in this parade is interesting to me insofar as it seems to repeat the displacement of the biographical subject that Bibb effects in his own narrative. If the box covers over or substitutes for Brown himself, then the appearance of Brown in the box displaces the representation of Brown the subject in the act of escaping with an image of escape itself. As I will discuss at greater length later, this is precisely the shift enacted in Brown's narrative.

Like Henry Bibb, the Crafts escaped by dissimulation, manipulating their bodies and demeanor to maximize their chances for escape.[86] Brown's case is slightly different, involving the withdrawal of his body into an enclosed space, the box, in which he is conveyed to safety. A similarly enclosed space plays a central role in yet another slave narrative, one perhaps more widely celebrated today than any other except Douglass's: Harriet Jacobs's *Incidents in the Life of a Slave Girl*. While Brown spent 27 hours traveling from slavery to freedom nailed up in a box, Jacobs spent seven years living in a tiny garret to escape the sexual advances of her owner. In both cases, the space marked out by the box or the garret is a peculiar space in relation to slavery, neither fully within slavery nor fully outside it. Brown in his box and Jacobs in her garret provide two alternative figures of fugitivity who foreground the *geography* of slavery and freedom by playing on spaces of inclusion and exclusion. Where I read Bibb as a figure of fugitivity who challenges the exclusive identities of subject and object by embodying escape itself, the containers that intervene in the escapes of Brown and Jacobs suggest yet another way in which the figuring of escape in slave narrative undermines the oppositions that structure slavery. As they withdraw into the enclosed spaces that allow for their escape, they are out of the reach of slavery and so no longer property, but neither are they propertied subjects.

The box and the garret are "elsewheres" where the stability of the separation and interdependence between property and subject breaks down. What is the relation of this elsewhere that allows for escape to the freedom that is the ultimate aim of escape? The freedom that is recognized and protected by the state is always the freedom of the self-possessed subject; such a subject cannot exist in this elsewhere. Therefore, Brown's and Jacobs's freedom is necessarily realized only by leaving these spaces. Yet the fact that they expose the possibility of this excluded and invisible elsewhere reopens the question of freedom itself. In these excluded and constrained spaces, Brown and Jacobs do not register as proper subjects; therefore, the question arises, what would freedom be absent this subject? These narratives may not be able to answer such a question, engaged as they are in the practical matter of emancipation within the terms of the subject. And yet they cannot help but raise this question, insofar as the very possibility of this elsewhere reveals the artificiality of the limits and conditions whereby the propertied subject appears as natural and neutral.

Brown's narrative is an example of one that critics such as James Olney would like to dismiss from literary consideration as entirely inauthentic. In its first edition, the narrative does not try to conceal the fact that Brown is not its author. It was published in 1849 under the descriptive and explanatory title *The Narrative of Henry Box Brown, Who Escaped from Slavery Enclosed in a Box Three Feet Long, Two Feet Wide, and Two-and-a Half Feet High, Written from a Statement of Facts Made by Himself. With Remarks upon the Remedy for Slavery. By Charles Stearns.* Olney singles Brown's narrative out for examination as one extreme of the spectrum of possible relationships between sponsor and narrator. Olney insists that in the case of Brown's narrative, we cannot consider Brown to be the author in any meaningful sense because "the preface and narrative are both clearly in the manner of Charles Stearns." [87] As a result, Olney concludes, "it may be that Box Brown's story was told from 'a statement of facts made by himself,' but after those facts have been dressed up in the exotic rhetorical garments provided by Charles Stearns there is precious little of Box Brown (other than the representation of the box itself) that remains in the narrative" (p. 161). It is interesting that Olney finds the only true representation of Brown in his narrative to be the sketch of the box that is appended. The image of the box takes the place of the image of Brown that would be represented by the conventional portrait found at the beginning of most slave narratives. The substitution of the means of escape for the one escaping, which I remarked in the case of the appearance of Ellen Craft in disguise at the front of the Crafts' narrative, is even more pronounced in the case of Brown. As I suggested earlier regarding the parade of Brown's box through the streets, the box is not simply the container that hides or transports Brown; rather, in each instance of its appearance, the box metonymically becomes Brown.

One is most forcefully struck by the ubiquity of this box standing in the place of Brown. Even his name incorporates the box, such that the man is literally synonymous with the means of his escape. It was not unusual for escaped slaves to take new names once they reached free states. The pervasiveness of slave catchers and bounty hunters made a change in identity prudent. And as both Frederick Douglass and William Wells Brown note in their narratives, a new name was the symbol of a new life. Slaves were most often known by the surname of their masters; the taking of one's own surname was thus the assertion that one was one's own master. Henry Brown's narrative contains no reference to his name either before or after his escape; but his narrative was published as the narrative of "Henry Box Brown." Thus, Henry Brown's new name is unusual in two respects: he retains his surname and takes another first name, and his new name symbolizes, not freedom, but the moment of escape.

A second edition of Brown's narrative appeared in 1852, this one titled *Narrative of the Life of Henry Box Brown, Written by Himself*. In this revision, the episode of escape in the box is even more prominent than in the first edition, emphasizing the extent to which Brown's story increasingly becomes the story of the box. Further bearing out the increasing weight placed on the box is the replacement of a flowery hymn of thanksgiving in the first edition with a popular-style song (sung to the tune of "Old Ned"), which Brown claims to have written to commemorate his escape. The song is in the form of a ballad, recounting the various stages of his journey in the box, and the chorus reads,

> Brown laid down the shovel and the hoe,
> Down in the box he did go.
> No more slave work Henry Box Brown,
> In the box by Express he did go.

Brown recounts in his narrative how, after his wife and children are sold to a slave trader, he resolves to gain his own liberty.[88] While praying fervently to God for help, Brown receives an inspiration: "suddenly, the idea flashed across my mind of shutting myself *up in a box*, and getting myself conveyed as dry goods to a free state."[89] A friend assents to accompany Brown's box to Philadelphia in order to be sure the box is kept upright and Brown does not suffocate. Brown describes the box he had made for the occasion:

> The box which I had procured was three feet one inch long, two feet six inches high, and two feet wide. On the morning of the 29th day of March, 1839, I went into the box—having previously bored three gimlet holes for air opposite my face and having provided myself with a bladder of water, both for the purpose of quenching my thirst and for wetting my face should I feel myself getting faint. . . . Being thus equipped for the battle of liberty, my friends nailed down the lid and had me conveyed to the Express Office. (p. 53)

Part of the thrill of this story is this image of being buried alive, nailed into a coffinlike box for what Brown describes as an excruciating 27-hour ordeal. Indeed, Brown plays on this imagery, equating the living death of his journey with the living death of slavery for all those enslaved. When his box arrives at its destination, his friends break open the box; "then," Brown says, "came my resurrection from the grave of slavery" (p. 57).

The simple narrative of death and resurrection is complicated, however, by the intervention of the box. Despite the resonance of box and coffin in this story, the box is in fact nothing like a coffin: its dimensions prohibit the laying out of the dead; instead Brown must curl up, knees to chest, to fit into its 3' × 2' × 2' space. This fetal position suggests that the box is also like a womb, in which Brown will slowly incubate into a free man. Through its various referents, the box successively reconstitutes Brown as corpse, as fetus, as first man.[90] However, the box is neither coffin nor womb but shipping crate. Brown is a peculiar cargo, not yet man, no longer slave, but something else. There is not a name or a category to represent Brown in this liminal space. Flight itself, as mediated by the box, removes Brown from the economy of mastery and slavery. Withdrawn from this economy, yet nonetheless in circulation, Brown's body becomes a substance that troubles the smooth circulation of persons and properties.

Brown plays on the confusion between sensible man and insensible object in his box: "Perceiving my box, standing on end, [a man] threw it down and then the two sat upon it. . . . I could now listen to the men talking and heard one of them asking the other what he supposed *the box contained*. His companion replied he guessed it was 'the mail.' I too thought it was a mail, but not such a mail as he supposed it to be" (p. 55). Brown's pun marks the way in which the introduction of *a male* is simultaneously a disruption of *the mail*. These observers little expect the mail to contain human cargo. Indeed, could there be any such suspicion Brown's escape would be blocked.

Brown's presence in the mail is disruptive, not only because he is using the mail to escape, but because as he shifts between subject and object of the postal system he troubles the status of the "postal subject."[91] The mail appears as a neutral technology of communication between subjects presumed to exist prior to their entry into the circuit of communication. But the subject is as much product as origin of this communication. Especially in the case of letters, the idea of a unique, private, original correspondence posits the biographical subject as its source in much the same way that a literary text is understood to point to an author, an individualized figure who is outside of and prior to the text. In this sense, the modern mail is like autobiography: a technology of subjectivity. It is also a technology of property. Bernhard Siegert argues that, beginning in the late eighteenth century, letters began to be understood as private correspondences expressing the personal thoughts and feelings, the "truth of the heart," of the sender: "words had an individual origin in thought. . . . Words were metaphors for ideas formed by the soul—every self thus became the subject of its own discourse a priori. Words were now the subject's private property: the pre-condition necessary for the existence of private letters."[92] The subject is presumed to precede this expression; what circulates in the mail is a representation that is the property of the subject, not the subject itself. Accordingly, the subject is understood to stand outside of and prior to the circulation of the mail.

But Brown's circulation in the mail is not as the product or the property of a prior subject. Brown, simultaneously agent and object of the act of mailing himself to freedom, disturbs the relation of prior, autonomous subject and property that is supposedly reflected in the system of the post. Brown can be delivered as subject only as a result of being sent through the mail; Brown's subjectivity depends on becoming the very mail that is supposed merely to represent the truth of a prior subject. Thus, where the subject is presumed to precede and stand apart from the mail, Brown's ultimate emergence as subject radically upends this relation. Brown is not an autonomous subject of the post; rather, he becomes a subject through the post. While Brown's delivery as a free man at the end of his journey affirms the postal logic of the subject by revealing an autonomous subject at the mail's terminus, his presence *as the mail* exposes the extent to which this subject is a product, rather than a precondition, of such subjectivizing technologies as the post.

The troubled and troubling status of Brown in the box continues throughout the journey to mark the space of the box as one difficult to locate or characterize in the terms of property, slavery, or subjectivity. Midway in the journey, Brown's box is transferred from a steamboat to a train:

> When the driver arrived at the depot, I heard him call for some person to help take the box off the wagon and some one answered him to the effect that he might throw it off. But, says the driver, "it is marked 'this side up with care.' So if I throw it off I might break something." The other answers him that it did not matter if he broke all that was in it; the railway company was able enough to pay for it. No sooner were these words spoken than I began to tumble from the wagon, and, falling on the end where my head was, I could hear my neck give a crack, as if it had been snapped asunder, and I was knocked completely insensible. (p. 55)

Brown is clear that something has indeed been broken by the rail workers' careless treatment of the box. The loss caused by such negligence, however, is not exactly the damaged goods that the workers anticipate. The damage to Brown's body results in the loss of consciousness, a literalized break with the past. Can the rail company hope to pay for what has here been lost? One might speculate that if the rail company had been responsible for damage to a slave, the slave's owner would be entitled to compensation for property damaged or lost. But what is in the box? Brown is no longer a slave, the property of another; yet neither is he a man who might sue the company in his own right for injuries sustained under their liability. The contents of the box at this moment is a blank, a consciousness "completely insensible."

If Brown has in the course of his journey become completely insensible, then we might say that there is no one, in the sense of a conscious being, in the box. While he is no longer a slave, as a fugitive in the box he cannot be a subject. There is barely room for his body in the box; the box is the smallest space in which his body may persist as body while at the same time being excluded from the regularized spaces of society. When his box arrives in Philadelphia, the friends who receive it are uncertain whether they will find their cargo alive or dead. Brown recalls, "I heard a man say, 'let us rap upon the box and see if he is alive,' and immediately a rap ensued and a voice said, tremblingly, 'Is all right within?' To which I replied,

'all right'" (p. 56). The phrasing of the question of Brown's status is peculiar, insofar as it is not addressed to Brown, the only one who might be able
to answer. If Brown were to suddenly burst through the door, rather than
arriving ensconced in a box, one might imagine the question to be "are you
all right?" But the interposition of the box unhinges the relation of identity
between Brown, Brown's well-being, and the contents of the box. Brown is
split between the one who answers, in effect, "yes, all is right within" and
the one who is "all right."

Perhaps it might be more accurate to say that Brown is fractured or
shattered by the box. By "shattering," I mean to suggest that the intervention of the box does not produce or reveal the "split subject" conventionally
described as the dialectical splitting internal to a self-conscious subjectivity (in a Hegelian or Lacanian sense), that is, the splitting of subjectivity
constitutive of subjectivity itself. Rather, this apparent splitting is of a particular sort, symptomatic of the status of the fugitive or of the space of the
box as outside the order of master and slave: there is no one to whom to address a question, no subject, insofar as subjectivity is assigned and ordered
by the categories of master and slave, to hear or to respond. Hence, the impossibility of addressing the question of well-being to its object.

The suspension of subject and object, of sensate man or insensate matter, is resolved in Brown's response, "all right." Not only is he all right,
having survived his ordeal, but all is made right in his simultaneous return
to the social order: his friends break open the box on hearing his voice,
and he "rose a free man." Emerging from the box, Brown is not only "res-
urrecting from the grave of slavery," he is equally returning to the realm
of subjectivity. What he is in the box is unclear and ambiguous; what he
is when he emerges from the box is unequivocal: a free man. The box is a
space outside, extruded by and excluded from the space of the social. Yet it
is only from the perspective of the box that one recognizes the limits of subjectivity marked out by the relation of slavery. The box is a bounded space
that, by being excluded from it, marks the constructedness and boundedness of the space of the social and the subject, which would otherwise
appear simply as neutral, natural, and static. When Brown rises from the
box a "free man," he reenacts the teleology of freedom that structures the
narratives of Douglass and Bibb. But the appearance of Brown *in the box*
remains puzzling. In the box, he is not a subject, nor is he free, and yet he is
somehow escaped from slavery. Brown's fugitivity is not the same thing as
freedom, and yet it bears some relation to freedom. There where there is no

subject, can there be freedom? And what sort of freedom would it be? The possibility of freedom, and the relation of freedom to fugitivity, is a central concern in the last slave narrative I want to consider, that of Harriet Jacobs.

## Harriet Jacobs's Loophole

Harriet Jacobs's *Incidents in the Life of a Slave Girl, Written by Herself* (1861) now holds pride of place as perhaps the most widely read piece of nineteenth-century American literature written by a woman. Since speculations that it was in fact a sentimental novel written by white abolitionist Lydia Maria Child were finally put to rest by Jean Yellin's publication of Jacobs's newly discovered correspondence in 1981, readers have viewed the narrative as exemplifying a specifically textual strategy of resistance and subversion that creates a powerful voice for the black woman from within the discursive constraints that have rendered her invisible. Jacobs's narrative has been shown to meld characteristics of both the slave narrative form and the sentimental novel, a literary innovation that creates a black feminist agency that resists simultaneously the oppressions of slavery and of patriarchy while insisting on the irreducibility of black women's experience to either their race or their gender.[93] Critics suggest that as author, Jacobs's manipulation of literary conventions "displays her power over the forms at her disposal."[94] Repeating the theme of empowerment in the interpretation of the narrative action, many readers have seen the pseudonymous "Linda Brent's" desperate actions to evade her master's reach as strategic subversions that assert her own agency.[95]

But Jacobs is far more equivocal about her empowerment than many of her contemporary readers seem to acknowledge. Carla Kaplan has suggested that to insist on Jacobs's textual triumph over her oppressors is to miss the point of the story: "Jacobs is at great pains to dramatize Brent's *inability* to 'subvert' her status, 'assault' her master's domination, wage 'effective' combat, or 'reverse' the power structures which bind her. This is the lived meaning of slavery for Linda Brent. It is this narrative's strongest indictment."[96] Although *Incidents* conforms overall to the teleological structure of slave narrative, which documents the transformational development from slave to free, Jacobs's circumspection over the possibilities of power or freedom as defined within the terms of the self-possessed individual opens a space within the narrative for a more critical examination of what freedom might mean.

Jacobs's narrative, like Douglass's, ends with freedom. Yet the relation of each to that freedom is markedly different. As I have already suggested, for Douglass the transformation is absolute and unequivocal: "I was now my own master. . . . It was to me the starting point of a new existence." [97] Jacobs too is free, but her nominal freedom is in fact severely constrained by her continued servitude: "The dream of my life is not yet realized. I do not sit with my children in a home of my own. . . . God so orders circumstances as to keep me with my friend Mrs. Bruce. Love, duty, gratitude also bind me to her side." [98] Legal freedom notwithstanding, the promises of possession and self-possession continue to prove elusive for Jacobs.

Like Douglass, Jacobs's freedom was finally secured through the intervention of friends—in particular Mrs. Bruce—who paid $300 to secure her freedom. But where Douglass's *Narrative* suppresses the commercial details of his freedom, Jacobs incorporates this transaction into her story. Douglass, once the sale has occurred, is pragmatic about its necessity and resolves to use the transaction as yet another rhetorical weapon in his assault on the institution of slavery: "I will hold up those papers before the world, in proof of the plundering character of the American government. It shall be the brand of infamy, stamping the nation, in whose name the deed was done." [99] Jacobs, in contrast, never consented to the purchase, and when Mrs. Bruce informs her that the deed is done, Jacobs is shocked and dismayed: "My brain reeled as I read these lines. . . . The bill of sale! Those words struck me like a blow. So I was *sold* at last! A human being *sold* in the free city of New York!" (p. 200). Where Douglass positions himself unequivocally as self-possessed, his own master, Jacobs emphasizes the continual ambivalence of her relation to property and hence also to the autonomous ideal of subjectivity at stake in Douglass's struggle with Covey. Douglass can only become such a subject by suppressing everything that would challenge, undermine, or complicate that subject's autonomy and authority. In contrast, Jacobs renders explicit the impasse that must be excavated from Douglass's silences and suppressions: "Contracts [i.e., legal relations of property] fail to alter her status or provide her real freedom, yet they remain her only meaningful hope for both protection and change." [100]

Within the context of a liberal polity founded on principles of property right, it is only as a propertied subject that Jacobs has any hope of rights, protections, or the future that she dreams of ("a hearthstone of my own, however humble" [p. 201]). But as a woman and a former slave, such self-possession is deeply compromised. Jacobs's story ends with a freedom marred by the price at which it has been attained, the "bill of sale" that re-distributes property and person such that Jacobs's freedom is in fact legally attained as Mrs. Bruce's purchase of Jacobs. Mrs. Bruce's insistence that she has paid for Jacobs, not to own her, but to free her offers only a little comfort. Jacobs's dismay at her bought freedom raises the question Doug-lass necessarily suppresses: where would a freedom not liable to the threat of purchase lie, and what would it look like? Douglass attempts to neu-tralize the ambivalence of the freedom available to him as self-possessed subject by availing himself of the power of Enlightenment rhetoric. In con-trast, Jacobs insists on the gap between the rhetoric of freedom and its material reality; forced by circumstance to be critical of the emancipatory promise of the self-possessed subject, Jacobs goes much further in explor-ing the limits, boundaries, and exclusions of the order based on property and contract. The persistence of the problem of property as the determi-nant of personhood in the last pages of Jacobs's narrative suggests that another freedom must escape this insidious economy.

Such an escape is indeed figured in Jacobs's narrative in what she de-scribes as a "loophole of retreat," which is not a flight to the freedom of the North (the conventional figure for the freedom of the self-possessed "free man") but a withdrawal into a space that is simultaneously interior to and outside of the economy of slavery. Others have remarked on the mul-tiple valences of the "loophole" in this narrative as a means of escape from slavery and particularly from the abusive power and sexual exploitation of Flint and Sands. These readers discover Jacobs's freedom in confine-ment, concealment, and the power to see and act without being detected.[101] But the nature of this loophole and its peculiar relation to the economy of slavery and subjectivity make such a univocal reading difficult to sustain, not simply because Jacobs's experience in the garret is also restricted, con-strained, or vulnerable, but because the space marked out by the garret is outside the realm of subjectivity, such that the freedom of the garret is purchased at the price of the loss of the authorized self.

Jacobs's retreat to the garret emerges in the narrative as a solution to the inherent contradiction between her disposition as property by Mr. Flint and the ties of love and responsibility that she maintains with her extended family despite the master's efforts to prevent them. In the narratives of Henry Brown and Henry Bibb, the narrators' desire to flee enslavement is at odds with their sense of obligation to their families; in each, slavery's re-fusal to recognize the kinship ties of the black family is ironically turned back on itself in that it provides the motivation and occasion for flight. Brown did not want to leave his family, but when they were sold away the only reason not to attempt escape was removed. Similarly, Bibb struggled to stay with his wife and, if he were to escape, to bring her with him; it is his owner's determination to sell him away from his wife as punishment that results in their separation and subsequently Bibb's successful escape. Thus, in these narratives, the idea of freedom seems necessarily individual: one gains one's freedom alone, echoing in fact the theoretical autonomy of the subject. Jacobs's strong ties to a relatively stable community centered around her emancipated grandmother, as well as her love and concern for her children, render even more acute the conflict between family and such a freedom.

Jacobs's continued sexual victimization and vulnerability make her desperate to escape from her lascivious master, but her solution is not autonomous flight. Given Flint's obsession with his "Linda," the chances of a successful flight are slim. Even if she could find her way north, she would constantly be hounded by his pursuit; the possibility for success of such an attempt is further lessened by the fact that he has effectively blocked every exit whereby she might flee to a place of freedom. Thus, instead of flight, Jacobs's family finds a way to secrete her in its innermost heart. Jacobs lives for seven years in the crawl space between the ceiling and the roof of a small storage shed attached to her grandmother's house. The space is hardly fit for habitation:

> Some boards were laid across the joists at the top [of the shed], and between these boards and the roof was a very small garret, never occupied by any thing but rats and mice. It was a pent roof, covered with nothing but shingles, according to the southern custom for such buildings. The garret was only nine feet long and seven wide. The highest part was three feet high, and sloped down abruptly to the loose board floor. There was no admission for either light or air. (p. 114)

In her garret, her "loophole of retreat," Jacobs has effected an escape without going anywhere, as if the surface of slavery looped back on itself and created a little pocket where Jacobs can be *in*, but not a part of, the goings-on of her community. It is, in fact, precisely because she is not anywhere within slavery, but in a pocket outside or alongside slavery, that her safety is guaranteed. The space of the garret is not a space similar to the space of slavery; rather, it is radically separate.

The force of slavery depended on its totalizing colonization of every space and every body; either thing or subject, either slave or free. The separation of places of work and habitation assigned to slave and free populations, the regulations governing modes of movement in public places and thorough-fares, and the continual surveillance of the enslaved and the refusal of any space of privacy or retreat were all mechanisms to enforce through spa-tial practices the fundamental opposition between the willful person of the master and the will-less property that is the slave. In contrast, the space of the garret is invisible, unsurveilled, unregulated. It is a space excluded by the space of slavery; and this very exclusion marks the limits of slavery's totalizing premise of opposition between person and property. Even when she sees Dr. Flint on the street outside, just a few feet away, she feels safe from his reach: "Had the least suspicion rested on my grandmother's house, it would have been burned to the ground. But it was the last place they thought of. Yet there was no place, where slavery existed, that could have afforded me so good a place of concealment" (p. 117). The ambiguity of the syntax of this last sentence is suggestive. On the one hand, it might read: here where slavery existed, there was no other place that could have afforded so good a place of concealment. But the sentence might equally be read as follows: there was no place at all in those places where slavery existed that could have afforded so good a place of concealment; and there-fore by implication, this place of concealment is not where slavery exists. The loophole of retreat has shifted into an elsewhere where slavery does not exist.

Michelle Burnham has suggested that Jacobs's loophole of retreat is like a loophole in the law, which allows one to evade the intention of the law without breaking its letter. Thus, Jacobs's loophole condition is according to Burnham "a simultaneous inscription and transgression of the law of slavery [such that] she is able to reverse the master-slave power relation."[102] I would suggest further that this legal dimension of the loophole is compli-cated and transformed by the loophole's literal, spatial dimension. Jacobs has broken the law of slavery by removing herself from the reach of the will of the master; but the effect of this lawbreaking is to remove her from the realm of the law altogether. In the garret Jacobs as fugitive is neither subject of nor subjected to the law of slavery. The legal sense of *loophole* im-plies an ambiguity or omission in a law, an "out" always rendered possible by the failure of the language of the law to achieve plenitude. But the else-where of the garret is not simply an inadvertent omission in the cataloging of places. Jacobs in the garret is "no place," a loophole whose relation to the law is not contiguous but rather disjunctive.

Is this loophole, as Burnham and others would have it, a "site of resistance"? I must confess that it is difficult for me to see it in such a positive light. The "elsewhere" of the loophole is not an actual place where Jacobs might safely live beyond the reach of slavery. It is at great physical and mental cost that she remains in the garret. Jacobs's descriptions of her experience are punctuated by the progressive atrophy and deterioration of her body. The lack of air, the lack of space, and the ravages of the seasons make her constantly conscious of her body and its continual discomfort. During her second winter in the garret, she comes close to dying: "I had a very painful sensation of coldness in my head; even my face and tongue stiffened, and I lost the power of speech. . . . [My brother] thought I was dying, for I had been in an unconscious state sixteen hours" (p. 122). The deprivation of air, space, and finally consciousness itself is the price of removing herself from the economy of master and slave. The elsewhere of the loophole of retreat is an elsewhere nobody, no *body*, can inhabit for long. If the loophole is an escape, it is not a triumph. Jacobs as fugitive cannot be reduced to property, but neither can she avail herself of the securities of person. Jacobs as fugitive is, from the totalizing perspective of slavery, "no thing" and "no one."

Jacobs's safety in the loophole is predicated on her exclusion from the social; the condition of her security is simultaneously the absolute deprivation of freedom. The unsustainability of this paradoxical circumstance marks the limits of a reading that would interpret her efforts to deflect Flint's attention as a reversal in the power relations between Flint and herself. If we view the loophole as merely reversing the relation between slave and master we miss the implications of the loophole as a (non)place outside slavery. But to say that there is no one in the space of fugitivity is not to say that nothing can happen. Jacobs is able to remain secure in this liminal space by effecting ruses that deflect Flint's attention. This activity does not reverse the power between master and slave; rather, it works to secure and maintain the garret as a space apart from mastery and slavery.

To make Flint believe she is residing in Boston, Jacobs writes false letters that appear to be written from that place and gives them to a traveling friend to post. The ruse is quite successful in convincing Flint that Jacobs has truly escaped to the North. He even goes so far as to write a letter to the mayor of Boston inquiring if he knows of her. Flint's delusion is the occasion for great relief because it causes him to stop looking for Jacobs close to home. In these letters, Jacobs appears to Flint in a virtual space, one in which she is visible but entirely inaccessible. For Jacobs, the letter is important, not for what the letter itself says, as we typically think of letters, but for what is on the envelope, seemingly irrelevant to the content of the letter. The letters that fall into Flint's hands, while neither addressed to him nor written to him, are in fact intended for his eyes and convey information only to him. The postmark on the envelope and the dateline within are the marks of a supposed authenticity that guarantee to Flint that these letters are what they appear to be, signs of the presence of Jacobs's body in other locations. But, in fact, these letters are written from an unlocatable elsewhere; the real point of origin is the no place of the loophole, while the virtual point of origin is an illusion — if Flint were to go to New York, Boston, or Canada he would not find Jacobs at all.

In my reading of Brown's narrative, I suggested that the logic of the post presumed that the subject stood outside and independent of the system of the mail — a logic called into question by the postal production of Brown as subject. Jacobs's manipulation of the mail to in effect throw her voice emphasizes yet another aspect of the subjectivizing function of the mail: addressability. For the post to operate, each individual must represent a unique, localizable address. Mail delivery requires both a name and a location for originator and addressee: it is the transmittal of a message from someone somewhere to someone else somewhere else. Jacobs's postal missives appear to establish and reveal her post. This is what Flint reads from the surface of the envelope: the return address is presumed to stand in for the subject who is the letter's origin. As the recipient of this correspondence, Flint's certainty that he is "here" is transformed into the certainty that, likewise, she must be "there." But Jacobs is not there; the ruse works to misdirect Flint's attention because the apparent logic of addressability becomes inverted. Jacobs's *virtual* appearance in Boston or Canada reveals the possibility that rather than the individual being simply represented by the address, as Flint assumes, the address produces the *effect* of an individual as origin. Thus, Jacobs's security in her loophole is the result of an ambivalent relation between individual and address, a relation that is assumed to move from the former to the latter but that may also move in the reverse direction. The false address projects her body into a virtual space, where in fact she is not. At the same time, her body is shielded from

Flint's discovery because the loophole is an elsewhere that cannot be addressed. Jacobs cannot receive the post in this loophole; outside the realm of addressability, it is a logical no place.

The circumstance of Jacobs's body in the loophole reinforces the significance of property in the determination of the subject. In her loophole, Jacobs is neither a slave nor a free subject, neither embodying the property of another nor possessing property in herself. Jacobs does not become free simply by withdrawing from slavery; rather, she must be reinserted into the economy of property, first as purchased (by Mrs. Bruce) then subsequently as potential purchaser (of a hearth of her own). Freedom is as much a problem as it is a solution at the conclusion of her narrative; that the promise of freedom in property might fail Jacobs leaves open the question of whether this is the only possible freedom. As Carla Kaplan notes, it is this failure that makes of the narrative an implicit call for political intervention: "Although Brent does eventually get out of her miserable attic hideaway, Jacobs does not escape the impasse this narrative so brilliantly renders. And that is the narrative's point. Her inability to do so makes further — or future — action on our behalf necessary." [103] The future action that slave narrative seemed to call for in its day was the end to slavery, an action wrenchingly achieved. Yet that cannot be the end, just as Jacobs insists that her freedom from slavery cannot be the end of her own story. The future of freedom is not only Jacobs's nineteenth-century future, it is our future as well. Jacobs's ambivalence in the last pages of her narrative suggests that freedom's future is as yet unknown, calling for further, and future, action.

## Fugitivity and Freedom

Fugitivity, as I have described it, is different from the freedom that appears again and again as the telos of the slave's journey. The latter is the freedom granted and protected by the state, the freedom of the citizen. If slavery is, as Justice Ruffin explained in *State v Mann*, the absolute negation of all possible freedoms, then this freedom in turn appears as the negation of slavery. Hence, the freedom of the citizen-subject, the freedom that Douglass celebrates, the freedom granted and protected by the state, appears to be the only possible freedom: freedom simple, absolute freedom. But if we look more closely, we see that this freedom is not simply the negation of slavery; such a freedom depends on slavery insofar as freedom and slavery define each other: one who is a slave is not free, one who is free is not a slave. Hence, this freedom is a freedom specific to a particular social order and to a particular understanding of the individual. As Douglass's claim to have become his own master suggests, this freedom incorporates and preserves the relation of property and proprietor that is fundamental to slavery and installs that relation at the heart of the subject. This is not to say that the privileges of this form of freedom are not worth seeking or that the value that slaves placed on freedom was misplaced. To be a social and political subject is to be a subject of and subject to the state. The freedom sought by the enslaved, the freedom that appears as the telos of the slave narrative, is the form of freedom proper to this subject. Like the space of Brown's box or Jacobs's loophole, one may be outside, but there one is not a subject; the outside is uninhabitable. Because freedom within the state is the only possible freedom of the subject, that freedom—characterized as (self-)possession—is the only form of freedom that registers as freedom, the only freedom that is recognized or protected.

From within the terms of the order of slavery and property, the social order of subjects regulated and regularized by the state, the freedom of the subject is the singular and unique alternative to slavery. But fugitivity interrupts this apparently totalizing opposition of slavery and freedom. Fugitivity exposes the interdependency of slavery and freedom by opening—however evanescently—onto an "outside" that cannot be reduced to either term. As neither the property of another nor propertied in the self, the fugitive does not register on the map of social relations. The space of the fugitive is, from the perspective of the state, no place. Thus, the fugitive remains withdrawn, invisible, unrepresentable from the perspective of proper subjects and objects of property. Where the state provides a framework for assigning each individual an address, a localizable identity that ensures both addressability and responsibility, the fugitive has no address, cannot be addressed. The fugitive evades the regularized and regulated paths of circulation—of goods, of persons, of information. Whether in perpetual motion, like Bibb, or still as death, like Brown, the persistence of the fugitive's body in those (non)places where no one can be reveals the mechanisms of the production and colonization of social space by exposing that space to its constitutive outside. Thus, while the fugitive can neither embody nor effect another positive form of freedom (because freedom within the state is only sustainable and recognizable as the freedom of the subject, which the fugitive by definition is not), the fugitive does expose that freedom of the subject, which appears as the only possible freedom, to its con-

stitutive conditions and limits. In this way, the fugitive poses a challenge
to any politics that claims freedom as its goal. Once we have recognized
the contingency of the form of freedom we are accustomed to understanding as freedom simple, freedom can no longer simply be a solution or a
goal. Rather, the question of politics must begin from an interrogation of
freedom itself and from an interrogation of the subject assumed to be the
ground of both politics and freedom.

Part of the propaganda function of slave narratives was to expose the
violence of slavery that was often hidden under the guise of benevolent
plantation paternalism. Justice Ruffin's ruling confirmed as legal fact what
the slave narrators described as implicit principle: that absolute force and
illimitable violence are the repressed conditions whereby a slave is made
and maintained as a slave. This violence marks and sustains the distinction between slave and free. Freedom implies rights in the body that are
protected by the state; the state offers no such protection to the body of
the slave. But beyond the violence that makes the slave a slave, there is
another violence specific to the condition of fugitivity. Fugitivity is not an
end, either for the slave narrative or for the subject. The fugitive will be
captured and returned to slavery, will become a free subject, or will per-
ish. The fugitive never remains fugitive; fugitivity is unsustainable. And
this unsustainability is decidedly corporeal, as in relation to the uninhabit-
ablity of the fugitive's space (the box or the "loophole") or the purchase
of Douglass and Jacobs to prevent their recapture. If the possible ends of
the fugitive are death, captivity, or freedom, then freedom seems the obvious choice. But from the perspective of fugitivity, this freedom is a forced
choice, demanded by the violence sustained on the fugitive body (recall
Jacobs's dismay at her freedom-by-purchase). The violence with which the
fugitive is confronted, a violence that enjoins the fugitive either to return
to slavery or to become a free (wo)man, exposes the fact that it is only
through violence that the opposition of "slave" and "man" appears totally
to account for the realm of possibilities.

If not only "slave," but also "man," are the products of force, then it appears that the outside marked by fugitivity is potentially disruptive of the
social order of slave and man insofar as that outside reveals the violence
that produces and sustains such order. However, it is clear that the outside
of fugitivity is not a positive, sustainable alternative to this ordering violence. The excruciating pain of Box Brown's 27-hour journey, the crippling
ordeal of Harriet Jacobs's seven years in the attic of a shed, do not appear as

positive utopias. The spaces of fugitivity are not ideals whereby the social might be measured or remade. Rather, they are precisely u-topic insofar as they mark the elsewhere of the social, which is at the same time an impossibility. This is what Diane Elam has called a "critical utopia," a utopia that serves as the "grounds of an exploration. . . . [It] is the literal utopianism of a 'no place' which undermines existing models of thought." [104] The distended fugitive body painfully exposes both the limits of the discursive order of property and person and the agonizing effects of any attempt to evade or surpass these orders. It is true that the self-possessed individual is an ideological fiction—but it is a fiction of sufficient power to enforce its appearance as natural through the more-than-systematic violence that exposes the bodies of Brown and Jacobs to their corporeal limits. The outside inhabited by the fugitive is not freedom but a painful elsewhere that serves both to expose the contingency of the totalizing appearance of the duality free/enslaved and to undermine the image of the freedom of the subject as absolute freedom.

Reading the corporeal topography of the space of fugitivity, one becomes increasingly skeptical of the blithe, celebratory invocations of the subversive powers of boundary-crossing, nomadism, or excess—all figures that *might* be mobilized to describe the space of fugitivity. The fugitive cannot in any way be read as representing some idealized absolute freedom of fluidity or boundlessness. Such a positive recuperation of fugitivity would absolutely miss the point of the fugitive's untenable relation to both slavery and freedom. The fugitive body does not escape the violence of order; what it does do is expose on its surface the violence necessary to preserve order, hierarchy, boundedness, propriety, and property. The fugitive reveals the extent to which the proper(tied) subject is a political achievement, "constituted by power . . . subjected and produced time and again" rather than simply the neutral agent of politics.[105]

The fugitive is neither a subject nor a political agent in any sense that can be recognized or accounted for within the political orders of the subject. This is why, for example, Jacobs's actions in the loophole ought not be taken as a sign of subjective agency. Thus, the fugitive body cannot simply be read as an oppositional agency or a force from the outside that would subvert, destabilize, or upset the existing orders of power. And if the fugitive does prove to be a potential or actual source of destabilization or subversion, these possibilities must be carefully thought in and through the conditions and circumstances of the fugitive body. The political imperative of the fugitive for us today, I am suggesting, lies in the way it forces us to confront the question of freedom itself. To raise the question of freedom is impossible so long as we remain under the sway of "the self-evidence of the common notion of freedom—which is always more or less that of a free will—coupled with the moral self-evidence of the necessity of preserving the rights of this freedom." [106] The space of fugitivity does not offer a positive alternative to the common notion of freedom so much as it exposes the conditions of self-evidence and clears the ground for exploring the mechanisms and exclusions of this self-evidence.

But while the fugitive cannot be understood as a figure of freedom, viewing the u-topia of fugitivity as the opening for an exploration of the question of freedom may provide us with some alternative directions for thought. Although I have suggested that the fugitive is by definition excluded from freedom (as the freedom of the subject), in fugitivity we may catch a glimpse of a freedom that cannot be assigned, appropriated, possessed, legislated, denied, or limited—all of these determinants, insofar as they subsume freedom to some higher power, make of freedom something less than free. Is there some freedom that is not determined as the free will that presupposes a subject as possessing freedom? This freedom might appear as a surprise, as the unexpected, as a freedom the delineations and forms of which cannot be predicted or determined. There is something of this in fugitivity, perhaps.

Fugitivity in itself cannot claim the position of subject. Where the subject demands recognition, rights, and protections, the fugitive remains exposed as a being without ground for claim. The groundlessness of the fugitive opens up a space of uncertainty, undecidability. The appearance of the fugitive, as being without ground, challenges the self-evidence of freedom as the right of the subject. For now, we can do nothing more than mark this possibility as an opening for thought. But at the same time, it must be acknowledged that such an opening is inherently risky. If we cannot be certain of the priority of the subject, we cannot know in advance what will constitute such ethically desirable ends as freedom, justice, or community. But if freedom is to be unconstrained, if justice is to be more than the application of law, if community is to be uncoerced, then it seems that we must necessarily be subjected to such uncertainty. Such uncertainty may feel threatening or disturbing to the ways in which we have become accustomed to thinking and acting. But I would argue that we need to learn to recognize the ways in which the comforts of certainty may be illusory. This is one of the lessons of the slave's testimony: the appearance of certainty and order—the natural order of white masters and black slaves—is produced and secured through violence. This violence, as it is differentially applied and experienced, must be understood not as incidental or extraneous, but as the very price and condition of certainty.

# 3. A Question of Justice

## *Chesnutt's Twins Across the Color Line*

The Civil War and the passage of constitutional amendments ending slavery and granting equal protection under the law to all citizens—newly defined as both white and black—are thought to have fatally ruptured the logic of slavery. Progress, opportunity, equal rights, advancement—these have been the watchwords of racial politics for over 100 years. Thus, it is somewhat shocking to learn that it was not until 1995 that the last state—Mississippi—finally ratified the Thirteenth Amendment abolishing slavery. Although by this time such a gesture is entirely symbolic (in practice, slavery ended in 1865), it invokes in an uncanny way a history commonly considered dead and gone.

## Accounting for Justice

Some local observers have suggested that the reason Mississippi refused to ratify the amendment originally was out of anger at the federal government for failing to reimburse the slave owners for their lost assets. By this account, it was not the enslaved but their tormentors who had suffered a historical injustice. Such a perspective suggests that the legacy of slavery persists in a particular system of human accounting. To render an account demands a principle of commensurability, a measure by which one may determine the balance due. Slavery relied on the untrammeled mechanisms of the marketplace to balance the potential profitability of a lifetime against the cost of flesh. The slave as property was a "labor commodity . . . both productive labor and value, a quantitative abstraction of exchange: the equivalent of three-fifths of a single unit of representational value."[1] The reduction of bodies, lives, and their potentials to an implicit table of equivalencies is claimed as a legitimate basis for justice—not for the enslaved, of course, but for the ones who claimed right to them and to their disposal. This was the framework in which emancipation could be viewed as theft, the uncompensated transfer of assets from slave owners to the slaves themselves. The freedom the slaves got could be valued on the open market: so much for a strong field hand, so much for an aging woman, and so on.

Neither Mississippi nor any other state received reparations for their "loss." But the idea that such a notion of loss and compensation is appropriate to the circumstances surrounding slavery reemerges today in other guises, for example, in the compensatory argument for affirmative action. Such an argument grounds affirmative action in "the claim to compensation for discrete and 'finished' harm done to minority group members or their ancestors."[2] Implicit in this view is the notion that the accounts could be settled once and for all, that the limits of responsibility would be the valuation and compensation of a discrete and finite harm. The untenability of such a static and economized view of history's impact on the present becomes clear as soon as one begins to attempt the accounting. Nevertheless, such a view has dominated current discussions of the future of affirmative action—and effectively undermined both its defensibility and its efficacy—as the legal focus has shifted "from rectifying the harm to Blacks to invoking legal protection for the rights of whites who are innocent of discriminatory acts, although they have benefitted from prior discrimination."[3]

The human accounting of slavery thus substitutes economic calculation for ethical accountability. Claims must be compared; responsibility, suffering, and compensation must be determined. This is the justice of the account, of calculation. As a basis for racial justice, such a system of accounting originates in the slaveholder's ledger, the written record of purchase, value, sale, profit, and loss. William Faulkner's vivid rendering of the McCaslin family ledgers in *Go Down, Moses*, in particular the section entitled "The Bear," hints at the violence of abstraction necessary to transform the tragedies of incest, rape, and suicide into economic transactions. This ledger speaks the truth in its very silence, revealing to the next generation the price in human lives and moral failures at which the present has been purchased. Ike seeks to settle up these accounts by fulfilling the will of the patriarch, Carothers McCaslin, to leave money to his unrecognized black sons and by repudiating his own part in this past by disinheriting himself and living alone in the woods, where he imagines it is possible to recover an illusory innocence. But Ike and the world around him are nothing but the product of this inescapable past. The accounts can never be fully balanced; the ledger can never be finally closed. Any accounting such as this cannot but leave a remainder. Faulkner suggests that if the sin of slavery was to seek to transform human beings into ledger entries, there is no principle of accounting that will balance out the scales.

Faulkner's accounts reveal another account between the lines, the silenced account of violence and violation that must be excluded and repressed in order to preserve the impression of accounts that will balance. The accounting principles of the ledger and their rules of commensurability promise justice in the balance; but this promised justice is exposed for sham by the gap between the letter of the ledger and what it does not or cannot say. The injustice of slavery could not be measured by slavery's accounts; justice could only appear outside the ledger, in the form of a resistance to submitting human life to the rule of equivalence.

Although slavery ended, the relations of domination and exploitation between white and black did not. Slavery gave way to a new mechanism of accounting, a new rule of commensurability, that, like the old rule of the ledger, revealed an incalculable injustice between the lines. This was the rule of segregation, a rule that in principle acknowledged the freedom and citizenship of black people while simultaneously insisting on their inherent separateness. The foundational racial division implicit in the courts' rulings to uphold the practices of segregation so long as they remain "separate but equal" instituted a new justice of accounting. Thus, the Civil War did not cancel the accounts of slavery so much as shift them into a new arena. After slavery, the justice of separate but equal proved again and again that it could only be a false justice of commensurability, a commensurability defined and enforced by the very law that claimed merely to reflect it. If, as Charles Chesnutt wrote in an 1899 letter to Walter Hines Page, "the Supreme Court of the United States is . . . a dangerous place for a colored man to seek justice," would it be possible to imagine another kind of justice?[4] Or was the problem of racial injustice, as Chesnutt's contemporary Albion Tourgée wrote, "one of those questions beyond remedy by any human means . . . [a question that] only God can handle."[5] In *The Marrow of Tradition* (1901), Chesnutt takes up the question of racial justice in the contemporary climate of crisis in an effort to open a space for a justice beyond the ledger's accounts.

## Riotous Twins: 'The Marrow of Tradition'

Chesnutt's major novel of segregation was not a commercial success in its own day and until quite recently inspired little serious critical comment. A look at the critical reception of this novel suggests that part of the reason for its relative neglect may be that its complex portrayal of the issues of racial tension and racial justice coupled with its seeming failure to take up any particular position unambiguously has forestalled the emergence of a critical consensus about its importance or its place in the African-American literary tradition. It has alternately been viewed as bitter, propagandistic, excessively harsh, or not harsh enough. At the novel's time of publication, the sharp view of the realities of white supremacy presented in it brought down the wrath of the white Southern literati: "from the South there came a storm of resentment and unfavorable criticism. One paper attacked Chesnutt bitterly for writing a book of lies and slander about the South. . . . Another characterized the book as utterly repellent to Southern sentiment and one calculated to do infinite harm to the South if widely read. . . . A leading Washington paper questioned the 'wisdom of such a book as it arouses bitter resentments in politics and personal relations.' "[6]

In contrast, while African-American readers could embrace Chesnutt's representation of the harsh reality behind the propaganda, it was unclear where Chesnutt stood in relation to debates about racial justice, which, at the turn of the century, revolved around the competing poles of accommodation and militant resistance. These two alternatives appear to be embodied in the characters of Dr. Miller, who counsels patience and gradual uplift, and Josh Green, who seeks a more immediate and violent resolution to the injustices of the moment. Critics have debated which of these best represents Chesnutt's own position, and the assessment of the novel has varied accordingly. For example, in the radical climate of the late 1960s, Addison Gayle praised the novel for inventing the "New Negro" in Josh Green, a working-class revolutionary. Writing about the same time, Amiri Baraka raged that Chesnutt was advocating, in Dr. Miller, "an acceptance of the idea of the superiority of the white man, or at least the proposition that the Negro, somehow, must completely lose himself within the culture and social order of the ex-master."[7]

More recent critics have left Chesnutt firmly in the camp of "ambivalence" and "unresolved dilemma," suggesting that Chesnutt could see no clear way out of the apparent political impasse of the turn of the century.[8] But this continuing controversy is in fact based in an implicit consensus. Although divided in their assessments of just what kind of political solution Chesnutt intended, readers have tacitly assented to the assumption that the novel is primarily motivated by two political concerns: to expose the violence and lawlessness of white supremacy and to intervene in black debates regarding the best course of future action.

I would not dispute the priority of these two concerns as forming the political core of Chesnutt's project in *Marrow*. But it seems to me that the attendant critical emphasis on the public politics of white supremacy as represented in the novel is necessarily only a partial reading. The fictionalized but accurate account of the Wilmington, North Carolina, race riot of 1898 has been, for Chesnutt's contemporaries and for readers ever since, the emotional and political center of the novel. One might therefore be surprised to learn that less than one-fourth of the novel actually is about the riot or events leading up to it. Critics have generally considered the episodes focusing on Olivia Carteret and Janet Miller, wives of the male protagonists as well as half-sisters, to be secondary elements in the novel's structure (if they mention them at all).[9] The remainder of the characters and plots are usually ignored. The critical excision of most of the novel is consistent with the view that it is primarily polemical and political in intent and that the remainder has little to do with the political question. The problem with this view is that it automatically assumes that the arena of politics is encompassed only by those masculine activities that bear on public life. But what of the major counterplot of the women, the story of white Olivia and her black half-sister Janet? Is this counterplot not also inextricably bound up with the political questions evoked by the conspiracy and riot? In their very marginality, Olivia and Janet become central. The novel opens and closes with Olivia and Janet and the problem of relation and recognition that binds them together and forces them apart. The tension between Olivia and Janet frames the narrative; as it enfolds and colors all the ensuing action, the problems raised by their complex relation are inseparable from the more recognizably political problems acted out in the race riot.

Olivia and Janet are figured throughout the novel not merely as sisters, but more specifically as twins. We might pause to ponder this emphasis on twinning as a metaphor for racial difference, a metaphor that reappears in other writings contemporary with Chesnutt, in particular Mark Twain's *The Tragedy of Pudd'nhead Wilson*.[10] The number two suggested by the twin is important; as twinned, it can neither be a question of a proliferating multiplicity nor of the oppositional relation of a simple binary. Unlike the mutually exhaustive terms of a binary opposition, the twoness of the twin does not mark a completion or an exclusion; the necessity of the second term is not a function of the content of the term itself but rather of the inconceivability of a simple oneness. Twoness here suggests a pure supplementarity without reference to any particular originary term. One cannot array these two in a hierarchical relation of original and copy, source and derivative. The logic of this twoness insists only that there is never one, always two. This is the twoness of the twin, a doubled one, separate and equal. The figure of the twin thus insists on a unity that can only be expressed as a doubling. The appearance of twinned characters that are distinguishable only in terms of an imperceptible blackness or whiteness suggests that this doubling is purely formal. The twins are not two different individuals but a single one that must necessarily be repeated with the distinguishing difference of race. Thus, the logic of the twin is in tension with the logic of racial division, which is that of hierarchy. That is, while on the one hand, in their social circumstances one sees that Olivia and Janet are necessarily separate and *unequal*, at the same time their twinning echoes the superficial understanding of the law of segregation—separate and *equal*.

In this twinning across the color line, the difference between black and white is figured not as cultural difference but as formal distinction. Chesnutt's emphasis on the physical similarity between Janet and Olivia forces the reader to acknowledge the arbitrariness of the racial distinction that separates them. At the same time, the twinning of the two women complicates the meaning of *same* and *different*. If the definition of a twin is another of the same, the only difference of twins is that there are two of them. A twin is a sameness that is different; a paradoxical conjoining of two that are supposed to be absolutely separate, absolutely opposed. The figure of the twin is thus a double that is incommensurable with itself; the twins are neither the same nor different. As such, the twin poses a challenge to the logic of commensurability, which I have suggested is the basis for justice conceived in the economic terms of the ledger's balance. While the ledger posits the formal equivalence and substitutability of its balancing terms, separate and equal, the twins are simultaneously *inseparable* and yet equal. If the color line functions in terms of such a twinning, we realize that the ledger's justice can only be secured by suppressing this originary doubling of race. The logic of the ledger suppresses the dependence of whiteness on blackness, formally disavowing their twinned relation and thus creating the appearance of whiteness as the origin and the same and blackness as derivative and different. Thus separated, black and white can be defined by the ledger as equal while at the same time rendering invisible the violence whereby such apparent commensurability has been purchased. It is the workings of this violence in the name of justice that Chesnutt aims to reveal.

Through the twinned relationship between Olivia and Janet, the novel addresses the racial division codified in segregation law, asking, what sustains identity in relation to the color line? What counts as difference? By focusing attention on the workings of the color line in the twinning of Janet and Olivia, I will suggest that the novel goes beyond criticizing the violence and hypocrisy of race politics. It does so in order to call the very notion of race politics into question by interrogating the categories of opposition and exclusion that are its necessary preconditions. Chesnutt, I will argue, leaves open the possibility of justice at the novel's conclusion, not by resolving the racial conflict in the fictional city of Wellington in a just manner that would rebalance the accounts, but by evoking an alternative justice in the complex relation between Olivia and Janet.

## White Supremacy and National Unification

At about the same time Chesnutt was writing *Marrow*, a new consensus was developing in historical accounts of the Civil War and Reconstruction that shifted the focus from sectional conflict and compromise to national crisis and reconciliation. As opposed to postwar accounts, which wholly blamed one side or the other, the Rhodes-Burgess Compromise accepted slavery as a necessary evil for which both North and South shared responsibility.[11] In an effort to move beyond the overt sectional biases of histories written in the 1870s, 1880s, and 1890s, the compromise view shifted its perspective from region to nation. In this view, the Civil War was neither the result of Northern aggression against the peaceful agrarian patriarchy of the South (the Southern version) nor a moral crusade originating in the North against an immoral Southern institution (the Northern version) but rather a national struggle to root out a painful national evil and restore the national body to harmony and unity. This new unified narrative imagines the Civil War as a temporary but necessary rupture in the unity of the nation. The nation is restored to wholeness by translating the earlier narrative of sectional rivalry and eventual Northern domination into one of national crisis and resolution.

The emphasis on the Civil War as the eruption of disunion and its conclusion and aftermath as the restoration of union effectively displaces the problem of national definition from social divisions of race to the regional divisions of North and South. The image of brother fighting brother in the Civil War was a common one, emphasizing the familial dimension of the war, its "civility." Once it had been represented as a family dispute, the war could easily be reinterpreted as a struggle internal to an already constituted, cohesive, racially homogeneous body. The tensions and conflicts embodied in the presence of racially marked others could be symbolically suppressed by rewriting all legitimate national conflict as the conflict expressed and resolved by the war. The remainder is outside the nation, illegitimate. From this perspective, the properly national problem has been the problem of white disunion; white reunion is equivalent to national union.

In relation to the narrative of white familial union, the racial divisions that remain are not relevant or important to the identity and unity of the nation. By rewriting the war as the final solution to the definition of the nation, any remaining conflict over rights or citizenship in the nation is extranational. The cultural and political reunification of the nation was predicated on the emerging view that race was not a national problem. Indeed, the refusal of the courts to interpret the Fourteenth Amendment as relevant to questions of individual racial discrimination left black rights in the hands of the states (which in practice amounted to a virtual abrogation of the apparent intention of the Fourteenth Amendment). Although many have interpreted the collapse of Reconstruction as a return to the economic and political structures of slavery, the shifting familial metaphor suggests otherwise. The plantation had been portrayed as the patriarchal family in miniature, with the white father ruling over his black children; on the other hand, as Walter Benn Michaels has suggested, the rise of Jim Crow "marks not a return to but a final repudiation of paternalist prewar race relations, casting blacks out of the family so that Northern and Southern whites . . . can finally become brothers." [12] Rising prejudice and violence against African-Americans at the turn of the century thus went hand in hand with a national narrative of union and reconciliation.

The imaginative force of a white imperium as portrayed in the vicious writings of white supremacists such as Thomas Dixon could only be sustained by disavowing the intertwined histories of black and white in the making of the nation. In the only slightly less fantastic narratives of turn-of-the-century revisionist historians, the sectional divisions between white Americans appear to have been reconciled into a unified nation after the abolition of slavery only by suppressing the persistent division of race. Consensus revisionism deflected the question of race into the realm of the extra-national; in contrast, in *Marrow* Chesnutt reinstalls the question of race at the heart of the nation. White Olivia and black Janet are half-sisters; their familial indivisibility is in constant tension with the line of racial division that divides them. The domestic geographical conflict of white Northern brother fighting white Southern brother is recast in *Marrow* as a domestic racial struggle of white sister against black sister. Whereas in Dixon's *The Clansman* the Northern and Southern white protagonists are, in Michaels's words, "as much alike as twins" and finally, under the aegis of national reunion, become brothers,[13] in *Marrow* it is the white and black sisters who are twinned. As Mammy Jane puts it, "anybody mought 'low dey wuz twins, ef dey did n' know better" (p. 106). In *Marrow*, it is not the Civil War but *race* that divides the family and the nation; the line of division is not the Mason-Dixon Line dividing North from South but the much more amorphous, and much more ominous, color line. The twoness of these twins at the center of *Marrow* suggests that the project of national (re)unification can succeed only by producing a phantasmic oneness (the nation) that is in fact predicated on the maintenance of a displaced twoness (black and white).

The novel presents a fictional but historically accurate rendering of the events leading up to the infamous Wilmington race riot of 1898. Wilmington was not the only arena of racial crisis in that year; 1898 also saw the United States flexing its imperial muscle in the Spanish-American War. Spain's defeat made the United States a colonial power in what was left of the Spanish Empire (most importantly, Cuba and the Philippines). The Spanish-American War symbolically completed the project of reunification by joining North and South in a specifically national struggle against a common enemy.[14] Similarly, the instigators of the Wilmington riot aimed to restore white supremacy by joining the various factions of white society in Wilmington against the "external enemy" of blackness. Although the racism of internal oppression and the racism of imperial conquest were intimately related, white supremacy was equally consistent with an anti-imperialist nativism that sought to shield the nation from contaminating contact with racially degraded or inferior others. It is against the purifying racialization of national identity implicit in the white supremacy movement that Chesnutt writes.

By placing racial division at the heart of an indivisible family, Chesnutt insists that racial division is not external to but at the core of the nation. Thus, Chesnutt's restoration of the repressed twoness that underlies the image of oneness works as an explicit counter to the nativist or supremacist vision of an America purified. Chesnutt reinstalls the division of race not as the relation of white America to its external other but as *the* domestic question itself. Events in Wellington, Chesnutt suggests, are driven by the same energies driving the course of the nation. Conversely, the resolution of the Wellington story has national implications, even at those moments when the plot has narrowed its focus to the domestic and psychological entanglements of two women.

## The Persistence of Twoness: Separate and Equal

The nation unified itself not only through a revision of the past but through a convergence of legitimation of racist practices and beliefs. Eric Sundquist puts it nicely: "In the legal rise of Jim Crow, the South received the blessings of a Northern court; in the cultural rise of Jim Crow, the North adopted Southern plantation ideology. The sections fed imitatively upon one another's racist inclinations." [15] This mutual accommodation culminated in the famous 1896 Supreme Court decision, *Plessy v Ferguson*, which codified the doctrine of "separate but equal" as the principle of legal racial segregation. Although *Plessy* passed with little notice at the time, the terms of this ruling distilled the tension between white racism and American democratic idealism that emerged after emancipation. In the idea of separate but equal, the principle of human equality that forms the rhetorical foundation of the nation could be reconciled with racial prejudice, discrimination, exclusion, and violence. The decision suggested that the existence of different races was simply a given and that therefore it was only natural that they should be arrayed in hierarchical order. In the Court's opinion, racial segregation merely reflected the natural order of the universe: to preserve the distinction and separation of the races was to preserve order. Separate but equal not only allowed for but insisted on the doubling of institutions, facilities, laws, and social and cultural practices to accommodate the two races uneasily cohabiting within the borders of the United States (a costly redundancy on which subsequent opponents of segregation sought to capitalize in lawsuits demanding separate facilities in the hope that the burden of the expense would prove fatal to the entire edifice). In symbolic and in material terms, the Supreme Court's assent to the concept of separate but equal codified twoness as the very principle of American social and political life.

Of course, this arrangement existed in the form of "Jim Crow" laws and customs long before its legality was affirmed by the Supreme Court. Contrary to current interpretations of this decision as a watershed moment in U.S. legal history, the *Plessy* decision was not shocking or even remarkable to turn-of-the-century white sensibilities because it conformed to conventional white supremacist wisdom and long-standing practice. In his classic account of *The Strange Career of Jim Crow*, C. Vann Woodward argues that the formal and informal systems of segregation in transportation, housing, schooling, and accommodation were developed long before the 1880s. Systematic racial segregation existed in the Northern, nonslave states prior to the Civil War. According to Woodward, it was only after emancipation that a system of physical segregation seemed necessary to white Southerners. Is this to say that the North was in fact responsible for segregation? Woodward's account of the history of racial segregation has been criticized in recent years as a quixotic attempt at Southern apology or accommodation by appealing to the Southern tradition of paternalism as a basis for an end to discrimination. This may be an accurate charge; nevertheless, I find Woodward's groundbreaking effort to historicize the development of racial segregation to be a very interesting approach to the relation between spatial politics and racial distinction.

As Woodward persuasively argues, slavery was a system requiring physical proximity, and often intimacy, between white master and black slave:

> In most aspects of slavery as practiced in the ante-bellum South . . . segregation would have been an inconvenience and an obstruction to the functioning of the system. The very nature of the institution made separation of the races for the most part impracticable. The mere policing of slaves required that they be kept under more or less constant scrutiny, and so did the exaction of involuntary labor. The supervision, maintenance of order, and physical and medical care of slaves necessitated many contacts and encouraged a degree of intimacy between the races unequaled, and often held distasteful, in other parts of the country.[16]

We can follow Woodward this far without arriving at the spurious conclusion that therefore Southern paternalism was more gentle, more accepting, or more humane than Northern segregationist racism. Woodward suggests that because the status of black people in the South was already fixed and regulated by slavery, there was little need for the restrictive measures of segregation proper (although of course there were no end of restrictive measures regulating the *behavior* of the slave). There were of course some free black people in the South, but as slavery came under increasing attack they were tolerated less and less. As Joel Williamson has argued, "free Negroes were a contradiction in an organic world in which whites were free and Negroes were slaves. In the last generation of slavery, the controlling whites exerted tremendous social pressure, largely successfully, either to drive free Negroes out of the South or else reduce them practically to slavery." [17] Thus, although every Negro was not a slave, *Negro* increasingly meant virtually nothing but "slave." As slavery came to be justified by recourse to the specifically racialized nature of the enslaved, "membership in the new social category of 'Negro' became itself sufficient justification for enslaveability." [18] Hence, the fundamental and irreducible difference between white and black under slavery was the relation to slavery itself: " 'Black' racial identity marked who was subject to enslavement; 'white' racial identity marked who was 'free' or, at minimum, not a slave." [19] This implicit identity between *black* and *slave* was reinforced by the emergence of the metaphor of "white slavery" as a basis for wage labor reforms between the 1830s and the 1860s. As David Roediger has suggested, the attacks on so-called white slavery implicitly reinforced the identity of black people with enslavement by protesting only the slavery of white workers; at the same time, the metaphor was unsustainable because it threatened the very whiteness of those workers by symbolically aligning them with the racial degradation of slavery.[20] In sum, in slaveholding states prior to emancipation, slavery itself marked and guaranteed the distinction between black and white. Slavery as a system of social order and hierarchy kept everyone in his or her place. To state explicitly the separation of those places would be redundant.

Segregation in Woodward's account functions as a substitute for slavery; wherever slavery is not, segregation quickly develops. Indeed, legal definitions of *Negro* did not begin to emerge until *after* the Civil War.[21] Segregation as a spatial practice of separation in effect serves to preserve the social salience of the referent for *Negro* when slavery no longer exists. The white racial privilege that served as a shield from slavery was transmuted, in the rise of legalized segregation in the 1880s and following, into privileges of access and movement that accrued only to whites. While these segregation practices are often attributed to white revulsion at racial mixing, William-son has suggested a far more pragmatic and cynical explanation: "Radicals wanted black people to have clearly inferior accommodations and to know that they were inferior. Like arbitrary disfranchisement, arbitrary relega-tion to always inferior facilities was a sign of where the power actually lay, and where it was likely to lie in the future." [22] Tellingly, the major excep-tion to such practices was domestic servants; although no longer enslaved, the relative status of black servants in relation to their white employers was relatively fixed.

Such deliberate intentions as Williamson proposes need not be adduced in all cases to account for the ongoing and, to the popular white mind, natural practices of segregation. Rather, such practices and the social per-ceptions that accompanied them served to maintain under the guise of the natural the exclusive boundary around whiteness and to sustain the settled expectations of white privilege. As Cheryl Harris notes, "whiteness pro-duced—and was reproduced by—the social advantage that accompanied it." [23] From this perspective, segregation and related taboos on miscegena-tion are not simply the legal expression of social antipathies. To locate racial revulsion as the origin of segregatory practices is to mistakenly naturalize the effects of a social system of distinctions and divisions and to relegate racism to the immutable realms of the eternal unconscious. Rather, segre-gation and the legal, social, and institutional contexts in which it operates function as mechanisms that contribute to the production, ordering, and control of racial identities.

While the *Plessy* opinion seemed to assume that separate facilities merely reflected a prior and natural division of the races, the suppressed tautology between legal racial distinctions and natural racial divisions re-vealed that racial separation was, in a very significant manner, racial dis-tinction. According to the Court, the Louisiana separate car law in question separated the races on the basis of a real, prior racial distinction and there-fore could not be construed as impinging on claims to legal equality. Justice Brown, writing for the majority, stated: "A statute which implies merely a legal distinction between the white and the colored races—a distinction which is founded in the color of the two races, and must always exist so long as white men are distinguished from the other race by color—has no tendency to destroy the legal equality of the two races, or to re-establish a state of involuntary servitude." [24] Brown suggests that because the races are already unequal and therefore separate, the law merely reflects this natural division. By insisting that the law merely reflects the nature of things, Brown implies that the law has nothing to say about the production and perpetuation of white privilege. "Separate but equal" as it appears in this ruling refers not to the person's social condition, which Brown suggests is beyond the purview of the law, but to his or her standing before the law. But, in fact, the law accorded whiteness a particular and privileged status. The value of whiteness and the presumption of exclusivity could be maintained only by strict policing of the boundary line, which the law effected by enforcing standards of legitimacy for the claim to whiteness.

Thus, Brown effects a powerful rhetorical reversal of the relation between racial distinction and law, effacing the law's role in the production of distinction. The result was to remove the question of the origin or functioning of racial distinction itself into the realm of the presocial and the prelegal. As Michaels notes, "the doctrine of 'separate but equal' affirmed racial distinction *as such*; it affirmed, that is, racial distinction independent of any other legal consideration. . . . Thus the absence of any difference *grounded* in law became powerful testimony to the irreducibility of a difference *reflected* in the law; legal equality became the sign of racial separation." [25] Only things that are inherently separate need be defined as equal. However, that very separateness only *appears* neutral; it is in fact predicated on, and maintained in order to protect, the property and privilege of whiteness.

The equal protection accorded to all citizens by the Fourteenth Amendment, it would seem, was an equality in form violently disjoined from fact. As Brown put it, the Fourteenth Amendment could "enforce the absolute equality of the two races before the law, but, in the nature of things, it could not have been intended to abolish distinctions based upon color, or to enforce social, as distinguished from political, equality." The Court's willingness to uphold the exclusivity of whiteness and to protect the privileges attendant on whiteness meant that no matter how much equality might be insisted on, every assertion of the natural distinctions of the races was in fact a naturalization of the constantly reproduced and reinforced racial hierarchy. The effort to disjoin social hierarchy from a theoretical legal equality is evident in the original phrasing of the ruling, which speaks of laws providing for "equal but separate" accommodations.[26] The subtle transmutation of "equal but separate" to the more familiar locution "separate but equal" exposes the truth of the matter.[27] *Separate* is the prior, more important term, and *but* qualifies the separation, implying that absent that qualifier, such a separateness would in fact be unequal. Thus, "but equal" serves to signal the very condition it hopes to negate, that separateness can be anything but *unequal*. The Supreme Court recognized as much when it acknowledged 60 years later in *Brown v Board of Education* that "separate educational facilities are inherently unequal." [28] That is, there is within the very principle of separation the implication of inequality.

## Justice and the Law

Eric Sundquist calls Charles Chesnutt's *Marrow* "the most important [literary] protest against the painful descent of America into harsh segregation." [29] In today's judicial climate, in which a supposedly color-blind justice operates to uphold the settled expectations of ongoing white privilege originally given legal force in the wake of *Plessy*, it is especially urgent that we revisit the scene of segregation and failed justice that Chesnutt takes as his literary object.[30] Writing in the period immediately following the Court's capitulation to the increasingly violent status quo, Chesnutt (a lawyer by training) could not but be affected by the gap between the law's promise of justice and the inherent injustices perpetrated in the name of rights and equality. The novel is punctuated throughout by episodes of prejudice, hypocrisy, and cynical political opportunism, reaching a climax in the riot that destroys the black press and the black hospital and restores white supremacy in the city. As Sundquist has suggested, Chesnutt's exposure of the machinations of mob rule dramatizes the extent to which "in the age of segregation the law became a cloak for violent seizures of power and, conversely, that the fabricated specter of black lawlessness was a cloak behind which white lawlessness might be hidden." [31]

Sundquist argues that the imitative structure of blackface minstrelsy is the ruling metaphor for Chesnutt's view of the law: in *Marrow*, Chesnutt reveals the trappings beneath the South's "performance" of plantation paternalism, which has been staged in order to gain Northern acquiescence to the restoration of white supremacy. As Sundquist remarks, "minstrelsy was the cultural mask for a national reunion built upon an escalation of racial discrimination and violence." [32] There is no question that Chesnutt aimed to expose the discrimination and violence hidden under the mask of lawfulness in the contemporary political climate. But what appears as justice, I will argue, becomes increasingly complex. On the one hand, justice is a fraud, a sham mask under which violence and domination continue unabated. But at times the same justice is in fact the vehicle for such violence; justice need not be violated in order to be violent. The collusion of justice and violence marks, I think, the limits of the sort of justice that often appears as the only justice, the justice of commensurability and retribution. The law of racial division and segregation is one that demands a justice of commensurability; this is the principle of separate and equal. In this justice, each term is defined as equal to, and substitutable for, the other. The conclusion of the novel, I will argue, is an extended meditation on the impossibility of balancing the accounts, of resolving commensurable wrongs, or of arriving at a justice of retribution. And in the representations of justice and the law leading up to this denouement, Chesnutt is at pains to expose the tautological violence whereby incommensurabilities are rendered equal before the law.

Despite white characters' repeated appeals to the law of the land and the "higher law" to justify courses of action, the law is always suspect in this narrative: the justice it promises neither punishes the guilty nor spares the innocent. One encounter with legal racial segregation is described in this novel; as the episode makes explicit, the terms of the law are not inevitable, and the law is anything but impartial. Returning home from Philadelphia, Dr. Miller meets his white colleague Dr. Burns in the train coming south. In Virginia, they must transfer from the sleeping car in which they have been traveling to a day coach. Burns chooses a seat for both of them, but Miller pauses: "Miller stood a moment hesitatingly, but finally took the seat indicated" (p. 52). Miller appears slightly ill at ease, noting carefully the movements of the conductor. Soon, the conductor confronts Burns: "did I understand you to say that this man was your servant?" [33] Burns's indignant response in the negative prompts the conductor to demand that Miller move to the colored car: "I'm sorry to part *friends*, but the law of Virginia does not permit colored passengers to ride in the white cars" (p. 53). The source of Miller's unease since entering the day coach is now clear and is made even clearer by the conductor's next words: "This is a day coach, and is distinctly marked 'White' as you must have seen before you sat down here. The sign is put there for that purpose" (p. 54).

Miller knows what neither the reader nor Burns notice; that this is a "whites only" car, as the conductor explains. In fact, as the conductor takes pains to note, there is a sign: "a large card neatly framed and hung at the end of the car, containing the legend, 'White,' in letters about a foot long, painted in white upon a dark background, typical, one might suppose, of the distinction thereby indicated" (p. 54). Burns's behavior on entering the car suggests that he did not see this sign; or rather, he must have seen it because the narrator emphasizes twice its large dimensions, but the sign is visible only to Miller. Burns cannot read the word *White* in reference to himself; Miller reads *White* because it excludes him and demands his absence. The word *White* interposes itself between Miller and Burns even before the invocation of the law. The sign does not name the law ("whites only" or "no colored passengers allowed in this car") but rather names whiteness, as the origin and aim of the law: to establish the exclusive definition of *white* and to maintain it.

Despite Burns's outrage, Miller is obliged to move to the colored car. The narrator's gloss on the signs in the colored rail cars suggests that the function of the signs is as much to name as it is to legislate the disposition of those so named: "The car was conspicuously labeled at either end with large cards, similar to those in the other car, except that they bore the word 'Colored' in black letters upon a white background. The author of this piece of legislation had contrived, with an ingenuity worthy of a better cause, that not merely should the passengers be separated by the color line, but that the reason for this division should be kept constantly in mind" (p. 56). Chesnutt suggests that if segregation is to have the desired social effects, division itself ("separate but equal") is insufficient. It is the naming, the production of the reason for division, that appears as the primary object of these cards. But if this is the case, then the logical reasoning from the natural division of the races to the reflection of this division in the social practice of segregation is effectively reversed: it is the function of segregation, Chesnutt implies, to create the color line as the basis for the principle of a fundamental racial division. The description of the cards suggests the tautological mechanism of this production of division. On both signs, the color of the letters corresponds to the color the word names. One might posit practical or psychological reasons for this: for example, illiterate people might understand the visible mark even if they cannot read the word. However, one might also consider these signs as enacting the condition of law. These signs effect the ideal identity of signified and signifier that continually fails in real life. On the signs, the word names what the word is. Both color and word are abstract and refer to nothing but each other: a facile circularity of definition. White is the color; the word *White* is white. The simple declaration of absolute, unambiguous difference enacted by the signs is meant to mirror a real difference of persons.

But instead, these signs reveal the law of the color line as a law that simultaneously names and creates a difference: what is the (legal) definition of a black person? A person who is (legally) defined as black.

Miller's encounter with the law of segregation on a railroad car is an oblique allusion to the *Plessy* case, a case likewise concerned with the effects of separate car laws. The court rejected Homer Plessy's challenge, arguing that "the underlying fallacy of the plaintiff's argument consists in the assumption that the enforced separation of the two races stamps the colored race with a badge of inferiority."[34] But what from the perspective of the judicial logic of separate and equal appears as fallacy is, in practice, a palpable fact. Chesnutt does not fail to illuminate the chasm between the superficial impartiality of law and its inequitable effects. When Miller is forced to leave the white car, Burns's outrage is met by the conductor's equanimity: "there's no use kicking. It's the law of Virginia, and I am bound by it as well as you. . . . The law will be enforced. The beauty of the system lies in its strict impartiality—it applies to both races alike" (pp. 54–55). The conductor's invocation of the logic of "separate and equal" is quickly undermined, however, when white Captain McBane uses the colored car as his own private smoking car and refuses to leave when Miller objects. In the face of the conductor's impartial law, McBane replies, "I'll ride where I damn please" (p. 58). The law appears to name difference impersonally and to legislate impartially the resultant division. But in practice, the effect of the law is to produce and sustain difference and division in order to uphold the resultant inequalities that are justified in the name of that division. The law is not merely a minstrel mask for the ongoing violence of white supremacy; the law enacts in its assumption and maintenance of the color line the very condition of white supremacy, that is, the protection of the exclusivity of whiteness. White cannot define itself as superior without a simultaneous definition of what counts as white, and what is excluded. White supremacy relies on the very possibility of division, constructing a line of delimitation that splits the social body in two: white and black, dominators and dominated. At the heart (the marrow) of the tradition of white supremacy is a splitting. Echoing this splitting at the core of white supremacy, *Marrow* is dominated by figures of twoness and the effort to impose unity: the story is replete with instances of doubling, splitting, disavowing, twinning, repeating. The subtle tension of a oneness (the "marrow of tradition") that can only be expressed as a twoness (the split of white and black) points toward the most difficult contradictions of this novel.

## White Wills: Politics and Property

*The Marrow of Tradition* was written in part as a particular political intervention in the extremely volatile arena of race relations at the turn of the century, as a counter to white propaganda accusing the black population of violence and lawlessness and hysterically decrying the terrors of imminent black supremacy. In her literary biography of her father, Helen Chesnutt writes: "Chesnutt had been very much affected by the savage race riot that had broken out in Wilmington, North Carolina, in the November election of 1898. He had friends and relatives in Wilmington and had received many reports of the trouble there. . . . Late in 1900, Chesnutt began to write a new novel based on the Wilmington riot. He thought that by this book he might stir up the thinking people of the country to a realization of what was taking place in the South."[35] In 1898, racial relations in the relatively integrated coastal city of Wilmington, North Carolina, were strained to the breaking point. In the elections of 1894 and 1898, white Democrat "redeemers" who had ruled the city and the state since the collapse of Reconstruction and the withdrawal of federal forces in 1877 began to lose some of their power to an emerging coalition of Populists, supported by poor whites who had become disenchanted by the elitist rule of the southern Democrats, and Republicans who leapt at the chance to regain power. In the wake of this power shift, the black citizens of Wilmington gained a certain measure of political power, although their political representation was hardly commensurate with their majority position in the population. For the Democrats, this small shift was tantamount to "Negro domination." In 1898, the black vote was crucial for Populist-Republican success; the Democrats could remain in power only by blocking the black vote. Key politicians and other public figures who dreamed of a return to the Old South began a campaign of racial inflammation and fear designed to force the black voters to stay away from the polls, either by law or by force. The strategy was a success: on election day, November 8, 1898, the Democrats defeated the Republicans by 6,000 votes.[36]

The next day, the white business and political leaders determined to run prominent black citizens and their supporters out of the city. Five hundred heavily armed white men gathered and marched into the black part of the city. After destroying a black-owned printing press in a fairly orderly fashion, the invading force quickly took on the character of a mob; shots were fired, and chaos broke out. Throughout the day, heavily armed groups of white men confronted any black person so unfortunate as to be out in the street, searching, beating, and sometimes shooting them. This "campaign for white supremacy" culminated in many dead (ten according to the Democrat-controlled papers, hundreds according to black observers), many more wounded, and a black exodus from the city. The previously powerful black majority was replaced by a small but growing white majority. *Riot* is perhaps a misleading term to describe the events in Wilmington, suggesting an uncontrolled uprising from the bottom of society. What happened in Wilmington was rather a calculated effort on the part of the most powerful members of society to use mob rule to secure their position and ensure the reign of white supremacy.[37]

Chesnutt had high hopes for the power of fiction to influence politics. In an effort to refute Thomas Dixon's inflammatory portrayal in *The Leopard's Spots* of the Wilmington riot as a defense of white womanhood against the rapacious attacks of black men, Chesnutt sent copies of his own novel laying bare the political conspiracy to members of the House of Representatives. As a call to action on behalf of racial justice, Chesnutt hoped *Marrow* would be "lodged in the popular mind as the legitimate successor of *Uncle Tom's Cabin* and [Tourgée's] *A Fool's Errand*."[38] Although Albion Tourgée today is not well remembered, his satiric portrayal of American racial practices was well known in its day. Tourgée is also interesting in relation to Chesnutt's consideration of the problems of segregation and justice in *Marrow*; it was Tourgée who had argued a brief before the Supreme Court in the *Plessy* case claiming that the light-skinned Homer Plessy had been harmed by the loss of his reputation for being white. Although this connection is oblique, Chesnutt's allusion to the *Plessy* case in the scene on the segregated train suggests that the arguments surrounding that case were not unfamiliar to him.

Where science and superstition located the perceived differential of character and worth in the "blood," Tourgée in his brief sought to establish the privileged status of whiteness elsewhere, in the property interest of reputation.[39] By defining the reputation of whiteness rather than whiteness itself as the question, Tourgée sought to challenge the lower court's ruling that removing Plessy to a colored car had not violated his civil rights. In its response, the Court agreed that whiteness was a property interest but one that could only be claimed by whites. Because Plessy was a colored man assigned to a colored car, "he has been deprived of no property, since he is not lawfully entitled to the reputation of being a white man."[40] While Tourgée had hoped that his argument would expose the absurdity of legal racial distinctions, the Court turned the argument around to further reinforce the arbitrary but unassailable claims of whiteness. As Allen Douglas suggests, "rather than reputation being property, enabling one to first enunciate a property interest and reap constitutional protection, courts insisted that any property claim in the self could only be made upon the basis of one's white reputation."[41] Property claims were implicitly racialized; the only legitimate basis on which to claim property in whiteness was whiteness itself. While the Court in this instance recognized whiteness only as a "traditional status-property,"[42] the relation between the property of status or reputation and other forms of property could hardly be denied. Whiteness was not merely race but race conjoined to privilege. So long as some could be excluded from whiteness, whiteness was, as Cheryl Harris remarks, "the predicate for attaining a host of societal privileges, in both public and private spheres."[43] Hence, whiteness was not only a privileged basis for property claims; as Harris has argued in detail, whiteness itself was (and is) property.

In examining the execution of two white wills in the story, Chesnutt scrutinizes the relation between property and the production and maintenance of white supremacy that remains implicit in the Court's reasoning in *Plessy*. The first will to appear in the story is that of Olivia and Janet's father, Samuel Merkell. Or rather, this will initially appears in the story as a will that has failed to appear. Merkell's will was never found, and Olivia continues to be tormented by the possibility that the illegitimate daughter, Janet, might have some claim on the inheritance that Olivia has received by default. In refusing to recognize Janet, has Olivia violated her father's will? Major Carteret reassures his wife that, even if a will leaving half of Merkell's property to Janet's black mother Julia, and thereby to Janet, were to be found, it would be neither legally nor morally binding: "Who was she, to have inherited the estate of your ancestors, of which, a few years before, she would herself have formed a part?" (p. 256). Carteret suggests that the will of the white father *must* be to disown his black children. Carteret implies that there is no crossing from that which is property (Julia as a part of Merkell's estate) to that which may possess property (Julia as inheritor of Merkell's estate). Whiteness served as a shield against becoming property under slavery; after slavery, whiteness continues to shield property from falling into the possession of those excluded by color from the status of property holders. The property line *is*, in this case, the color line. While the law after slavery has established black people as citizens, and therefore as individuals to whom property rights cannot be denied, the reality of social relations and especially of property rights in the novel suggests that the continuing principle governing black property is that articulated as legal precedent *before* slavery: the black man or woman has no rights the white man or woman is bound to respect.

In the 1857 *Dred Scott* decision, the Supreme Court collapsed the distinction between free and enslaved blacks and concluded that no black, whether free or not, could be considered a citizen of the United States. As a result, no black person had any legal rights that needed to be recognized or protected:

> The question is simply this: Can a negro, whose ancestors were imported into this country and sold as slaves, become a member of the political community formed and brought into existence by the Constitution of the United States, and as such become entitled to all the rights, and privileges, and immunities, guarantied by that instrument to the citizen. . . .
>
> We think . . . that they are not included, and were not intended to be included under the word "citizens" in the Constitution, and can therefore claim none of the rights and privileges which that instrument provides for and secures to citizens of the United States. On the contrary, they were at that time [i.e., at the time of the drafting of the Constitution] considered as a subordinate and inferior class of beings, who had been subjugated by the dominant race, and, whether emancipated or not, yet remained subject to their authority.[44]

As Don Fehrenbacher points out, the crucial phrase here is "whether emancipated or not." The refusal to grant slavery itself as the distinguishing sign of status makes the relevant factor not actual enslavement, but race (as the sign of former or potential enslavement): "All blacks, according to his view, stood on the same ground. Emancipation made no difference. The status of the free Negro was fixed forever by the fact that he or his ancestors had once been enslaved." [45] *Dred Scott* was explicitly refuted by the collective emancipation effected by the Civil War, and the enacting of the Fourteenth Amendment granting citizenship, and its attendant rights, to anyone born within the United States. But despite this apparent reform, it was the principles of *Dred Scott* rather than the Fourteenth Amendment that informed the legal, political, economic, and social disfranchisement of blacks following the end of Reconstruction in 1877. Insisting that the Fourteenth Amendment had added no new individual rights but had only furthered the protection of existing rights, the courts left the definition and enforcement of "equal rights" in the hands of the states. The effect was, of course, to institute what Tourgée called the "legal condition of subjection to the dominant class, a bondage quite separable from the incident of ownership." [46] In *Plessy*, as Eric Sundquist has argued, the court anachronistically invoked the prewar abrogation of black civil rights as the status quo, "recreat[ing] caste distinctions that violated American principle, the legacy of the Civil War, and the process of Constitutional amendment." [47]

Of course, I am not suggesting that black people could not or did not hold property; for example, Dr. Miller is the owner of the Carteret mansion. But in the disposition of the white wills, Chesnutt suggests that where property might be contested, the logic of the *Dred Scott* decision continued to prevail after the war in the actual functioning of the law as applied by white custom. This becomes clear in the novel when Aunt Polly reveals to Olivia the ambivalent circumstances under which Olivia's claim to the entirety of Merkell's inheritance was established. On Olivia's father's death, Aunt Polly threw Julia and her daughter Janet out of the house: "If I had n't been just in time, Olivia, they would have turned you out. I saved the property for you and your son! You can thank me for it all!" (p. 129). Her words cause Olivia to suspect that there is more to the story than she has been told; but when she questions Aunt Polly, Polly becomes evasive: "Why do you want to know? You've got the land, the houses, and the money. You've nothing to complain of" (p. 132). Polly's equivocal affirmation of Olivia's right to the inheritance causes Olivia to suspect that the property she inherited from her father is not so properly hers as she had formerly assumed. But this does not make it any less hers. When Olivia discovers later that Aunt Polly hid a will and a marriage certificate that would have legitimated Janet, the only appropriate response to this deceit is, as Polly puts it, "enjoy yourself, and be thankful!"

Olivia has persuaded herself that because Janet is illegitimate, she need feel no compunction in keeping the inheritance to herself. When she finds a will leaving Janet $10,000, she burns it; if it is only a question of the property rights of an illegitimate daughter, Olivia feels justified in denying that she had any. By "every rule of law and decency," all her father's property ought to descend to her own son Dodie. But the discovery of a marriage certificate effectively legitimating Janet as the legal daughter of Julia and Samuel Merkell puts Olivia in something of a quandary. She cannot deny to herself that the marriage was legal, and hence that Julia's child Janet was legitimate, but she has destroyed the will. In the absence of a will, the disposition of Merkell's estate is governed by the law of inheritance: "Under the law, which intervened now that there was no will, the property should have been equally divided" (p. 266). Hence, where Merkell's will was initially subverted by Olivia's determination to refuse to recognize his miscegenational liaison as valid, now the will is one-upped by the law, which not only gives Janet the right to some of the property but to fully half. But the letter of the law is interrupted by Olivia's further reflection: "If the woman had been white, — but the woman had *not* been white, and the same rule of moral conduct did not, *could* not, in the very nature of things, apply, as between white people!" (p. 266). The "very nature of things" upholds the line between black and white. For Olivia, no matter what will or law may decree, the fact of Janet's blackness negates the property claim she might have had on Merkell's inheritance. The implication is that an incontestable property claim, outside the realm of the law, upholds the position of the white race; to give it to the black race is to undermine white supremacy and to undermine the separateness of whiteness itself.

Merkell is not the only white man whose will is circumvented when it leaves some property to a black man or woman. Shortly before his death, Mr. Delamere made a new will leaving all his property to Dr. Miller's hospital. General Belmont suppresses this will, "justified by the usual race argument: . . . Mr. Delamere's property belonged of right to the white race, and by the higher law should remain in the possession of white people. Loyalty to one's race was a more sacred principle than deference to a weak old man's whims" (p. 235). White property is by rights of race loyalty exclusively white; white property is proper to whiteness as it sustains the identity and enclosure of the race. To send white property across the color line is to call into question not only the legitimacy of white property (derived from the extraction of black labor) but also to risk a breach in the line separating whiteness from blackness. To preserve the "very nature of things," property can no more cross the color line than can person.[48]

## Twins

While Olivia seeks to retain the inheritance entirely for herself as a symbolic (and material) repudiation of any connection or obligation to Janet, Janet continues to haunt her. Janet persists as a painful reminder of the injustices of the past that have meted out to Olivia everything and to Janet nothing. Olivia struggles to forget this past and to disavow her own culpability. To acknowledge the truth of the past, and its embodiment in Janet, threatens to deprive Olivia of everything she holds dear, not simply the material inheritance that she claims as her right but more importantly the very whiteness that is the foundation of her identity as well as her position in society and her claim to property.

## IDENTITY AND DESIRE

As Olivia's identity emerges in the novel, it is constructed entirely around the repudiation of any relation to Janet and the refusal even to recognize her. Throughout the novel, Olivia is simultaneously repulsed and obsessed by Janet. Although they do not meet until the final chapter, Janet repeatedly appears to Olivia like a silent, reproachful apparition. Does Olivia's paranoid obsession with Janet represent, in the tradition of gothic romance, "the fearful, phantasmic rejection by recasting of an original homosexual (or even merely homosocial) desire"?[49] If this is the case, Olivia's desire is simultaneously incestuous, miscegenational, and homosexual; a multiplied violation of virtually every social taboo but at the same time, a virtual repetition of the convoluted patriarchy fostered on the slave plantation. To recognize her obsession as desire would be to expose this twisted history to a scrutiny it could not bear and to risk losing the certainty of distinction and differentiation that seems to guarantee the stability of patriarchy and white supremacy. But the turmoil of their intertwined histories is never far below the surface, and as Janet realizes—and Olivia is only vaguely aware—there is a destructive force between herself and Olivia that cannot simply be denied, one rooted in the "unacknowledged relationship" between Janet and Olivia, a "malignant force" (p. 77). The malignancy of their unacknowledged relationship perpetuates the tradition of violence and violations produced in the wake of slavery. The sign of this malignancy is the color line, which simultaneously joins and separates Janet and Olivia as twins. The violent and arbitrary order of race gives Janet and Olivia their respective identities; but, at the same time, the price of maintaining this order is revealed by Olivia's constant paranoia and the continuing threat to Dodie's life. The order that seems to result, a patriarchal, racially hierarchical order, is only apparent; the illusion of order can only be sustained by refusing to acknowledge her twin, refusing to confront the possibility that her identity, her apparent oneness, is in reality a suppressed twoness.

Olivia is especially alarmed at the fragility of her own whiteness, a whiteness constantly threatened by her repudiated relation with Janet. In particular, she fears that to recognize Janet as her sister would call her own whiteness into question: "She shuddered before the possibility that at some time in the future some person, none too well informed, might learn that her father had married a colored woman, and might assume that she, Olivia Carteret, or her child, had sprung from this shocking *mésalliance*, — a fate to which she would willingly have preferred death" (p. 270). If Janet's blackness poses a risk of contamination to Olivia's whiteness, then it is only in opposition to Janet's blackness that Olivia's whiteness is assured. While Olivia contrasts death with being mistakenly identified as black, and chooses the former over the latter, she also implicitly equates the two. From the perspective of white supremacy, blackness is itself a kind of ontological nothingness that might be termed a "living death."[50] But it is also the case that Olivia's identity *is* her whiteness; to be exposed to the contiguity of her own whiteness with Janet's threatening blackness is itself a kind of death, a loss of that determining aspect that makes Olivia secure in her Olivia-ness. If Olivia's whiteness is called into question, what then is Olivia? Throughout the narrative, the figures of death and doubling are never far removed from each other. The double threatens to expose the incompleteness of the one — this is its "death threat." Suppressing the double is the only means of warding off this threat. What is at stake for Olivia in her continued refusal to acknowledge Janet is her very life; but the price of attempting to preserve the precarious autonomy of her whiteness by repudiating her double is high. In the last pages of the novel, it appears that Dodie's life — and implicitly the lives of future generations — will be the toll exacted for the rigorous maintenance of the color line.

Janet's intense desire for Olivia's recognition is the mirrored reverse of the threat of death posed by the double. But where Olivia disavows her dependency by clinging to the illusory wholeness of whiteness, Janet experiences the incompleteness of herself in the presence of her double as a debilitating sense of loss and an overwhelming desire for the recognition she hopes will negate that loss. Despite Janet's central role in the familial plot, less than two pages of the novel are devoted to Janet's point of view prior to the last chapter. This condensation of her character emphasizes its singular dimension as embodying, almost to the exclusion of all else, desire for recognition. Although she knows that the social barriers between them do not allow her to expect anything else, "when the heart speaks, reason falls into the background, and Janet would have worshipped this sister, even afar off, had she received even the slightest encouragement" (p. 66). Her passionate desire for a sign from Olivia brings sisterly devotion into the realm of an almost erotic obsession. When Olivia finally does blurt out the truth, though, in the novel's final scene, Janet discovers that the recognition she has always dreamed of brings her no satisfaction: "Janet had obtained her heart's desire, and now that it was at her lips, found it but apples of Sodom, filled with dust and ashes!" (p. 328). The image of apples filled with dust suggests a promise that, once fulfilled, proves empty of the pleasure it offered, a "hollow, disappointing, specious thing."[51] Janet has dreamed that Olivia's recognition would restore her to her proper name and her proper place, that it would make her complete. Yet when the recognition she had longed for finally comes, it fails to give her anything more than what she already had: a respectable name, a good place in the world, and material security. But the figurative apples of Sodom also evoke the transgressive nature of Janet's desire for Olivia. Like the sins of Sodom, the recognition that crosses the color line between the two and joins them as one threatens the collapse of social boundaries. If Janet and Olivia are kept separate as black and white, their joining in mutual recognition disrupts both black and white and evokes some unnameable and uncontainable other. It is against this eruption of the unnameable that Olivia struggles throughout the narrative; but as I will argue that the novel's conclusion suggests, the future can only come from the realm of some such unnameable.

GUILT AND JUSTICE

In terms of both their father's property and Janet's desire for recognition, Chesnutt's position is clear: Olivia's status and privilege are the result of theft. Although Olivia is deeply troubled by her dawning conscience, the perpetuation of this crime is the necessary price of her whiteness. In his portrayal of Olivia's guilt and Janet's desire, Chesnutt suggests that the exclusive privilege of whiteness is the ill-gotten gain of a crime for which blackness must suffer the consequences. The relation between twinning, theft, and guilt is played out in a darkly comic vein in a sideplot that involves the dissolute Tom Delamere donning blackface and posing as his father's faithful manservant and former slave, Sandy. Tom's imitation of Sandy is so perfect that he wins first prize at a "cakewalk," an entertainment staged for visiting Northerners in order to give the visitors "a pleasing impression of Southern customs" (p. 117). Sundquist suggests that this cakewalk, read as a minstrel performance of Old South plantation ideology for the entertainment and edification of Northerners, might be viewed as Chesnutt's central metaphor for the current racial state of affairs. If "the vaunted 'reunion' of North and South at the close of the century was predicated upon northern acquiescence in southern control of the 'Negro problem,'" then "minstrelsy was the cultural mask for a national reunion built upon an escalation of racial discrimination and violence."[52] Such outrages as the Wilmington coup could continue so long as the North continued to smile and tap its toes to the South's minstrel staging of "all's well."

But where the blackface minstrel is understood to stand in for and efface an absent black other, Tom cannot be so easily separated from Sandy. The efficacy of Tom's performance is linked to the narrative twinning of Tom and Sandy. Chesnutt presents Tom's appearance as Sandy as a doubling rather than as an imitation. Insofar as they are related through twinning rather than imitation, Tom and Sandy become a unit that is constitutively split in two. This twinning relation thus displaces the alternative relation of original and imitation in which the former is viewed as primary and autonomous and the latter as secondary and derivative. The constitutive splitting of twinning insists that there is never autonomy; where original claims priority over imitation, twinning evades the question of priority. In the relation of original and imitation, the imitation produces the superficial effect of a twin or double. Thus, where imitation produces the effect of doubling, there remains an autonomous original. In contrast, the originary twinning of Tom and Sandy is the condition for Tom's subsequent imitation of Sandy. Here, doubling is the source of the possibility of imitation, such that there is no original, singular one that can exist apart from its double. It is the originary and constitutive division of the color line that enables the twinning between Sandy and Tom and that serves as the basis for the possibility of Tom's imitation. Sundquist argues that in such imitative practices as minstrelsy or passing, "the true threat of imitation lay in its destructive effacement of the authorized, legislated racial differences of segregation."[53] But the function of twinning in *Marrow* seems quite the opposite: where imitation suggests the color line is a fragile fiction, twinning positions the color line as the foundational social fact.

Twinning, I have suggested, is formally predicated on the symmetry of the color line; but in both cases—Olivia and Janet as well as Tom and Sandy—the consequences of this twinning fall disproportionately on either side. One night when, unbeknownst to Sandy, Tom has stolen his Sunday coat to dress up in minstrel blackface, Sandy is on his way home and encounters a frightening apparition: "As it seemed to Sandy, he saw himself hurrying along in front of himself toward the house. . . . 'Ef dat's me gwine 'long in front,' mused Sandy, in vinous perplexity, 'den who is dis behin' here? Dere ain' but one er me, an' my ha'nt would n' leave my body 'tel I wuz dead. Ef dat's me in front, den I mus' be my own ha'nt; an' whichever one of us is de ha'nt, de yuther must be dead an' don' know it' " (p. 167). The appearance of his double poses a perplexing problem for Sandy, of complex epistemological and ontological dimensions. If I am doubled and the other is me, then who am I? And how do I know who I am if I am not myself but someone or something else? Or, as Sandy asks Tom (now out of disguise) when he gets home, "ef I wuz in yo' place, an' you wuz in my place, an' we wuz bofe in de same place, whar would I be?" (p. 168). For Sandy, the recognition of himself in another threatens the loss of his own identity: if that is me, who am I? But Sandy's logic quickly moves from mere confusion to an ominous foreshadowing of the consequences of thus losing his identity to another. He reasons that if the other is me, I must be my own ghost; but if one of us is a ghost, then the other — that is, I — must be dead. Indeed, the violence latent in Tom's theft of Sandy's clothes and face explodes to the surface when we discover that Tom has taken up the disguise of blackface to rob Aunt Polly. When she dies of fright, the murder is pinned on Sandy.

If, as Sundquist suggests, the cakewalk stands in Chesnutt's novel for the cloaking of white violence under a staged performance of plantation harmony, then "Tom's [doubled] doubling of Sandy splits the cakewalk function perfectly in two: Tom portrays Sandy on the one hand as the minstrel darky, and on the other as the black criminal."[54] But it is also the case that the twinning of black and white effected by Tom's minstrelsy splits crime and profit neatly in two. Where the thief is in theory both criminal and profiteer, the color line neatly divides guilt and gain. The twinning of Tom and Sandy repeats the property structure of the twinning of Olivia and Janet: white property is gained and kept at the expense of black property or, in Sandy's extreme case, black life. Eric Lott has suggested that white minstrelsy worked to displace anxieties about the plundering of black culture and the appropriation of black labor.[55] Chesnutt does Lott one better, representing Tom's thievery as doubled: he steals once from Sandy and again from Polly. The desire for and theft of blackness that Lott locates as the contradictory impulse of minstrelsy is transmuted into blatant criminality. But in the realm of the color line, crime and punishment are effectively disjoined when the judicial response to the discovery of the crime is to interpret Tom's performance as fact.

A white mob quickly convicts Sandy of the crime and determines that a lynching is the only justice. The redistribution of guilt and responsibility that makes Sandy guilty for Tom's crime suggests the relation between the doubling of the color line and the execution of justice. The complacency of white "friends" in the face of Sandy's imminent lynching bears out the suspected injustice of the law. Dr. Price refuses to interfere, arguing, "If [Sandy] is innocent, his people can console themselves with the reflection that [Aunt Polly] was also innocent, and balance one crime against the other, the white against the black" (p. 194). Is the balance that a white death should be paid for with a black death? Or that a black crime justifies a white crime? In either case, what is repressed in this judicial balance is that white innocence is purchased with black guilt and that Polly and Sandy are both victims of *white* violence. In this ominous calculus, guilt and innocence are wrested from the realm of actions into the arena of identities. The law that defines guilt becomes the color line that defines race: separating the guilty from the innocent is the same as separating the black from the white.

The collusion of the law with the quick racism of the mob is not, Chesnutt suggests, accidental. When Sandy's employer, Mr. Delamere, attempts to persuade Judge Everton of Sandy's loyalty and innocence, the judge also refuses to intervene. As judge, he speaks with the voice of the law: "He admitted that lynching was, as a rule, unjustifiable, but maintained that there were exceptions to all rules, —that laws were made, after all, to express the will of the people in regard to the ordinary administration of justice, but that in an emergency the sovereign people might assert itself and take the law into its own hands" (p. 193). Judge Everton suggests that because the law in form is nothing but the will of the sovereign, the sovereign may assert its will in violation of the content of the law. In liberal political theory, the question of sovereignty is crucial to the claim of legitimacy for law and justice. Under theoretically ideal conditions, the people as a collective are identical with the sovereign power, such that the law that governs the people is (by definition) the will of the people. This is the basis for the theoretical justification for the force of law being necessary to carry out the people's will. Rousseau, for example, follows this line of reasoning concerning the "social contract," which would "force the people to be free" by following their own sovereign will as embodied in law. In Chesnutt's refiguration of the law as the undergirding of white supremacy, Judge Everton's easy identity of sovereign and law comes under scrutiny. Everton implies that the law establishes and guarantees the identity of sovereign and subject, and if it fails to do so, it is a failure of law, not of sovereign will. As Rousseau puts it, "the sovereign, by the mere fact that it exists, is always all that it should be."[56] In contrast, the "sovereign community" as Chesnutt portrays it is one forged in violence, lawlessness, and exclusion.

Rousseau argues that the object of the law is to "force the people to be free," that is, to force the individual to obey the general will, which is directed toward the common, and therefore also the individual, good. Chesnutt reveals that this law produces a "legitimate" sovereign only by drawing a line delimiting who is named by that sovereignty: the color line. Chesnutt's vision of the law reveals the distance between force and freedom: one part of the population asserts or realizes its freedom through the use of force against another group of individuals, those who inhabit the state but do not count as "the people." The aim of the law is not justice but the maintenance of the line distinguishing the sovereign people from others. The formal justice of this law is reduced to violence and destruction. If there is to be another justice, one that saves rather than destroys, it must come from someplace beyond this law.

## 'Fiat Justitia'

Olivia imagines that she is protecting herself and her family by repudiating the stain of racial impropriety represented by Janet's existence. The sins of the past, however, are not so easily forgotten. Olivia explicitly connects the continuing danger to Dodie with the presence of Janet: "Twice within a few weeks her child had been in serious danger, and upon each occasion a member of the Miller family had been involved. . . . Olivia felt a violent wave of antipathy sweep over her toward this baseborn sister who had thus thrust herself beneath her eyes" (p. 107).

Olivia blames Janet's person for her own discomfort and the danger to her child. Yet it is Olivia who has in fact harmed Janet, by refusing to recognize her and by conspiring to disinherit her. Despite her efforts to ignore or avoid Janet, Olivia cannot escape the danger Janet embodies, the danger of Olivia's own culpability and the frightening possibility that Olivia will be subject to retribution. Increasingly haunted by the moral and social dilemma presented by Janet's unacknowledged relation to her, Olivia has a dream that depicts one possible outcome. She is drowning in the sea, holding her child and struggling to keep his head above water. She sees a boat approaching:

> Straight toward her it came, and she had reached out her hand to grasp its side, when the rower looked back, and she saw that it was her sister. *The rec-*

*ognition had been mutual.* With a sharp movement of one oar the boat glided by, leaving her clutching at the empty air. . . . The rower, after one mute, reproachful glance, rowed on. . . . Herself floating in the water, as though it were her native element, she could no longer support the child. Lower and lower it sank. (p. 268, emphasis added)

The exchange of looks in this dream seems to balance Olivia's repudiation and disinheritance of Janet against Janet's opportunity for revenge. Justice is done, it would appear, when Janet rows on, leaving Olivia alone just as Olivia has left her. But an alternative reading is also possible: Dodie's death seems the direct result of the *mutual* look of recognition, the restoration of a unity between the divided twins. The dream makes explicit the stakes for which Olivia has been playing in her struggle to deny her tie to Janet. In refusing to confront the truth of her sister, Olivia is not only struggling to preserve her own identity, she is also forestalling the recognition of the wrong that has been done to Janet and her own culpability in that wrong. The dream suggests that the cost to Olivia will be much higher than simply restoring to Janet her name and inheritance.

As the novel makes clear, the nature of Olivia's wrong to Janet cannot be isolated to the relationship between them. Although they are a generation removed from the wrongs of slavery, slavery continues to influence the course of events. Hazel Carby has suggested that slavery necessarily lurks beneath the surface of much African-American writing that does not take slavery as its explicit subject: "Slavery haunts the literary imagination because its material conditions and social relations are frequently reproduced in fiction as historically dynamic; they continue to influence society long after emancipation. The economic and social system of slavery is thus a pre-history (as well as a pre-text to all Afro-American texts), a past social condition that can explain contemporary phenomena."[57] In *Marrow* slavery is the key term necessary to explain the conflicts of the narrative as well as the suppressed subtext of the twinning relation between Janet and Olivia. Julia, Mammy Jane reveals, was once Samuel Merkell's slave. Thus, although in subsequent discussions of Julia's relation to Olivia's father the fact that she was initially his slave will be suppressed, it is this fact that underpins that relationship. Just as the import of Olivia's relation to Janet extends beyond the boundaries of their particular circumstance, Olivia's wrong against Janet cannot simply be canceled out by recognizing her as her sister or even by restoring to her the inheritance that is her due.

As Olivia's dream reveals, recognition of Janet, and thereby of the wrong that has been done her, will be costly. The depth of wrong is that of slavery itself. With recognition comes redress, and as Olivia only dimly realizes to recognize the magnitude of the wrong of slavery would do more than call the legitimacy of her own world into question. It would also bring down a wrathful retaliation none would survive: "through the long centuries there had been piled up a catalogue of wrong and outrage which, if the law of compensation be a law of nature, must some time, somewhere, in some way, be atoned for" (p. 266). Although this passage seems to call for a compensation for the wrongs and outrages of slavery, the magnitude of those wrongs cannot but call the very principle of compensation into question. The wrongs of slavery are beyond counting; a justice of retribution would wreak endless revenge. If there is to be a future, it cannot be a future determined by vengeance for the monstrous wrong of slavery. The remainder of the novel is concerned, I would suggest, with precisely the questions of justice and the future. The riot marks the perpetuation of the wrongs of slavery into the present; in its wake, the Carterets and the Millers come face to face, and the question of what sort of justice will govern their relation becomes the question of whether there is to be any future at all.

The Wellington riot, the narrator wryly comments, "was a one-sided affair" (p. 298). Bands of armed whites roam the streets, threatening and often shooting at any black they meet. Miller's son is killed by a stray bullet. Although Dodie remains at home, safe from the rioting, his life is also endangered. He develops a severe case of the croup, and in the confusion set off by the rioting the only doctor left in the town who might save his life is Dr. Miller. Carteret goes to Miller's home and begs him to save Dodie. Miller refuses: "I cannot go with you. There is a just God in heaven! — as you have sown, so may you reap" (p. 320). As Miller has lost his son in the rioting, a "just God" would decree that he has no obligation to save Carteret's son. Carteret cannot argue: "Miller's refusal to go with him was pure, elemental justice; he could not blame the doctor for his stand" (p. 321). Hence, as the title of the chapter remarks, "*fiat justitia*," let justice be done. The scales of justice seem even: Carteret is responsible for Miller's son's death in the riot, and Miller in turn refuses to save Carteret's son from a certain death.

The scene of compensatory justice acted out between Miller and Carteret is repeated in the confrontation between Janet and Olivia in the final chapter. At last they meet face to face; in this confrontation toward which the novel has been building from the beginning, the signal themes of doubling, death, desire, and recognition all come together. Olivia is frantic at the thought of Dodie's death. When Carteret tells her that Dr. Miller has refused to come, she rushes to his house in the hope that she can succeed in persuading him to change his mind. At last, these two women stand face to face: "The two women stood confronting each other across the body of the dead child, mute witness of this first meeting between two children of the same father. Standing thus face to face, each under the stress of the deepest emotions, the resemblance between them was even more strik- ing than it had seemed to Miller when he had admitted Mrs. Carteret to the house" (p. 326). The doubling of the two is emphasized here, counter- posed to the singular points of their common father and the dead child that justice has decreed they ought to share. The question of segregation and division has insinuated itself into this most private scene, and Dodie's life hangs in the balance. If justice will be done, Dodie must die.

In her frantic desperation, Olivia blurts out the truth that she had deter- mined to conceal: "You *are* my lawful sister. My father was married to your mother. You are entitled to his name, and to half his estate" (p. 327). Janet is not moved: "Now, when this tardy recognition comes, for which I have waited so long, it is tainted with fraud and crime and blood, and I must pay for it with my child's life!" Olivia finally acknowledges that this is the just outcome: "And I must forfeit that of mine, it seems, for withholding it so long. It is but just" (p. 328). Justice will be done when each act is met with its double, an eye for an eye, a tooth for a tooth. The justice of law in the final scene is a justice of symmetry and doubling. This is the formal struc- ture of "separate but equal": it is the law that separates and the law that promises equality.

The violently compromised justice that would demand Dodie's death is not, however, the novel's last word. As I have already remarked, the penulti- mate chapter is titled "*Fiat Justitia*," connoting the judgment of the law; the final chapter, in contrast, is named "The Sisters," suggesting that the extralegal ties of familial obligation, charity, or mercy are the final court of appeal. The justice of the law is based on the separation between Janet and Olivia, the line of color that divides them and provides the grounds for can- celing out the death of one son with the death of the other. Beyond that jus- tice is the family connection of sisters, between whom no clear line of sepa- ration or difference can be drawn. Janet claims as her right the refusal to save Dodie; but her next words supplement the retributive justice of the law with a gift: "But that you may know that a woman may be foully wronged, and yet may have a heart to feel, even for one who has injured her, you may have your child's life, if my husband can save it!" (p. 329). This shift from the symmetry of justice to the *asymmetry* of the gift marks the insufficiency of justice to heal the death spiral set into motion by slavery. Justice cannot end the narrative; in the cycle of violence, justice only produces death.

*Marrow* does not conclude so much as it disappears. Janet commands Miller to go with Olivia to save Dodie; the novel ends abruptly with Miller being called up to Dodie's room. Many questions remain: Does Dodie in fact survive? Do Janet and Olivia reconcile? Does Carteret realize his hypocrisy? Does Miller restore peace to the town? What happens after the riot? The absence of resolution of any of the conflicts raised in the narrative has led several critics to conclude that Chesnutt was trapped by the contradictions of his day and could not imagine any resolution to the continuing violence of racial enmity. Chesnutt's political intervention seems to stop short of envisioning the restoration of racial justice. But is it possible to read disappearance itself as the solution to the problem of race posed by the novel? If we look carefully at the circumstances in which the narrative ends, it seems that the disappearance that characterizes the last page is not simply a stuttering failure to conclude but is in fact extremely purposeful.[58] Although all of the problems and characters disappear in the novel's ending, this ending is entirely directed toward the one character who has never really appeared: Dodie.

At the end of the novel, one might conclude that Janet's happiness and her son's life have been sacrificed so that Dodie, the white baby, may live. Is this, then, a sign of the inevitable triumph of the white race? Such an apparent capitulation to the inevitability of white supremacy seems perplexing given the widely shared view of Chesnutt's novel as a powerful condemnation of the politics of segregation. On the other hand, there are those who continue to reiterate an earlier assessment of Chesnutt as seeking white acceptance rather than black power. Most recently, Sally Ann H. Ferguson has pointed to Chesnutt's nonfiction, in particular "The Future American," to argue that "while the critics romantically hail him as a black artist championing the cause of his people, Chesnutt, as his essays show, is essentially a social and literary accommodationist . . . [who seeks] above all, to prompt white acceptance of color-line blacks."[59]

In "The Future American," which appeared serialized in the *Boston Evening Transcript* in 1900 (the year before the publication of *Marrow*), Chesnutt advocates a scheme of large-scale racial amalgamation as the solution to America's racial problem. This future amalgamated American race would be predominantly white (as was the population) but would be able to make no claims to racial purity because it would have absorbed and assimilated the blood of Indian and black. The result would be an end to racial struggle: "There would be no inferior race to domineer over; there would be no superior race to oppress those who differed from them in racial externals. The inevitable social struggle, which in one form or another, seems to be one of the conditions of progress, would proceed along other lines than those of race." [60] In the latter observation, Chesnutt anticipates the conclusions of Gunnar Myrdal's landmark study of racism, *An American Dilemma*. But where Myrdal has conceded the inevitability of racial division and seeks only to eliminate what he called the "habit" of racial prejudice, Chesnutt seems to imagine the possibility of eliminating the very division that is the basis for racial distinction, and thus racial prejudice. One is struck by Chesnutt's extremely mechanical understanding of race as presented in this essay; in his mathematical calculations of the effects of racial crossing only blood is at issue. Questions of culture and the complexities of racism do not arise. Moreover, Chesnutt does not balk at the idea that black and Indian *ought* to blend in and be absorbed; implicitly, it is *their* difference that stands in the way of national harmony. The "Future American" theory, Ferguson suggests, "implicitly celebrates white skin . . . [and] ignores the immediate obstacle of racism as well as undercuts the self-esteem [dark-skinned African-Americans] need to combat [racism] daily." [61]

Chesnutt is more complicated, I think, than such a characterization would allow. While the "Future Americans" of the eponymous essay seem based on a hopelessly myopic view of racial realities, the conclusion of *Marrow* also points toward a future American but this time in a manner finely attuned to the question of justice and the possibility of an end to violence. It is, I would suggest, through the figure of the baby Dodie that the narrative works its way toward an alternative future. Although the narrative begins and ends with the question of Dodie's life in the balance, one could hardly call him a character in any conventional sense. In fact, the Carteret heir appears as studiously devoid of subjectivity or personhood. There is the matter of his name or rather his names. He is christened "Theodore Felix," but this twice-proper name is quickly dispensed with: "Having thus given the child two beautiful names, replete with religious and sentimental significance, they called him — 'Dodie' " (p. 12). The proliferation of names around this baby's body presages the questions of identity and legitimacy that will dominate the narrative. "Dodie" neutralizes the staunch masculinity of "Theodore," replacing it with an infantile sexlessness. As baby Dodie does not reach even his first birthday in the course of the narrative, he remains both outside sex and outside language: outside, that is, those circuits of relation and meaning that would provide him with a subjective identity. Thus, when the narrative's ending is entirely directed toward the saving of Dodie's life, we must ask what it is that is being saved here because to say simply "Dodie's life" is to ignore the fact that when it is a question of Dodie, there is really no one there.

Despite the absence of Dodie as character or subject, he dominates the familial portion of the narrative, and the crises that repeatedly threaten his life punctuate the plot in a rhythmic counterpoint to the rising political crisis that grips Wellington. The threat to Dodie's life at the culmination of the narrative brings the novel full circle, rhyming the opening scene of Dodie's birth. At birth, Dodie has been marked with the sign of tragedy. He is born with an ominous mark on his body, a mole on his neck that the superstitious Mammy Jane interprets as a sign of bad luck:

> Had the baby been black, or yellow, or poor-white, Jane would unhesitatingly have named, as his ultimate fate, a not uncommon form of taking off, usually resultant upon the infraction of certain laws, or, in these swift modern days, upon too violent a departure from established social customs. It was manifestly impossible that a child of such high quality as the grandson of her old mistress should die by judicial strangulation; but nevertheless the warning was a serious thing. (p. 10)

"Judicial strangulation" is a circumlocutory reference to lynching, an increasingly less uncommon form of "taking off" (i.e., dying) at the turn of the century. For a black, yellow, or poor white baby, the mole would signal a warning that the child's fate was to die violently at the hands of a lynch mob. Such a threat is tempered by the baby's whiteness; thus, Dodie ought to be spared the judicial strangulation that is all the justice there is for those not so fortunate as to be marked white. Yet judicial strangulation, it turns out, is never so far off. The mole's silent threat is borne out in the course of the novel: in the last scene, Miller must decide whether to save Dodie from the suffocation brought on by the croup. Thus, Miller's determination that it would be just to let Dodie die in exchange for the death of his own son is itself a form of judicial strangulation, the same justice that has threatened to lynch Sandy as a balancing of white innocence against black. In both cases, justice is another name for the violence of retribution; and while we may be more sympathetic to Miller's anger, Chesnutt insists that his justice is no less violent than the justice of white supremacy.

Although Dodie has no real present, the past and the future cross in his body. Mammy Jane interprets the mole as the bodily expression of a supernatural malignancy, lurking in Dodie's future. On the other hand, the narrative suggests that this malignancy is a malignancy of the past, one that has erupted into the present to endanger Dodie's life. As the truth about the past that binds Olivia to Janet is slowly revealed, the danger to Dodie that is marked by the mole becomes explicitly linked to the evil circumstances engendered by slavery. Like the memory of slavery, the dangerous effects of the mole may fade for a time, but its malignancy will always return: "the mole . . . neither faded nor went away. If its malign influence might for a time seem to disappear, it was merely lying dormant, like the germs of some deadly disease, awaiting its opportunity to strike at an unguarded spot" (p. 105). The ominous mole marks Dodie with the sins of the past; but his indeterminate blankness makes him also the empty field in which the course of the future will be decided.

Olivia's fear of the dream of Dodie's sinking under the weight of Janet's gaze is reawakened by her fear of the dangers to come in the imminent race riot. The danger to Dodie's life, which has until now been connected only with Janet's relation to Olivia, expands to encompass the dangers surrounding the plotting of the white conspirators and their plans to take the town by violence. Chesnutt's explicit connection of Olivia's treatment of Janet, the conspiracy to restore white rule, and the racism of national imperial expansion suggests that the forces threatening Dodie are simultaneously familial, local, and national. Otherwise an empty cipher, Dodie is the central figure through which pass the narrative trajectories of identity, desire, recognition, and death: in Olivia's fear of Janet, in Janet's desire for Olivia's recognition, in Miller's calculation of the scales of justice, in the race riot itself, Dodie's life is at stake. Thus, Dodie's body functions as the space where the sins of the past will resolve themselves (or will fail to resolve themselves) into the possibilities of the future.

The ambiguity of Dodie as a narrative figure for sin, injustice, and possible redemption resists an interpretation of the ending that would see Dodie's survival as effacing blackness in favor of whiteness. Dodie's future is not the future of white supremacy but the possibility of any national future that can resolve the injustices and violence of the past. This is not a reconciliation of black and white that would sustain a division between blackness and whiteness that is itself the tragic legacy of slavery. Rather, the effect of another justice after the justice of recognition and retribution aims to restore a national future by *effacing* the line of difference that has produced division and doubling. But to efface this line of difference is also to efface all that it has produced; hence, the disappearance rather than the resolution of the characters, black and white. Olivia and Janet, Carteret and Miller, exist only *as* black and white, produced within the terms of racial division. Dodie embodies a future that is not representable from within the terms of racial difference or racial identity. Thus, the narrative's ending can point toward a utopic future only by disappearing; that future is an elsewhere that cannot be comprehended or represented in the terms then available. As Chesnutt's characterization of Olivia's white paranoia makes clear, there is no whiteness without blackness; Olivia's whiteness can only be sustained through the persistent repudiation of her implication in Janet's blackness. Whereas in "The Future American" Chesnutt describes the nation's future as the absorption of black into white, in *Marrow* Dodie's blankness is the *negation* of both black and white. Thus, *Marrow* ends not with gradual transformation or amalgamation but with an absolute rupture.

The conclusion of *Marrow* seeks a way out of the fatal logic of the double that has structured the nation's history as well as that of the Millers and Carterets. If the official oneness of national unity is based on the displaced splitting of race, the resolution of this violent contradiction can neither be the supplanting of one false unity (racial homogeneity) by another (antiracist pluralism) nor the replacement of oneness (racist exclusion) with a truer twoness (antiracist separatism). Justice, *Marrow* suggests, must lie in the excess of a gift that cannot be calculated or accounted for. What will this justice look like? We cannot know; it can only be presented as an opening onto uncertainty. The future marked by Dodie's unrepresentability is a future beyond unity, beyond symmetry, beyond doubling, beyond the structures of identity and difference engendered by the color line.

## 4. The Epistemology of Race

### Knowledge, Visibility, and Passing

Olivia and Janet, Charles Chesnutt's twins across the color line, split the racial body neatly in two. The stability and certainty of Olivia's whiteness, I argued in the previous chapter, depends on her *not* recognizing Janet as her double, on her insisting on the priority of the racial difference that divides them. Thus, what is at stake in Olivia's struggle against Janet is the very preservation of the color line. Throughout his writing career, Chesnutt continued to be interested in the color line, in the absurdities of a social system of classification and identification that insisted on an absolute difference between white and black, even as it warily acknowledged the existence of certain bodies that seemed to violate the very possibility of distinction. The arbitrariness and also the power of racial classification were important to Chesnutt both in his fictional writings and in his own life. Although he did not deliberately take advantage of his light-skinned appearance, he was sometimes mistaken for white; he describes one such episode in his diary of 1875 (he was 17): "Twice today, or oftener, I have been taken for 'white.' . . . I believe I'll leave here and pass anyhow, for I am as white as any of them. One old fellow said today, 'Look here, Tom. *Here's a black as white as you are.*' "[1] Donald Gibson suggests that at the center of Chesnutt's ideas about race and his own racial identity lies a paradox, the same paradox I will suggest is at the heart of race passing. As Gibson remarks, "[Chesnutt] indicates the disparity between illusion and reality, perception and knowledge. He deals with the enigma of the thing that is

what it is not, and is not what it is."[2] Between the "perception" of whiteness and the "knowledge" of blackness, an abyss opens up, an abyss that
threatens not only confusion but the very orders of being. What chaos will
ensue when a thing is what it is not and is not what it is?

While Chesnutt was not the first African-American writer to focus on
the social and psychological circumstances surrounding passing, *The House
Behind the Cedars* broke in important ways with several conventions common to the various forms of mulatto fiction that had preceded it. While
Rena Walden returns to her race, refusing finally to pass into the white
world, her brother John insists to the end that he is white. John Walden
stresses the priority of perception and self-identification in the determination of his own race. As he contends, "a Negro is black; I am white, and
not black."[3] Appearance, for John, is all there is. As William Andrews
suggests, Chesnutt's novel seems to ask why "people who look as white
as 'whites' and whose cultural affinities and socioeconomic goals mirror
those of 'whites' [should] be automatically condemned as racial impostors
for simply *being* what to all appearances they actually are—white men and
women."[4] Why, indeed? In insisting on the priority of affinity and appearance over the convoluted logic of blood, Chesnutt seeks to short-circuit the
contradictions and complications of the idea of race as it is subject to legal
definitions, social codes, and physical signs. While Chesnutt's solution ne-
glects the constructedness of both affinity and appearance, he broaches a
problem that continues to plague the contemporary politics of racial identity. The problem at the heart of the modern idea of race, the problem signified by the ambivalent bodies of such passing characters as Rena or John,
is that legal, physical, and social identities might fail to coincide, leaving
open the gaping question of where the truth of race in fact resides.

## Deception and Alienation

In *An American Dilemma*, sociologist Gunnar Myrdal gives a working
definition of passing: "For all practical purposes 'passing' means that a
Negro becomes a white man, that is, moves from the lower to the higher
caste. In the American caste order, this can be accomplished only by the
deception of the white people with whom the passer comes to associate and
by a conspiracy of silence on the part of other Negroes who might know
about it."[5] To pass is, for Myrdal, to disguise oneself, to simulate whiteness, to conceal the truth under a false appearance—this is the common-

sense understanding of passing. The one who passes is, in this common understanding, really, indisputably black; but the deceptive appearance of the body permits such a one access to the exclusive opportunities of whiteness. Common sense dictates that passing plays only with appearance and that the true identities underlying the deceptive appearances remain untouched. This has been the accepted understanding of passing, both on the part of social scientists who attempted to study the phenomenon and literary critics who sought to understand the significance of literary representations of passing.

What has been the significance of passing in American culture? In a survey of scientific studies, accounts in the popular press, and creative representations of race passing in American literature and culture, John Bayliss plots a trajectory of popular interest in race passing that emerges in the late nineteenth century, rises through the first decades of the twentieth century, and gradually falls off in the 1950s. Most of the social science research—what little there is—dates from the 1940s, 1950s, and 1960s, lagging somewhat behind the popular fascination with the phenomenon. Bayliss mentions fifteen black-authored and eleven white-authored passing narratives written between 1900 and 1960. Press accounts of passing begin to appear in the 1920s as case histories, and "the succeeding decades saw continued exposés of passing, not so much to promote witch hunts as to provide good copy for muckraking."[6] The *Index to Periodical Articles by and About Negroes, 1950–1959* (the first decade for which this index was compiled) lists seventeen articles under the heading "Passing," with titles like "I refuse to pass," "My father passed for white," and "Secret life of an ex-Negro." A handful of Hollywood films of the 1940s and 1950s took up the theme of passing, including *Lost Boundaries* (1949), *Pinky* (1949), *Imitation of Life* (1959), and *White Nurse* (1959). However, the ending of legal segregation and the transformations in racial politics of the 1960s made the theme of passing politically irrelevant. Passing disappeared from popular racial discourse and representations. By the 1970s, discussions of passing were by and large confined to literary studies of passing fiction.

Given the extent to which the theme of passing stimulated such vibrant imaginative activity, one might be surprised to discover that despite the imaginative force and the cultural anxiety surrounding the possibility of crossing the color line, virtually nothing beyond the anecdotal is known about the magnitude or distribution of actual race passing in the United States at any time. The reason is obvious, however: the very condition of possibility for passing is secrecy, making it an extremely difficult object for traditional empirical study. The consequences of the gap between the (white) need to know and the (black) refusal to tell resulted, in early studies, in some very peculiar research methodologies and a great deal of conjecture. In what is perhaps the most comprehensive examination of passing from a social scientific point of view in the early part of the century, Louis Wirth and Herbert Goldhamer admit that the secrecy surrounding passing makes it almost impossible for them to know anything with certainty.[7] As James Conyers, a sociology student attempting a study of passing in 1962, discovered:

> There have been no basic studies of the occurrence of passing among Negroes since they have become a "new" political and economic force in the United States—the last twenty years [i.e., since the 1940s]. Furthermore, many of the studies undertaken prior to that time were indirect, fragmentary, and often impressionistic. Some of the statements were based upon mere guesswork.[8]

Conyers was unable, in his own study, to move beyond the conclusions of Wirth and Goldhamer twenty years before. As Conyers put it,

> In view of the scanty data available concerning the practice of passing in the United States, it is not possible to state with any degree of certainty what the consequences of this practice have been.[9]

Without data or methodology adequate to the task, early efforts to illuminate the murky terrain of race passing relied in part on the literature of race passing, which came to stand in for a cultural phenomenon that evaded direct study. Wirth and Goldhamer cite James Weldon Johnson's *The Autobiography of an Ex-Coloured Man* as giving evidence of the psychological motivations and experiences of one who passes.[10] Other researchers drew evidence from anecdotal and personal accounts published in both the black and white press. Seeking a more scientific grounding for his assessment of the effect of passing, Conyers gained access to the unpublished results of what appears to be an unprecedented study of sixteen passers in Los Angeles.[11] Conyers concludes his summary of the findings by noting, "although the size of this study was small and questions of a more psychological nature were not asked, it is a commendable piece of research. . . . It lets us know in a very real sense that the phenomenon of passing is itself an actuality and *not a fictitious creation of the novelists*."[12]

Clearly, passing is not "a fictitious creation of the novelists." But the possibility that some white observers might attempt to contain passing by relegating it to the realm of fiction suggests that the possibility of passing is indeed disturbing to the stability of the racial hierarchy. What is equally interesting to me in these studies is the implicit substitution of cultural representations of passing for the actual occurrence of passing, a happening that proved in any event inaccessible to the scientific gaze. While the eclipse of empirical data by cultural accounts might be viewed with deep suspicion in most scientific inquiries, here it happens almost unthinkingly. Further, that both literary critics *and social scientists* would align passing research with novelists rather than with actual people who might be passing suggests that the importance of passing in the early twentieth century was less as a sociological phenomenon than as part of a cultural imaginary of racial difference and racial division. There is no doubt that many people passed, some casually for a limited time or a particular purpose, some permanently. Their stories remain private, however, the subject of familial debate or anecdote but not publicly registered or recognized. As Adrian Piper notes, "in the African-American community, we do not 'out' people who are passing as white in the European-American community."[13] Thus, while the individual decision to pass has profound effects on that individual and on those around her or him, at the same time this actual occurrence of passing, the lives and experiences of individuals who pass, is culturally invisible.

Much of the sociological literature of passing attempts to understand what we might term the psychology of passing: what drives one to pass; how the passer deals with the deception, isolation, and alienation; and so on. It may be tempting to read passing narratives such as Johnson's *The Autobiography of an Ex-Coloured Man* as a psychological exploration of the passing experience; but given the gap between the historical experience of passing and the sociological and cultural representations of passing, I would suggest that the meaning of passing for those who passed is not necessarily the same as the meaning of passing as it appears in the context of a public and popular discourse around passing. In the following pages, I want to focus on the ways in which the literary representation of passing in Johnson's *The Autobiography* and Nella Larsen's *Passing* work within the discourse of race passing to undermine the dominant understanding of racial identities and racial knowledges.

## *"Blood" and the Crisis of Representation*

Michel Foucault's analysis of the relations between the production of knowledge and the operations of power is a useful starting point for considering the relation between racial identity and racial knowledge. As Foucault argues, power is not simply the force wielded by some over others; power is deployed through and in terms of the production of the order of the world as knowledge. As David Goldberg puts it, "the categories that now fashion content of the known constrain how people in the social order at hand think about things. Epistemological 'foundations,' then, are at the heart of the constitution of social power." [14] Power is multiple and multiplied, working simultaneously through the epistemological power to name and evaluate, through the subjectifying power that interpellates individuals into particular social locations as agents of power and knowledge, and through the regulative power to enforce the order so named. The production of racial knowledge is inseparable from the production of racially marked subjects and the racial ordering of society; each provides the conditions for the other. As Foucault suggests, "The exercise of power perpetually creates knowledge and, conversely, knowledge constantly induces effects of power. . . . It is not possible for power to be exercised without knowledge, it is impossible for knowledge not to engender power." [15] But racial knowledge is simultaneously the basis for ordering the social world and is precariously exposed constantly to its own artificiality, especially during instances of conflict, as for example when the legal system is called on to adjudicate competing claims. [16] As a result, the authority of scientific knowledge to uphold the certainty of racial difference is both powerful and fragile; the power of this knowledge will remain invisible and unquestioned only so long as body, law, and perception all fit neatly together.

The modern epistemology of race hinges on the relation between visibility and truth. Common sense decrees that the phenotypical differences we associate with different races are a physical fact; and while we may disagree about the significance of this fact (for example, whether it has cultural, medical, or psychological circumstances), the fact itself, the visible and therefore, it would seem, undeniable differences between black and white, continues to function invariably as the basis of any claim to racial knowledge. But can we take that visibility so much for granted? Against the seemingly irrefutable "thereness" of the visible, we might construct an account of the history of vision, visibility, and their attendant knowledges. Robyn Wiegman asks, "does 'the fact of blackness,' as Frantz Fanon terms Western racial obsessions, lie in the body and its epidermis or in the cultural training that quite literally teaches the eye not only how but what to see?" [17] If we are to take seriously the idea that race is not a biological fact but a cultural fiction, then we must confront not only the fictionality of the biological way of understanding race but also the fictionality of the cultural way of seeing race. This is not to say that empirical variations from person to person in skin tone or any other morphological feature are not real but rather that the fact that we see them as elements of racial marking must be considered as an aspect of the cultural production of visibility.

We can chart several shifts in Western racial knowledge between the seventeenth and nineteenth centuries: from a geographical classification of human beings to one based on bodily (and primarily skin) classification;[18] from a view of skin color as variation to a view of skin color as the basis of classification; from a view of superficial differences superimposed on a human species considered to be morally and physically homogeneous to a view of the essential heterogeneity of the species despite superficial similarities (as, for example, the decline of the monogenesis thesis in favor of polygenesis)[19]; from a view of the body as a superficial sign to a view of the body as the exterior expression of a deeper organic truth of the organism.[20] In this shift to a modern, biologized understanding of race, skin color becomes visible as a basis for determining the order of identities and differences and subsequently penetrates the body to become the truth of the self. As a result, Wiegman argues, "the concept of 'race' [undergoes] significant transformation, losing the kind of fluidity it achieved in natural history as a product of climate and civilization, as a variation within the human species, to become a rather stable and primary characteristic for defining the nature of the body, both its organic and ontological consistency."[21] Race is on the skin, but the skin is the sign of something deeper, something hidden in the invisible interior of the organism (as organic or ontological). To see racial difference is therefore to see the bodily sign of race but also to see more than this sign, to see the interior difference it stands for. Thus, the modern conception of racial identity maintains an uneasy relation to the visual; the visible marks of the racialized body are only the signs of a deeper, interior difference, and yet those visible marks are the only difference that can be observed. The body is the sign of a difference that exceeds the body. The modern concept of race is therefore predicated on an epistemology of visibility, but the visible becomes an insufficient guarantee of knowledge. As a result, the possibility of a gap opens up between what the body says and what the body means.

In both popular racial discourse and in law throughout the nineteenth and much of the twentieth centuries, "blood" has been the primary figure joining the visible surface of the body with its inner truth. Eva Saks has argued that until the 1970s, the order of racial definitions in the United States was symbolically represented through miscegenation law, which regulated intermarriage between black and white and therefore also regulated the definitions of black and white. Miscegenation law "upheld the purity of the body politic through its constitution of a symbolic prohibition against the dangerous mixing of 'white blood' and 'black blood,' casting social practices as biological essences." [22] Saks suggests that in miscegenation law, "white blood" is invented as a metaphor for heritable title to whiteness, a title that is rendered null should there be any hint of "black blood." Whiteness thus becomes property in the legal heritability of such white blood. The problem, however, was and is that blood could only be an imperfect metaphor for the social relations it was meant to signify:

> Miscegenation law's identification system, based on the metaphor of blood, was committed to the separation of *looked like* (possession of whiteness without legal title to it) from *was* (good title to whiteness). . . . To substantiate blood, to substantiate what is neither a mimetic description nor a tangible entity but instead a semiotic figure, is impossible. Caught in an epistemological loop, courts were led right back to social codes based on appearance, which was where the problem had begun.[23]

The possibility of a paradoxical mismatch between being and seeming becomes the central anxiety of miscegenation law. In what Saks calls an "epistemological loop," neither being nor seeming can be unequivocally established as prior. Rather, being and seeming circle endlessly around one another, such that each is what it seems to be and each seems to be what it is. Thus, the disruption of epistemological certitude when being and seeming cannot be made to coincide threatens the collapse of the entire order.

This is the epistemological context in which the passing body takes on a particular charge. While the mulatto challenges the myth of racial purity, the figure of the passing body goes a step further, challenging the stability of racial knowledge and therefore implicitly the stability of the order that has been constructed on that knowledge. The mulatto body transgresses the boundedness of whiteness and blackness, illustrating the arbitrariness of the boundary. But the passing body is even more threatening, putting whiteness, blackness, and boundary—in short, the entire basis of social order—into question. In the figure of the passing body, the signifiers of race are unloosed from the signifieds; the seemingly stable relation between representation and the real collapses, and representation is suddenly dangerous and untrustworthy. If, as Wiegman suggests, "the 'logic' of race in U.S. culture anchors whiteness in the visible epistemology of black skin," [24] the possibility of a breakdown between the visible and its internal meaning occasions the threat of the collapse of whiteness itself. This emphasizes the asymmetry of blackness and whiteness, an asymmetry perfectly described by the so-called one drop rule defining blackness. Although many states recognized intermediate classifications between white and Negro such as mulatto, quadroon, person of color, and so on, in the decades before the Civil War, gradually these multiple categories gave way to a more rigid binarization of black and white.

The modern definition of white began to solidify in the 1850s and came to be characterized in terms of the one drop rule, which in subsequent decades prevailed socially throughout the United States and in many states stood as the legal definition of *Negro*. The rule can be characterized as follows: one is white if *all* one's ancestors are white; one is black if *any* of one's ancestors are black.[25] This asymmetrical definition of white and black in this period in America produced what Joel Williamson has called "invisible blackness": "Well before one was down to the single drop of African blood, that heritage was lost to sight. Centuries of miscegenation had produced thousands of mulattoes who had simply lost visibility, so much did color and features overlap between those who were mixed and those who were purely white."[26] Thus, although whiteness certainly could be described in terms of its visual characteristics, whiteness could not be "invisible"; whiteness then is the absence of both visible and invisible blackness. But if whiteness depends on the absence of something that cannot be perceived, then whiteness becomes increasingly precarious. The possibility that the body, which is meant to reflect transparently its inner truth, may in fact be a misrepresentation and that its meaning may be illegible threatens the collapse of the system of racial ordering and separation on which the hierarchical distribution of social, political, and economic opportunity is based. Thus, the stability of discrete racial identities is based not only on visibility but on knowability.

The relation between knowability and visibility is one way of comparing the mulatto figure and the passing figure. In representations of the passing figure, visibility interrupts knowability. In contrast, despite the mulatto's ambivalent appearance, I would suggest that in representations of the mulatto, knowability and visibility are made to converge. The mulatto theme is based on the possible ambivalence of racial identity; conventionally, the mulatto is torn between two worlds, the black and the white. For those who sought to uphold the rigid separateness of whiteness, the mulatto was meant to exemplify the inevitable tragedies that would ensue should the color line be broached. On the other hand, for those who perceived racial classification as arbitrary and oppressive, the mulatto could be represented as revealing the artificiality of the color line. While the implicit critique of the color line embodied in the mulatto might be a powerful one, in practice several strategies existed for recuperating the mulatto as evidence of the necessity of racial order rather than its negation. Lisa Jones's description of this cultural tendency is compelling: "Vessel of desire and pity, martyr or redeemed heroine, the tragic mulatto has been a Hollywood standard since the silent era. . . . Miss Tragedy is the morbid personification of integration. Those raging bloods of hers will explode one day, as will America's if it keeps mixing up bloodlines. Mono-race communities are the only place to find love and shelter. Don't cross the tracks." [27]

Historically, the idea of the mulatto emerged in the United States at the same time as the development in the nineteenth century of the polygenesis theory that hypothesized separate human races (as opposed to the earlier thesis of a single human family differentiated by rates of development and influenced by variable factors such as climate and geography). As I noted in Chapter 1, the term *mulatto* was initially coined to refer to the sterile mule, the progeny of a mating between two diverse species. Thus, the mulatto's presumed sterility was (tautological) evidence of the assertion that white and black were indeed separate and distinct. Although crossing was possible, as evidenced by the undeniable existence of mulattos, white racist thinkers insisted that these mulattos were doomed to disappear and therefore posed no real threat to the continued discrete separation of the races. In social and legal practice, the principle of hypodescent simply defined mulattos as black and returned them discursively to the black side of the color line. Thus, although the mulatto might seem to be the embodiment of racial impurity, the fact that only whiteness was defined as purity meant that anything other than whiteness could potentially be recuperated as a confirmation of the superiority and purity of whiteness. Popular belief was also able to reconcile the apparent gap between the mulatto's being and appearing by developing a complex typology of visual markers that would assure classifying observers that they would know one when they saw one. In mulatto fiction, there is always a telling mark that reveals the truth of the drop of black blood: a peculiarity of complexion or feature that will reveal its secret to the truly discerning eye. No matter how faint the bodily mark, its existence assures that appearances are in fact not deceiving, that ambivalent appearances simply require more subtle forms of interpretation.

In contrast, the passing theme insists that knowability and visibility may diverge in unsuspected and uncontrollable ways. The passing theme foregrounds, not the status of the color line, whether seen as absurdly and violently artificial or as natural and necessary, but rather the collapse of the continuity between representation and identity, appearance and being, as they are supposedly determined along the color line. Although the one who passes is technically a mulatto, I would argue that it is not his or her "mulattoness" that is the issue in passing narratives; rather, the issue is the problem of reconciling identity to appearance, an epistemological problem of restoring order and certainty when the conditions of certainty fail to hold. What is unique in the passing narratives that I will be concerned with in this chapter is that, unlike the so-called tragic mulatto who is ultimately revealed to be truly black, the passing figure evades any singular judgment, suggesting the possibility of an irrecuperable chasm between representation and identity or between appearance and an unreachable truth.

In the cultural experience of passing, there are two kinds of black bodies: those whose dark color reveals unequivocally their blackness and those whose visible ambivalence puts them in a more tenuous and unstable relation to blackness. Thus, attention to passing as a site of disruption in the racial order may seem to imply for some a privileging of the body closest to whiteness, leaving the dark-skinned to the realm of the static and unchanging. For this reason, I must emphasize again that what is under consideration is not the experience of real people but rather the literary figure of passing as it lends itself to multiple readings. My intention in this chapter is to call into question the grounds of distinction between white and black, and between white-appearing blackness and black-appearing blackness, by focusing on the interrelation between vision and knowledge. From this perspective, it is no more natural to define the narrator of *The Autobiography*, with his few drops of black blood, as black than it is to define his childhood friend "Shiny" as black. The very visibility of blackness, a visibility that seems so commonsensical in the modern world as to need no explanation, is itself a part of, not prior to, the epistemology of racial difference. If the figure of passing challenges the principles and the power of this racial epistemology, then the implications of this challenge are not limited only to those in between. Historically, the continued power of the

color line has not been a result of any particular location or distinction between black and white but rather the result of the possibility of making any
such distinction. Hence, the power of the literary representation of passing
is in its figuration of the breakdown of the very basis on which distinction,
certainty, and order rest.

The potentially disruptive force of the passing figure is hinted at in the
publisher's preface to the first edition of James Weldon Johnson's *The Autobiography of an Ex-Coloured Man*, in which the writer notes that "these
pages . . . reveal the unsuspected fact that prejudice against the Negro is
exerting a pressure which . . . is actually and constantly forcing an unascer-
tainable number of fair-complexioned coloured people over into the white
race." [28] Is this the nervous voice of a white writer or the warning voice of a
black writer? It is not known who wrote this preface; perhaps it was Johnson himself. But whichever tone we hear, the message is clear: the white
race is not the white race that it seems; it has in fact been infiltrated by an
unknowable black presence. This is an "unsuspected fact"; "they," those
fair-complexioned colored people, might be anywhere, might be anyone.
Apparent whiteness is no guarantee of true whiteness. There is no longer
any way to tell the true whites from the impostors. This uncertainty, which
might be seen on one side as paranoia and on the other as opportunity, is
exactly the point of passing.

## X-Subject: 'The Autobiography of an Ex-Coloured Man'

In this interpretation of passing, I am departing from the conventional
reading, in which passing is cast as a metaphor for alienation and the
search for identity. In general, the reception and interpretation of literary
representations of passing in the twentieth century has been based on the
premise, consistent with the idea of a social order structured around fixed
racial identities, that the narrative representation of black passing for white
is about coming to terms with black identity as it is distinct from white
identity. This reading is exemplified in Michael Awkward's summary of the
passing plot, with specific reference to the two novels I will be considering
here, *The Autobiography of an Ex-Coloured Man* and *Passing*: "These texts,
which narrativize variations on the formula 'tragic mulatto,' effectively em-
ploy notions of the differences between being and seeing, between (racial)
essence and appearance, positing, each in its own gender-specific manner,
that passing for white ultimately is unsatisfying because of the psychic

impossibility of ignoring black biological imperatives and cultural connections." [29]

In Awkward's reading, passing plays on the transgression of racial boundaries but ultimately reinforces the premise of a racial essence underlying identity. Appearance may not coincide with essence, Awkward implies, but for the writers of these passing narratives, there is a racial essence, a real, inescapable truth of racial being (simultaneously biological and cultural) beneath the potentially deceptive surface of appearances. Awkward's traditional and commonsensical interpretation of passing begins by assuming the very terms I want to call into question: the priority of being over appearing, the production of appearing so as to coincide with a presumed being, and, behind them both, the assumption of the racial subject as the bearer of a racial being.

Passing for white *is* unsatisfying for the narrator of Johnson's *The Autobiography*, but it is not, I will argue, because of the irresistible compulsion of some racial essence, biological or cultural. Rather, *The Autobiography* scrutinizes the process of racial subjectification, both in terms of the production of the modern subject as the project of autobiography, and in terms of the breakdown of specifically *racial* subjectification, signaled by the "X" of the Ex-Coloured Man. The decision to write a (fictive) autobiography is not insignificant: the genre of autobiography historically bears a particularly close relation to the Western ideal of the rational, autonomous subject. Traditional theories of autobiography take the subject as both the source and the object of representation of autobiography. Georges Gusdorf, for example, claims that "the autobiographer strains toward a complete and coherent expression of his entire destiny . . . [requiring] a man to take a distance with regard to himself in order to reconstitute himself in the focus of his special unity and identity across time." [30] The aim of autobiography, in this view, is not historical truth but "the truth of the man, for it is first of all the man who is in question." [31] Johnson does not challenge the implicit metaphysical underpinnings of autobiography directly, as for example "postmodern" autobiographies have done. Rather, Johnson's version of autobiography substitutes the "X" of crossing out where the name should be, the name that would indicate the subject whose life is in question. Thus, this autobiography has violated the very condition of autobiography at the outset, leaving a gaping hole where the originary subject of autobiography ought to be. [32]

The problem of the originary subject plagues Johnson's novel from beginning to end. Throughout *The Autobiography*, the narrator's *I* never gains a proper name; the only truly proper names in the narrative are place-names.[33] Characters are named by common nouns that describe the character (Red, the Texan) or relate her or him to the narrator (my mother, my millionaire). Often, this denomination is even further distanced from the character by being placed in quotation marks (the "widow," "Shiny"). This might be taken as further evidence of the secrecy surrounding the act of passing. But alternatively, it might be taken as pointing to a suspension of the subjectivizing function of the name. The name assures the continuity of responsibility and agency over time and, within a patriarchal society, indicates the relations of familial belonging that locate and specify the subject in relation to others. The name mediates between momentary sensations or relations and the necessity of social continuity and coherence over time. As Lacan puts it, "the name is the time of the object."[34] While the name seems simply to reflect the continuity of the subject through time, it is the name itself that gathers together the strands of time, generating and guaranteeing the continuity of the subject under its aegis.

By assigning one proper name to a heterogeneous cluster of events, memories, and affects, this proper name appears simply to name a pre-existing subject (just as the genre of autobiography claims to represent, as Gusdorf puts it, the truth of the man). But the stability and identity of the subject are not inherent in the subject; rather, they are secured by the functioning of the proper name. By refusing proper names to the characters that populate *The Autobiography*, Johnson has diffused the air of temporal continuity that is presumed to give psychological and historical depth to the subject. Instead, the characters are like pieces on a playing board, playing out particular and discrete narrative functions in relation to the narrator.[35] And if this is the desubjectivizing effect of substituting common nouns for proper names in relation to the secondary characters of the novel, it must be noted that the effect is that much more powerful for the main character, who goes unnamed and can be referred to only in the negativizing mode of "ex-." In talking about this unnamed character I have been sorely tempted to substitute a name, "Ex-Coloured Man," for example. But in asserting such a name in the place of insistent namelessness, the critic risks repeating the gesture of positing a coherent and continuous subject in the place where, Johnson will insist, such coherency and continuity come under scrutiny. In the spirit of Johnson's insistence on unnameability, then, I will refer to the protagonist as "the narrator."

In the fully racialized society of the United States, racial identity is an integral part of personal identity, as inextricable and powerful as gender identity. Howard Winant's description of the "impermeability" of racial identity gives a good sense of what is at stake in the social fiction of race: "U.S. society is so thoroughly racialized that to be without racial identity is to be in danger of having no identity. . . . Indeed, when one cannot identify another's race, a microsociological crisis of interpretation results." [36] Winant might be glossing Johnson's title; the substitution of "Ex-Coloured Man" where the name of the subject of autobiography ought to appear effects the double negation of identity—of race, and again, inextricably, of the self—that Winant suggests is at risk when racial identity cannot be taken for granted. Here, I would propose reading "ex-coloured" not as a temporal event, being first colored and then not, but as a superimposition of X and *colored*, effectively negating both terms of the racial binary: colored negating whiteness, X negating colored, thereby rendering impossible both whiteness and blackness without restoring by default the relation of opposition that is presumed to prevail between them (as in the one drop rule). And it is with the attendant "crisis of interpretation" that *The Autobiography* confronts us if we are able to resist the temptation to immediately substitute a proper and properly raced subject in the place of the unnamed and unnameable one who resists both racialization and subjectification.

## *Passing Through*

The race passing plot of *The Autobiography of an Ex-Coloured Man* is embedded in a narrative line structured by the narrator's passage through the North, South, and Europe. As the narrator tells the story of his life, from his birth in an unnamed town to his current life as an anonymous white man in New York, he lays out two trajectories of travel: a psychological journey through whiteness and blackness and a physical journey through the United States and Europe. These two trajectories, the psychological journey of passing and the physical travel through the United States and Europe, are linked by more than narrative coincidence. *The Autobiography* does not take place in any fixed locale; rather, it traverses multiple locations. The narrator takes us on what one critic has called "an endless journey" [37] through Savannah; Connecticut; Atlanta; Jacksonville; New York; Paris; London; Amsterdam; Berlin; Boston; Washington, D.C.; Richmond; Nashville; Atlanta; Macon; and finally New York. He is perpetually homeless, traveling light, following at a whim whatever opportunity or adventure fate brings him. He is never so much *in* a place as he is, to turn a phrase, passing through. The coincidence of the thematics of geographic mobility and race passing is not accidental. Practically, if one is to pass, one must go somewhere else, where one's identity is unknown.

Signaling a more important connection between geographic mobility and race passing is the fact that the very word *pass* contains the trace of its origins in movement. The term *passing* as used with respect to race means to be taken for or to be accepted as, where one thing is substituted for another. However, several other meanings are layered into this term. In particular, *passing* can refer to different forms of movement: to pass an object from place to place, for example, or to be oneself passing from place to place. The conjunction between substitution and movement is revealed, in the case of race passing in the United States, in the implicit reference to a metaphoric geography of race: one crosses, or passes, over the color line dividing black and white. The narrator's perpetual movement suggests that the geography of race as it emerges in the figure of passing is not just metaphoric; passing is the continual motion of crossing the color line. Indeed, the priority of motion over position might be read in the novel's title; the prefix *ex-* that qualifies the narrator's racial identity signals not only temporal negation, as in *formerly*, but also spatial removal, as in *out of* or *outside of*. In fact, I would suggest that passing as it figures in the novel must be sustained as perpetual motion rather than discrete event.

At stake in the distinction between passing as discrete event and passing as perpetual motion is the very identity of the narrator and the implicit question posed in the title: namely, whether there can be any racial identity whose authenticity is not compromised by the "X." Henry Louis Gates Jr. argues in his introduction to the 1989 Vintage Books edition of *The Autobiography* that the narrator's movement "between Black and white racial identities is intended to establish the fact that such identities are entirely socially constructed" (p. xvi). Socially constructed identity seems here to connote an identity easily altered or cast off: according to Gates, the narrator is "white *and* Black, at his whim and by his will" (p. xviii). I find this dressing room model of racial identity somewhat unsatisfactory in relation to what is represented in the novel as a much more troubled relationship to both blackness and whiteness. Although the narrator is able to decide whether he will be taken by others as being black or white, he does not ever claim to be simply black or white, and there is always an uncomfortable dissonance between what others take him for and his own sense of himself. For others, the narrator appears as white and black; but, for himself, he feels neither white nor black.

The narrator's childhood whiteness is implicitly characterized as a condition of ironic mis-recognition. This whiteness is represented retrospectively; thus, the narrative understands the narrator to be not-white even before the narrator-as-child is marked as colored. When, for example, one of the black boys in school is provoked into throwing a slate at the white boys, the narrator is strongly affected: "I was very much wrought up over the affair, and went home and told my mother how one of the 'niggers' had struck a boy with a slate. I shall never forget how she turned on me. 'Don't you ever use that word again,' she said, 'and don't you ever bother the coloured children at school. You ought to be ashamed of yourself' " (p. 15). As in all autobiographical recollection, the narrator is split between present and past, between the *I* who experiences the event and the *I* who narrates it. Yet here that temporal splitting is explicitly marked as a displacement along the color line. The original whiteness of the narrator is necessarily inauthentic because it can emerge narratively only as already contaminated by the knowledge of not-whiteness. But the narrator is no more originally black than he is originally white. His blackness is also a copy, a specular image of the blackness he observes in others.

The narrator's childhood emergence into racial consciousness is simultaneous with his emergence into self-consciousness. The narrator relates that as a child in Connecticut he had little consciousness of race but played with the white children, until one day in school his teacher singled him out in class as colored. The principal entered the classroom and "for some reason said: 'I wish all of the white scholars to stand for a moment.' I rose with the others. The teacher looked at me and, calling my name, said: 'You sit down for the present, and rise with the others' " (p. 16). Barbara Johnson points out that, here, the racial difference between the narrator and the white students is produced through textual repetition.[38] As both black and white, the narrator will "rise with the others." The difference for Johnson lies in the hierarchy of the terms *black* and *white* veiled by the repetition, which gives them a false air of equality. But the symmetry of the narrator's relation to the terms of blackness and whiteness—each time he rises "with the others"—indicates that he does not really belong on either side. At the same time, the teacher's act of producing by naming the narrator's racial identity is based on a constitutive confusion between identity and difference: when he is told to "rise with the others," we must read this as indicating simultaneously "the others" who are the others included in the group of the same and the others who are different.

When the narrator rushes home to confront in his mirror image the signs of this truth as written on his face, the spectacle of display staged by the teacher for the principal and other students—in which the narrator suddenly takes center stage as the star of a race drama of which he has been ignorant—is repeated as a specular confirmation through which the narrator must come to know the lesson the teacher has made him learn. As his face is reflected back to him, he sees what the others see, but what he sees has been transformed by this new knowledge. This is the first and only view of the narrator provided the reader, and it is a striking one: "I noticed the ivory whiteness of my skin, the beauty of my mouth, the size and liquid darkness of my eyes, and how the long, black lashes that fringed and shaded them produced an effect that was strangely fascinating even to me. I noticed the softness and glossiness of my dark hair that fell in waves over my temples, making my forehead appear whiter than it really was" (p. 17).

The narrator describes the conventional "tainted whiteness" of the mulatto, whose dark hair and eyes traditionally signal to the reader the mark of black blood that, no matter how faint, the logic of race demands be rendered visible. Noticing these features for the first time, the narrator sees himself with a new vision. From one perspective, we might conclude that he had never before been able to read properly the truth written on his features; and in a conventional tragic mulatto tale such a conclusion would be supported by the reader's prior knowledge of the signs that the protagonist only gradually learns to recognize. But in the case of *The Autobiography*, the visibility of a hidden blackness is simultaneous with the knowledge of this hidden blackness. As the narrator's self-identity is achieved through the mediation of the mirror image, this scene of recognition simultaneously creates the self, names the self as black, and splits the self between eye and image. This scene might be read as a classical example of the process of the assumption of subjectivity in what Jacques Lacan calls the "mirror stage." Lacan's description of this process emphasizes that the specular identification that translates the mirror image into a reflection of the self must also always be an alienating *mis*-recognition. The identification of the self with an image external to the self provides a basis for identity by substituting the coherent *image* of the other for a complex, unstable self. Visibility, then, is central to the process of identification. But we should remember that racial visibility is a part of, not prior to, the social production of racial meanings. Hence, the narrator's coming to see his own image reflected in the visible difference of others repeats the process whereby each comes to locate her- or himself within the order of racial identities. Thus, it is not accidental that the narrator's mirror scene occurs at precisely the moment of racial identification; subjectification within the realm ordered and known in terms of racial epistemology is necessarily racial subjectification.

In the psychoanalytic theory of the development of the subject, the successful completion of the mirror stage is marked by the identification of the self with the image. However, for the narrator, the image remains alien and distant. Although the narrator has been identified, both for himself and for others, as colored, he is plagued by his inability to translate that identification into a feeling of identity. In sharp contrast to the supposed naturalness of racial feeling, the narrator presents his becoming colored as an autodidactic course of deliberate self-transformation. He reads everything he can about the life and achievements of his newly acquired race, devoting himself to *Uncle Tom's Cabin* and Frederick Douglass and casting aside his former white heroes, King David and Robert the Bruce. On graduation from high school, the narrator chooses Atlanta College, a black institution, over Harvard, in part to satisfy his "peculiar fascination with the South" (p. 51). Descending south to Atlanta in a pointed inversion of the journey north, which is a central plot device in much African-American narrative, the narrator experiences his first brush with "coloured people in large numbers" (p. 55), but he encounters them more as a tourist in search of the curious and exotic than as his own people.

Atlanta disappoints; rather than the "luxuriant semi-tropical scenery which [he] had pictured in [his] mind," the narrator finds "a big, dull, red town" (p. 52). He is repulsed by the "unkempt appearance, the shambling, slouching gait and loud talk and laughter" of the colored people he encounters in the streets of Atlanta but is relieved to discover that they are "of the lower class" (pp. 56, 55). The class distinction that the narrator insists exists between himself and these "lower classes" allows him to remain a spectator, consoled that he is not one of them. He takes the most pleasure in the stereotypical. He is thrilled to breakfast in the boardinghouse of a benevolent "mammy" figure: "Scrupulously clean, in a spotless white apron and coloured head-handkerchief, her round face beaming with motherly kindness, she was picturesquely beautiful" (p. 59). This is what the narrator had hoped for, *Uncle Tom's Cabin* (which he believes to be "a fair and truthful panorama of slavery" [p. 42]) come to life: "When I had finished, I felt that I had experienced the realization of, at least, one of my dreams of Southern life" (p. 59). Yet this dream is not one of recovering or returning to his own authentic cultural roots but rather of being an active spectator to the spectacle of stereotypical representations of African-American culture given life in popular theater and literature.

The culmination of the narrator's geographical descent into blackness is achieved in Jacksonville, where he is welcomed into the cultured black middle class: "Through my music teaching and my not absolutely irregular attendance at church I became acquainted with the best class of coloured people in Jacksonville. This was really my entrance into the race. It was my initiation into what I have termed the freemasonry of the race. I had formulated a theory of what it was to be coloured; now I was getting the practice" (p. 74). The narrator's patient translation of theory into practice belies the mythical power of blood to make him colored. As opposed to the popular belief that black blood will always show itself through appearance or manner, the narrator suggests that blackness is acquired as a bodily discipline through study and repetition. His transformation into privileged insider accentuates his position as outsider; he must be initiated into the race because he is not truly of the race. Indeed, it is this very move from outsider to initiate that is promised to the reader in the 1912 preface: "the reader is given a view of the inner life of the Negro in America, is initiated into the free-masonry, as it were, of the race" (p. xl). By juxtaposing the preface with the narrator's own description of his entry into the race we can see the extent to which the narrator is deliberately positioned in the same spectatorial position as the reader. If both the implicitly white reader and the not-white narrator can be "initiated into the free-masonry . . . of the race," then on the one hand racial identity is rendered inessential, but, at the same time, the narrator's claims to have become or to be colored are increasingly suspect. The preface has positioned the reader as a spectator who will, through the eyes of the narrator, "glimpse behind the scenes of this race drama which is being here enacted" (p. xl). But, in fact, the narrator is just as much a spectator as the reader.

In the final pages of the novel, the narrator describes the circumstances leading to his current position as an "ordinarily successful white man" (p. 211). At first, passing as white and the material success it makes possible are a "capital joke" that he has pulled off on the racially exclusive white world. But his joke loses its punch when he falls in love with a white woman.

The possibility of consummating his whiteness by joining himself to "the most dazzlingly white thing I had ever seen" (p. 198) raises the specter of exposure and discovery. What begins as a fear of being caught out of character gives way to a paranoia that something invisible to himself will give him away: "I began to doubt myself. I began even to wonder if I really was like the men I associated with; if there was not, after all, an indefinable something which marked a difference" (p. 200). In fact, there is an "indefinable something which mark[s] a difference," but it is not the tangible something of appearance, behavior, or character. Rather, it is the mark of difference itself, the empty signifier of race that the narrator cannot shed: "This was the only time in my life that I ever felt absolute regret at being coloured, that I cursed the drops of African blood in my veins and wished that I were really white" (p. 205). A feeling of duty impels him to divulge his secret. But even in the moment of confession the narrative resists naming or fixing the identity of the narrator: "I told her, in what words I do not know, the truth" (p. 204). But note that the "truth" can only be told by a not-telling; the truth is told in "words I do not know." The true, authentic identity of the narrator can only be told as *not*-being: the narrator does not name the truth because the truth (an authentic, single, essential racial identity) *is not*.

Thus, I would suggest that the action of passing can be read as characterizing both the narrator's assumption of whiteness and his assumption of blackness. If this is true, then it becomes increasingly difficult to localize the action of passing or to measure the success of passing against some otherwise knowable or stable pre-passing identity. The narrator himself seems torn between viewing his own blackness as either deception or truth. In the final pages of the novel, the narrator again repeats the formulation of racial non-identity as spectatorship, balanced against the blood-bound imperative of racial identity: "Sometimes it seems to me that I have never really been a Negro, that I have been only a privileged spectator of their inner life; at other times I feel that I have been a coward, a deserter, and I am possessed by a strange longing for my mother's people" (p. 210). The narrator's own refusal to decide between these two alternatives broaches the central epistemological dilemma raised in the novel: once we suspend the commonsense reading of *The Autobiography* as being about a black man who passes for white, we are constantly faced with the difficulty of determining what is passing and what is not.

And if it is difficult to ascertain the boundaries of passing, then it is equally difficult to determine in any particular instance who is meant to be an "insider" and who is being positioned as the "dupe."[39] Insider and dupe cannot be distinguished on the basis of identity because either black or white can play the role of dupe; rather, in *The Autobiography* insider and dupe can only designate epistemological positions. The dupe is always the one who does not see passing, while the insider is the one who sees passing everywhere. For example, we can read an episode such as the Jacksonville entry into the race either from the position of dupe or from the position of the insider: either the narrator is learning to appear to be what he really is or he is assuming an appearance that does not correlate with or reflect any deeper truth. In other words, in the Jacksonville episode, we can read the narrator either as being black or as passing for black. Neither of these readings takes absolute precedence over the other because the triangular structure of passing necessarily provokes both of these readings simultaneously. The drama of passing plays out precisely the confrontation between these two epistemological perspectives, which, for the players, appears as the confrontation between appearance as truth and appearance as falsity. But from a critical perspective that does not align itself with either passer, dupe, or insider, passing appears as the figurative expression of the breakdown of any mechanism whereby one might adjudicate claims of truth or falsity. Is the narrator black? Is he white? The answer to each seems to be simultaneously yes, no, and it depends. The assumption that there is some true being that lies beneath and corresponds to appearance relies on the very gap between appearance and being that it presumes to have abolished, leaving open always the possibility that such a gap can be wrenched further open to reveal a play of appearances disconnected from true being.

Passing effects a sort of epistemological contagion, spilling out beyond the boundaries of the narrative proper. For passing to be passing, someone must recognize it as passing; hence, the necessity of a knowing spectator. Narratively, such a spectator may be provided within the framework of the episode of passing, or alternatively the reader her- or himself may serve as the knowing spectator who witnesses the effects of passing on the dupe. Thus, there is always passing within the text and passing between text and reader. One might ask, however, whether the reader is necessarily an insider; in the case of *The Autobiography*, the reader might just as easily be played for the dupe. Such a possibility further complicates the stability of any assertion of truth: if it is the reader who is being fooled, then the reader's chances of restoring certainty to some semblance of the real in the text are significantly diminished. The problem of what the reader knows is in fact central to the history of the novel's publication and reception.

In its first publication in 1912, *The Autobiography of an Ex-Coloured Man* appeared anonymously. While neither Johnson nor the book's publishers actively attempted to deceive the public about the book's status or origin, readers were left to draw their own conclusions. Some readers took it as true autobiography, the actual narrative of the anonymous author's life. Johnson's biographer, Eugene Levy, believes Johnson intended the work to be taken in this way. Levy points to a letter to a college friend in which Johnson writes, "when the author is known, and known to be one who could not be the main character of the story, the book will fall flat." [40] What would it mean for the book to "fall flat"? In the original preface and first pages of the novel, the reader is implicitly positioned as white; it is a white reader who is offered the "glimpse behind the veil," and it is the white reader to whom the narrator confesses his crime and his guilt because it is primarily in relation to whiteness's claim to purity that the narrator's passing for white might be taken as a crime. The preface promises to transform the reader into an insider, to provide the reader with the previously hidden knowledge of both black life and the mysteries of passing. Hence, if it is known that the true author is not recounting actual experiences of passing, does Johnson mean that readers will discount the authority of the depiction of passing? That is certainly one way the novel might fall flat; but, alternatively, perhaps Johnson means that the novel will fall flat in the way a joke falls flat. If the novel is not an authentic revelation of truth but rather an exercise in deception, then for the insider who recognizes the deception, the novel might be seen as a joke put over on the white reader who takes at face value those glimpses of black life. Then the black reader becomes the knowing spectator of a theater of passing performed at the expense of the duped white reader, in which what is passing is not the black narrator passing for white but the narrative of fiction passing for anthropological truth. Are the glimpses behind the veil ironic comments on the narrator's alienation from his cultural identity? Are they well-intentioned efforts on Johnson's part to increase intercultural understanding? Are they meant to fool the outsider into believing he or she is getting the real thing? These questions cannot be answered definitively any more than can the question of the narrator's true racial identity.[41]

I have suggested several ways in which the narrative itself works against the simple black-passing-for-white logic of passing and its attendant model of race as the expression of a prior, proper identity. The prevalence of the interpretation of passing as black passing for white is the basis for the most common and widely accepted critical evaluation of the novel, namely, that it is a modernist tragedy about the alienation of the subject as experienced in terms of racial community. In Robert Stepto's reading of *The Autobiography*, for example, the narrator's troubled relationship to his blackness as culture or a sense of history is a tragic failing. Stepto's interpretation focuses on the narrator's failure to recognize his proper heritage and tradition.[42] As for Stepto, for Lucinda MacKethan the novel represents an ironic revision of key figures and forms of the African-American literary tradition: we should read the narrator's opinions on class and race as ironic because they are based in his own "illiteracy," his "inability to 'read' himself in his presentation of his past." [43] In their presumption of an authentic originary blackness from which the narrator has fallen, both Stepto and MacKethan repeat the cultural logic of race and passing: by posing the narrator's blackness as fixed, they imply that passing for white can only be a deviation from his real identity as black.[44]

It seems to me, however, that while the narrator claims to be really black, the terms of blackness and whiteness as they emerge in the narrative belie the possibility of identity or authenticity that would allow the narrator to *be* black *or* white. As the novel unfolds, the narrator's relation to blackness is shown to be as inauthentic as his relation to whiteness; rather than being both black and white, or either black or white, he is in fact neither. While he may copy blackness or whiteness, the copy is always contaminated by its very inauthenticity. It is in this circulation of contaminated copies that we discover the true originality of Johnson's portrayal of passing. In the cultural logic of passing, passing follows from identity. Unlike the cultural logic of passing defined as a deception opposed to the true identity hiding underneath appearance, Johnson suggests that there is no authentic, original identity that could be hidden or imitated; there are only copies and copies of copies that give the impression of originality. In effect, it is identity that follows from passing. Identity is not what we are but what we are passing for. This is the source of the epistemological crisis I referred to at the outset; not only that the body named as black passing for white is not what it appears to be but that such a body, the passing body, exposes all appearance as absolutely disjoined from the being, the depth or invisible essence, that is supposed to be expressed, represented, or reflected in appearance.

## Racial Discipline: Transgression and Guilt

The narrator cannot *be* black or white; his appearance as black or white is produced through the imitation of the blackness or whiteness of others.

The narrator's necessarily inauthentic relationship to any racial identity suggests that the arbitrariness of the terms of racial embodiment and the absence of any real referent for blackness or whiteness make spectatorship and imitation—what we might call mimetic spectatorship—the constitutive structure of race. Race is supposed to be the truth of the body; but the narrator's continual passing reveals that the body can neither be nor have such a thing as race. Nevertheless, within the narrative the subjective indeterminacy implied by mimetic spectatorship is countered by a continual social pressure on the narrator to corporealize race. In order for race to function smoothly to order relations, produce norms and expectations of behaviors, and regulate or restrict access to different forms of power and privilege, it must be produced as an irrefutable bodily marking.

The narrator cannot escape the social imperative of the "drops of African blood" in his veins; whatever its empirical status, it is this blood that bars him from the status of "really white." Nevertheless, the color with which this blood marks him is not something that can be identified or characterized. It has the same theoretical existence as a geometrically defined point, which exists as a position without having any substance. The narrator's tenuous relation to the race to which he must belong reveals the fissure at the heart of the logic of racial identity and racial difference: the mark of blackness, one drop of black blood, neither is nor produces any content of blackness. Blackness is the signifier of an arbitrary but culturally indelible marking, a position rather than a thing. As such, it is empty, a placeholder in the social order, without content. The narrator cannot *be* black because there is nothing there to be. This assertion should not be confused with the racist claim that blackness is ontological blankness and whiteness is ontological plenitude. The narrator cannot *be* white either. My point is that the modern epistemology of race posits a distinctive being, an essence if you will, as the basis for racial distinction, and yet at the extreme this essence is revealed to be nothing more than the distinction itself.

For the narrator, the essential difference between black and white is marked by the drop of blood, and insofar as this drop of blood is nothing but a mark, the essential difference between black and white is tautologically determined to be what is at the same time the condition of their distinction and the mark of the distinction itself. Put another way, the essential difference between black and white is only the fact that black may be distinguished from white. Every other difference may disappear; black and white may be identical in everything, and still the difference between black and white remains as simply the insistence that they are not the same.

The shift in perspective that I am suggesting here from racial difference as cultural difference to racial difference emerging in terms of and along the distinction marked as the color line traces its genealogy to a dissident approach to the study of ethnic groups, associated primarily with the work of anthropologist Fredrik Barth. In contrast to today's emphasis on cultural diversity and cultural relativism, Barth's fieldwork in the 1960s led him to argue that the focus on overt cultural forms as the determinant of ethnic identity rested on a flawed premise because cultural forms did not always differ between groups, and might change over time, while ethnic identity remained constant. He argued instead that the characteristics of ascription and self-ascription were the most important factors in defining and maintaining an ethnic group. The primacy of the role of ascription shifts the critical focus from the "cultural stuff" (forms, values, and institutions) to the boundary that defines the group. The shifting of critical focus from content to boundary makes impossible and irrelevant appeals to authenticity as a signal of ethnicity. Difference thus refers not to some reality (which then serves as a basis for making determinations of authenticity) but to positionality. Regarding differences between groups, Barth notes that "we can assume no simple one-to-one relationship between ethnic units and cultural similarities and differences. The features that are taken into account are not the sum of 'objective' differences, but only those which the actors themselves regard as significant."[45] That is, the contents on either side of the boundary may be, at the extreme, exactly the same, and yet the boundary may persist as the expression of some arbitrary, but socially significant, mark—for example, that of blood.

But, as Barth recognized, the fact that a boundary such as blood is arbitrary in no way means that it is illusory or that its power is not real. Despite the novel's insistence that the narrator's blackness is an empty mark and not an expression of what he is, either essentially or culturally, he is never completely free from the structure and strictures of his racial identity as black. The relation of racial identity to the body can only be paradoxical: while *The Autobiography* makes evident the absurdity of the determination of racial identity based on blood, and thus effectively insists that racial identity be dis-embodied, at the same time the narrator experiences the re-embodiment of race as, in this case, an undeniable, irreducible fact of blood. Even as his body cannot be located as the truth of his race, it becomes the site and the source of racial discipline and racial subjectification: "I cursed the drops of African blood in my veins and wished that I were really white" (p. 205). Once the one drop rule has defined the bodily location of the line separating black from white, the arbitrary condition for blackness becomes an irresistible fact. As the one drop rule is instantiated both in judicial law and social practice, it appears to take the demarcation between black and white as given and to legislate only the rules for each side. But, in fact, it is the application of the one drop rule that produces black and white, calling into being a distinction by naming a difference. The "drops of African blood" that make the narrator, in society's eyes, a colored man have no meaning outside this law of difference; the mark is completely arbitrary but, as it functions in terms of the law, absolutely irresistible.

In *The Autobiography*, the force of the implicit but pervasive law of racial identity is everywhere present. It is for this reason that the narrative of race passing, a deliberate violation of this law, takes the form of a confession. But even as the narrator compulsively confesses, the confession is not of any particular crime but rather of a perpetual state of guilt. On the first page, the narrator sets the stage for the confession that follows: "I know that in writing the following pages I am divulging the great secret of my life, the secret which for some years I have guarded far more carefully than any of my earthly possessions" (p. 3). The stakes of this confession are raised as the narrator continues to compare himself with a compulsive, paranoid outlaw: "I feel that I am led by the same impulse which forces the un-found-out criminal to take somebody into his confidence, although he knows that the act is likely, even almost certain, to lead to his undoing" (p. 3).

The overwrought expression of a sense of transgression and guilt in the introductory paragraph perhaps seems out of proportion to the acts he has committed; that he might fear discovery is understandable, but that he might feel he has become a criminal would seem to grant a certain legitimacy to the power of whiteness to exclude, a legitimacy that the narrative challenges throughout. But perhaps we should not be surprised that a confrontation with a social principle that has all the force of law should produce a pervasive sense of guilt. One need not have committed any crime to feel guilty. Like the pedestrian who feels a pang of guilt when passing by the police officer, or the motorist who suddenly checks her speed when she has spotted a police car in the rearview mirror, the narrator's existence within the law makes him already implicitly guilty before the law. In effect, he is guilty, not because he has passed for white, but because his very existence has violated the law of racial division. Within the logic of race, he must be either black or white. But, as I have suggested, he is trapped in a paradox: he lives under the imperative to be the blackness his blood has marked him as being, but because this blood that marks his race is nothing but a mark he must fail.

While whiteness sustains its own boundedness and exclusiveness by insisting on its own purity and projecting all impurity onto blackness, the narrator brings to the surface the necessary failure of racial identity to ever be what it says it must be—a failure shared by blackness and whiteness. He has transgressed or perverted the natural order, not because he has moved from one position in that order to another, but because his inauthentic (and therefore guilty) relation to every position upsets the very naturalness of that order.

The pervasiveness of a disproportionate guilt suggests that the perversion or transgression is not confined to race alone. To begin with, passing is specifically linked to sexual transgression via the intermediary figure of miscegenation.[46] Passing evokes miscegenation in two ways: the racially ambiguous body recalls the act of miscegenation, and the invisibility in that body of a potentially contaminating blackness threatens to perpetuate the "crime" of miscegenation. The taboo on miscegenation is certainly the most historically visible link between the racial and the sexual as systems of discipline operating through the definition of bodily norms and the pathologization and punishment of deviation from those norms.[47] I would expand on that link by suggesting that if passing is a perversion of the natural order of race, then becoming perverse in relation to race spills over into a more diffuse, and sexually charged, perversion.[48] As Eva Saks has suggested, the joining of two racially disparate bodies in the "miscegenous body" threatens to broach the full range of social boundaries: racial, sexual, political, legal, and representational.[49] But if we consider the figure or the threat of miscegenation as it functions as a discursive locus for the expression or containment of cultural anxieties regarding order and difference, then it is not miscegenation itself, but the collapsing of boundaries that miscegenation enacts, that is threatening and therefore defined as perverse. For this reason, the tension of transgression in *The Autobiography* is seldom where one expects to find it; his technically miscegenational marriage, which would seem to be the worst of his transgressions, is not presented as such in the narrative. While the transgression of passing is inseparable from the transgression of miscegenation, the crime that the narrator compulsively confesses is not simply this final miscegenational affair.

The novel begins by rhetorically linking the secret of passing with sexual transgression. The tension of keeping the secret alluded to in the opening of the novel is magnified in terms of an erotics of self-exposure: "I know that I am *playing with fire*, and I feel the *thrill* which accompanies that most *fascinating pastime*; and, back of it all, I think I find a sort of *savage and diabolical desire* to gather up all the little tragedies of my life, and turn them into a practical joke on society" (p. 3, emphasis added). However, telling the secret will not expiate the guilt. If the narrative is driven by the desire to tell the truth, that desire is never satisfied.[50] The uneasiness of release is suggested by the immediate diffusion of these images of "fire" and "thrill" into "a vague feeling of unsatisfaction, of regret, of almost remorse, from which I am seeking relief, and of which I shall speak in the last paragraph of this account" (p. 3). The promise of a powerful erotic charge implied by the opening frame seems to dissipate in the narrator's subsequent reluctance to discuss his romantic life. Joseph Skerrett's conclusions about the reticence of Johnson's *Along This Way* might just as well apply to the implicit critical consensus regarding *The Autobiography*: "*Along This Way* is not one of those autobiographies in which the author 'tells all' in a rush of breathless confessional prose. Johnson was too reticent, too Victorian for that sort of thing. His is a public story of a public life: the private life—love, sex, marriage—and most of the stronger emotions are only glimpsed if seen at all."[51]

In *The Autobiography*, the heterosexual narratives of "love, sex, and marriage" are pale, almost perfunctory. The women whom the narrator presents as love objects are curiously sterile, even more unspecified than the other nameless characters who people the book. Unlike the empty conventions of sentimental romance that produce the female characters, the male characters are central, powerful figures who dominate the narrative.[52] As Cheryl Clarke has demonstrated, this text lends itself particularly well to a homoerotic reading that focuses on the numerous scenes of intimate homosociality, in particular the narrator's relations with his father, his work- and playmates in the cigar factory and the gambling club, and his millionaire patron.[53] But this homoerotic desire is never recognized or realized. We might read the erotics of these relations as energized by the slippage between identification and desire or between wanting to be a wealthy white man and wanting to have a wealthy white man, insofar as, by the end of the novel, the narrator has become like the father and the millionaire, wealthy and white. But I think that the perhaps tempting conclusion—that the narrator has failed to read or recognize his true (homosexual) desire in the same way that, as Lucinda MacKethan suggests, he fails to read the signs of his true heritage or recognize his true racial identity—risks reverting to the cultural logic of passing that posits some identity, racial and sexual, as essential and irreducible. There is a significant interplay between sexual transgression and racial transgression in *The Autobiography*; as Clarke remarks, "in the murder of the widow and the lynching of the black 'wretch,' Johnson links sex and race as transgressive awareness that can potentially result in destruction."[54] But what exactly is the nature of this link? As I will argue in greater length in relation to *Passing*, the epistemological crisis marked by passing is the occasion for the complex enfolding of multiple transgressions each in the other.

The narrator's condition of guilt is not a mark of the moral condition of the narrator; rather, it signals the power of the law of sexual and racial propriety to punish those who deviate from its prescriptive norms of boundedness and separation. Although the impossible demand of this law is ever present in the narrator's feelings of alienation and failure in relation to both whiteness and blackness, nowhere is its force more powerfully expressed than in the scene of lynching witnessed by the narrator. Lynching, as commentators since Ida Wells have insisted, is a practice of bodily discipline designed both to contain the black population politically and socially by the immanent threat of violence and simultaneously to produce for the white spectators the spectacle of blackness as bestiality and degeneracy. But the true function of lynching as a form of political terrorism was masked by the ideological association prevalent at the turn of the century between rape and lynching. In particular, the white Southern defense of the practice of lynching in the face of Northern criticism relied on the irrational and emotional power of the charge of rape. In the popular white imagination, as expressed in films such as *Birth of a Nation* or as manipulated by the conspirators in *The Marrow of Tradition*, lynching became inextricably linked with the specter of black violation of the sanctity of white womanhood.[55] Thus, as Hazel Carby has noted, "while accusations of rape were made in only one-third of all lynchings, the cry of rape was an extremely effective way to create panic and fear. . . . The North conceded to the South's argument that rape was the cause of lynching; the concession to lynching for a specific crime in turn conceded the right to lynch any black male for any crime: the charge of rape became the excuse for murder."[56] Hence, miscegenation and lynching are ideologically two sides of the same coin. Just as miscegenation is the crime in which all the anxieties and absurdities of white purity and the color line are embodied, lynching is the symbolic and bodily response to miscegenation's threat to whiteness and racial separation.

Thus, it is not coincidental that this scene of lynching holds a prominent place in a drama of racial passing. It is this scene that prompts the narrator's final, precipitous flight from the South to a new life as a white New York businessman. In addition to finding the spectacle horrifying, he is gripped by a "great wave of humiliation and shame" (p. 187) at "being identified with a people that could with impunity be treated worse than animals" (p. 191). The narrator's response seems cowardly and disloyal; but I would suggest that identification and loyalty are complicated in this scene by the implicit threat directed at the narrator. Inasmuch as he identifies with the victim, he too is symbolically disciplined. If lynching has historically served as the most extreme form of bodily discipline for policing the boundaries of racial hierarchy, then in this lynching scene the narrator comes face to face with the demand, and the violence, of racial discipline. It should be noted that the bodily discipline of race staged in this lynching repeats and refines the bodily discipline of the narrator's primal scene of racial identification. The teacher's admonition that the narrator should not stand with the white children but should "rise with the others" forcibly places the narrator's body as a spectacle of racial difference in what can be read from the perspective of this latter scene as a milder version of the spectacular racial discipline of lynching. While the narrator's final flight into whiteness might be judged opportunistic or selfish, it seems to me that we might alternatively read this flight as a (necessarily futile) attempt to escape the violent reach of the law that demands from him that he be what his blood says he must be.

To read *The Autobiography* without resorting to the critical fallacies involved in pronouncing moral or sociological judgment on a fictional character, we must take the narrator not for what the cultural logic of passing decrees him to be, a truly black man passing for white, but for what the narrative presents him as—unnameable. Johnson refuses to resolve any of the epistemological doubts raised by the narrative, as though he realized the power of the demand that each individual possess a certain and ascertainable racial identity and set out deliberately to write a narrative that would violate precisely that principle. Sartre once wrote, "the nature of consciousness simultaneously is to be what it is not and not to be what it is." [57] In this knot of being and not-being, the fact of identity, the mark of the law that continually produces identity as codified difference, coexists in a tangled tension with the necessary inauthenticity of the experience of that identity. That Johnson's narrator cannot *be* either white or black need not be read as a personal, subjective failure; rather, the narrator's failure and his guilt point to the constitutive failure that is, in the terms given by the modern epistemology of race, the very condition of racial identity.

## Nella Larsen's 'Passing'

In *The Autobiography*, the certitude of racial knowledge is challenged through an exploration of the self-knowledge of the narrator. In Nella Larsen's 1929 novel *Passing*, the question of racial knowledge, of who knows what, of what they know, of how they know it, is shifted from the subject's knowledge of the self to the subject's knowledge of the other. In *Passing*, the indeterminacy raised by the specter of passing exposes racial identity as a contingent relation based on recognition and knowledge. As Irene explains to her white friend Hugh Wentworth, "nobody can [tell if a white-appearing person is passing]. Not by looking." "Not by looking, eh? Meaning?" "I'm afraid I can't explain. Not clearly. There are ways. But they're not definite or tangible." [58] Race becomes a difference that cannot be described, located, seen, or distinguished in any "definite or tangible" way. Race, we might say, is not a nothing-at-all, but a *something* that says nothing. In *Passing*, we see Barth's emphasis on difference as ascription rather than "stuff" taken to its limit. The black professional and cultural elites of Harlem have little need for the white world. The black world of Harlem is just like the white world outside. Aside from the racism that continues to mark the power of racial hierarchy, racial difference itself is represented as a purely formal difference, nearly an absurdity, one that would seem comic were its effects not so powerful and, in the end, tragic. "Tell me honestly," Clare asks, "haven't you ever thought of passing?" Irene answers, "No, why should I?" (p. 160).

Irene's insistence that she has no desire to pass is given the lie by the fact that at the very moment when she denies it she is in fact passing, enjoying tea in a segregated Chicago hotel. But while she may be able to deny the significance of her own acts, her encounter with Clare is like an explosion, sending shock waves into every corner of her previously placid existence. There is something about Clare—or, rather, there is something about Clare as she embodies the figure of passing—that makes her simultaneously dangerous and desirable, fascinating and repulsive. Although the representation of Clare in the novel seems to support the traditional deception model of passing, I would suggest that in Clare and the disruptions of knowledge and desire that she sets in motion we see a further development of the disruptive effect of passing in relation to the discipline and order of racial knowledge that characterize the action of *The Autobiography*. The epistemological structure of Clare's passing does not resolve into the triangular structure of insider and dupe. Clare's husband, John Bellew, seems to play the dupe in the first part of the novel, and yet his is a knowing unknowing; his affectionate nickname for her, "Nig," speaks even as it denies the impossibility of that racial purity on which he has staked his own claim to whiteness.[59] At the same time, while Irene seems to be an insider, her own growing uncertainty and suspicions about Clare place her increasingly in the position of dupe, although importantly we never know what relation Irene's suspicions bear to the truth. If the dupe mistakes seeming for being and the insider recognizes being despite seeming, Clare's passing seems to allow for neither of these interpretations. Rather, Clare's body marks, not simply the gap between being and seeming, but the widening of that gap into an abyss that threatens to obliterate absolutely the comfort of security and certainty.

The gap that Clare opens between seeming and being cannot be described or named; outside the orders of categories and identities, it is manifested in the inarticulate expression of laughter. When Bellew explains the nickname "Nig" by insisting that Clare is getting darker and darker and that "if she don't look out, she'll wake up one of these days and find she's turned into a nigger," he bursts into laughter. While Bellew's "Hello, Nig!" seems to name the truth of passing, Irene's response to Bellew's knowing ignorance complicates this truth by exposing a suppressed but uncontrollable disorder beneath the mannered pleasantries of the Bellew home: "Irene, who had been sitting with lips tightly compressed, cried out: 'That's good!' and gave way to gales of laughter. She laughed and laughed and laughed. Tears ran down her cheeks. Her sides ached. Her throat hurt. She laughed on and on and on, long after the others had subsided" (p. 171). All in this scene save Bellew are aware that the order of race on which he has staked the purity of his familial line is in fact illusory. Although Irene's laughter initially reinforces the triangular structure of passing, marking with her laughter the absurdity of Bellew's position as dupe, this laughter seems to take on a life of its own, violent and uncontrollable. This hysterical laughter points toward a moment of breakdown in the structuring order of race. Irene laughs because she cannot speak; laughter is the only possible expression of this circumstance. Thus, her uncontrollable laughter exposes chaos glimmering just beneath the surface of order and regularity.[60]

It is not simply a question of Irene knowing something to which Bellew is oblivious. Rather, the laughter exceeds Irene's intentions, signaling, even as it cannot name, a space "outside" the ordering identities of race. I suggested earlier the arbitrary, contingent character of the law of race, which raises an empty mark, one drop of black blood, to the sign of difference. This law produces identity by requiring each individual to embody either white or black. Difference, within this law, is reduced to the difference between these two terms. This law of identity and difference is a contingent structure that relies on the apparently natural, necessary status of a posited, arbitrary difference. There is no subject-position outside the either/or of race, no place from which to speak. That which is outside this order cannot be named or known: the naming that is the condition of knowledge or truth is determined by the law that produces identity and regulates difference. The incursion of difference that cannot be assimilated into identity bubbles up as inarticulate laughter.

The possibility or impossibility of language becomes the sign in this scene of the regularizing function of race. Irene's unnameable, inarticulate laughter gives way to a barely concealed fury: "There was a brief silence, during which she feared that her self-control was about to prove too frail a bridge to support her mounting anger and indignation. She had a leaping desire to shout at the man beside her: 'And you're sitting here surrounded by three black devils, drinking tea'" (p. 172). Unlike her laughter, the fury is articulate and definite; it has a content, a truth, which she must decide whether or not to speak. Her anger takes the form of rage and shame at finding her race insulted and vilified and being unable to respond. Thus, her anger reestablishes the orderly exclusions of race that place her in opposition to Bellew: Irene and Clare as black, Bellew as white. Irene's apparent race loyalty in this scene is less a loyalty to the dignity of her race than it is a loyalty to the very principle of race, insofar as it is the condition of order, predictability, and security in her life. The alternative is the uncontrollable, the irrational, the unpredictable, as embodied in hysterical laughter.

## The Eruption of Desire

Before she meets Clare, Irene lives in a carefully controlled oblivion, wanting what she has, having what she wants. This is the self completely adequate to itself, neither needing nor wanting the supplement of an other: transparent, autonomous identity. But Clare's passing body becomes for

Irene the site of a rupture in the orderly structure of transparent identities. Irene's memory of her reunion with Clare begins with an image of complete satisfaction and wholeness. Overpowered by heat during her shopping expedition in Chicago, she retreats to the roof of the Drayton Hotel and orders tea. This tea emblematizes all of Irene's fantasies of wholeness and completion, of satisfaction completely adequate to desire. "The tea, when it came, was all that she had desired and expected. In fact, so much was it what she had desired and expected that after the first deep cooling drink she was able to forget it" (p. 147). For Irene, desire is limited to that which can be satisfied. A satisfied desire is a forgotten desire. She reinforces this sense of control over desire as her thoughts turn to her boys and the gifts they expect her to bring. "Why was it that almost invariably [her son Ted] wanted something that was difficult or impossible to get? Like his father. For ever wanting something that he couldn't have" (p. 148). Implicit in Irene's musings is a contrast between her husband's dissatisfaction, which derives from wanting what he cannot have, and her own satisfaction, the result of wanting only what she can or does have. Irene's solitary thoughts are interrupted by the sudden appearance of Clare, whom she has not seen in many years. Irene is deeply unsettled by this meeting; Clare ruptures her satisfied, if illusory, feeling of wholeness or self-sameness by disrupting her carefully constructed correspondence between her own desire and what she has.

Irene's fascination with Clare begins with the ambiguous complexities of passing: "It was as if the woman sitting on the other side of the table, a girl that she had known, who had done this rather dangerous and, to Irene Redfield, abhorrent thing successfully and had announced herself well satisfied, had for her a fascination, strange and compelling" (p. 161). This strange and compelling fascination is in marked contrast to the forgotten satisfaction emblematized in the tea. Meeting Clare produces a wedge between desire and satisfaction: all of a sudden, Irene realizes the possibility of wanting something she does not have. Clare asks her, "haven't you ever thought of 'passing?'" Irene answers promptly: "No. Why should I? . . . You see, Clare, I've everything I want. Except, perhaps, a little more money" (p. 160). This "except" exposes a fissure in the continuity between having and wanting that forms the basis of Irene's sense of stability. Clare's passing produces an ambivalence, an instability, in structures of sameness and difference that underwrite Irene's feelings of satisfaction and identity. In the most simple terms, we might say that although both Clare and Irene are "black," Clare has introduced a difference into this sameness by passing for white. More importantly, Clare's passing undermines the basis of distinction between black and white through which Irene's world has been ordered, thus suspending the criterion on which sameness and difference could be determined. For Irene, and for others who come into contact with Clare, Clare's passing unleashes a crisis of knowledge, judgment, and desire.

In the face of Clare's daring, Irene's carefully controlled suppression of uncertainty and desire crumbles. Irene muses to Brian, "it's funny about 'passing.' We disapprove of it and at the same time condone it. It excites our contempt and yet we rather admire it. We shy away from it with an odd kind of revulsion, but we protect it" (p. 186). Like her feelings about passing, Irene's feelings about Clare waver between attraction and repulsion. Angry, determined to push Clare away, Irene always succumbs to the temptation to draw her closer, despite herself. For example, following the episode with Bellew in Clare's drawing room, Irene receives a letter from Clare. At first, she is determined not to read it, but she can't help herself, she is overpowered by Clare's attractive force: "She became possessed of an uncontrollable curiosity to see what Clare had said about yesterday" (p. 177). When Clare insists on visiting Irene in New York despite Irene's refusal to answer her letters, Irene is determined to "tell her at once, and definitively, that it was no use, her coming" (p. 194). Her resolve dissolves in an instant when Clare enters and "drop[s] a kiss on her dark curls. Looking at the woman before her, Irene Redfield had a sudden inexplicable onrush of affectionate feeling" (p. 194). Irene is "possessed," she is ruled by "uncontrollable," "inexplicable" feelings: Clare exerts an attractive force over Irene over which Irene has no conscious control, no conscious understanding. Unable to confront the possibility of the attraction of desire, Irene must repress its source, leaving her unable to explain what keeps drawing her back to Clare.

The erotics of this relation are the focus of Deborah McDowell's reading, an extremely influential interpretation that forms the preface to the Rutgers University Press combined edition of *Quicksand* and *Passing* and has been perhaps the single most important factor in the recent revival of interest in this novel. For McDowell, the "safe" theme of passing is a "protective cover underneath which lie more dangerous sub-plots," particularly, the implicit story of "Irene's awakening sexual desire for Clare" (p. xxvi).[61] McDowell was the first to recognize the complex erotics of the novel in terms of a protolesbian relation of desire between women. Unfortunately, this recognition comes at the price of a separation of the emergence of this desire from the narrative of race passing. The "passing" of the novel's title implies for McDowell "false, forged, or mistaken identities." McDowell suggests the novel "takes the form of the act it describes" (p. xxx), that is, the dangerous sex plot is passing as a safe race plot. Thus, McDowell implies, the sexual plot is the true identity of the novel, and the race passing plot is its false, forged identity.

McDowell's uncovering of a protolesbian plot underneath the race passing plot might lead one to conclude that race operates independently of sexuality or gender. Having acknowledged the importance of Irene's desire to this novel, however, might not we consider that desire as a part of, rather than disguised by, the passing plot? In her reading of *Passing* in *Bodies that Matter*, Judith Butler takes the position that "not only is it unnecessary to choose whether this novella is 'about' race or 'about' sexuality and sexual conflict, but . . . the two domains are inextricably linked, such that the text offers a way to read the racialization of sexual conflict."[62] Butler's reading of the power and fragility of white masculinity as well as the operations of desire and disavowal between Bellew and Clare, on the one hand, and between Irene and Clare, on the other, reveal the "inextricable links" between race and sex. But I think that we need to go carefully before concluding, as Butler does in the passage just quoted, that *Passing* exposes the "racialization of sexual conflict." Despite her critique of "psychoanalytic feminism" for deriving every other form of difference from sexual difference, for Butler sexuality maintains a priority and a reality that is not attributed to race. This assertion is supported by the different metaphors she uses to distinguish homosexuality from blackness. Butler writes: "the muteness of homosexuality converges in the story with the illegibility of Clare's blackness" (p. 175). For Butler, homosexuality is mute, repressed, a powerful presence that is struggling to come to the surface. This would suggest that sexuality is what gives a charge to passing; sexuality, not passing, creates the danger in the text that ends in Clare's death. From such a perspective, blackness is illegible, unreadable, a sign that says nothing. There is nothing to read in blackness, while homosexual desire is a real plenitude. But why should sexuality be any more real than race? Neither has any existence, any substance, or any meaning outside the social relations in which each is defined and operates. For Butler, race is second to the first question, that of the ordering structures of sexuality. I think this implicit bias is primarily the product of her larger project, which is to consider the possibilities and limits of psychoanalysis in relation to race; thus questions of desire, sexuality, and gender are to a certain extent necessarily prior. And I think she succeeds in demonstrating the extent to which the analytical priority of sexual difference in much psychoanalytical theory "assumes that sexual difference is white sexual difference, and that whiteness is not a form of racial difference" (p. 182). Nevertheless, I find the relation between "passing" and "queering" as Butler reads them in the novel to be troubling.

While Butler makes a strong argument for avoiding the temptation to separate race from sexuality and while her reading makes a persuasive and powerful case for racializing our theories of sexuality, she reads passing as the occasion for something else: namely, queering. *Queering* is defined as "a term for betraying what ought to remain concealed" (p. 176). Does she intend here to redefine or redeploy the idea of "queerness" in such a way as to evade the identification of "queer" with the violation of heterosexual norms? Because *Bodies that Matter* concludes with a meditation on the term *queer* in relation to sexual identity politics and gender performativity, this does not seem likely. Thus, we ought not lose sight of the sexual charge of queering when Butler concludes that "*in the last instance*, queering is what upsets and *exposes* passing; it is the act by which the racially and sexually repressive surface of conversation is exploded, by rage, by sexuality, by the insistence on color" (p. 177, emphasis added). But it seems to me that in both *Passing* and in *The Autobiography of an Ex-Coloured Man*, the idea of exposure and its implied opposite, concealment, are troubled by the very presence of passing. In the figure of passing, the basis for certainty, whereby one would be able to tell definitively and indisputably the difference between concealment and exposure, has been displaced.[63] Clare's passing is not simply deception; insofar as it disrupts the grounds of certainty and security it sets in motion the convoluted and often dangerous desires that threaten to explode the surface of convention. This is not to conclude that the terms should be reversed, such that race is anterior to sexuality; rather, passing disrupts all anteriority, revealing the impossibility of either exposure or concealment.

## Suspicion and Knowledge

As Irene's desire for Clare becomes more intense and more threatening, McDowell suggests that she "project[s] her own developing passion for Clare onto Brian."[64] But in addition to discovering in Irene's jealous suspicion a deflection and disavowal of her own desire, Irene's suspicions raise once more the question of the relation between passing and knowledge. Irene criticizes Clare for tactlessly coming to a party to which she was not invited, but Brian confesses that he in fact invited her. Irene responds with shock and anger:

> Irene cried out: "But Brian, I—" and stopped, amazed at the fierce anger that had blazed up in her.
> Brian's head came round with a jerk. His brows lifted in an odd surprise. . . .
> . . . that little straightening motion of the shoulders. Hadn't it been like that of a man drawing himself up to receive a blow? Her fright was like a scarlet spear of terror leaping at her heart.
> Clare Kendry! So that was it! Impossible. It couldn't be. (p. 217)

There is nothing more than this: a turning head, a lifting brow, a drawing up of the shoulders. Surely not definitive proof of her husband's infidelity. If we assume for the moment that knowledge, as it is understood by modern scientific empiricism, is based on the certainty accorded to presence, palpable evidence, something there, then Irene's suspicion is the contrary of knowledge, based entirely on absence: "Nothing. She had seen nothing, heard nothing" (p. 223).

This "nothing" echoes the nothing of racial difference in the scene of passing, as Irene explains it to Hugh Wentworth, that "something" that is "not definite or tangible" but that assures Irene that she can tell the difference between black and white. In both Irene's knowledge of racial difference and her knowledge of her husband's infidelity there is nothing definite, nothing there to see or hear, but nevertheless this nothing functions as a something, telling and showing even as it remains mute and invisible. An empirical nothing has become something, and their interchangeability suggests that the knowledge of something, knowledge based on presence, is not so far from the suspicion of nothing, which we might view as a knowledge based on absence. Irene's suspicion is as powerful as a certainty: "life had changed, lost its colour, its vividness, its whole meaning. . . . Knowing, stumbling on this thing, had changed her" (p. 218). Suspecting functions for Irene in the same way as knowing: each is indistinguishable from the other. The repeated slippage between suspecting and knowing calls into question the possibility of empirical certainty on which a distinction between these terms might be based. A nothing can be neither exposed nor concealed, and yet it has the power to transform Irene's vision and, in the final scene, to destroy Clare.

It is Clare who is the cause of these suspicions, the source and site of the nothing that becomes for Irene a suspicion with all the force of certainty. The emphasis on the nothing at the heart of Irene's suspicions about Brian's fidelity is repeated in the scenes that mark Bellew's emerging suspicion about his wife's identity and activities. Irene encounters Bellew while shopping with Felise Freeman, a darker woman. Bellew at first greets Irene, but then he notices Felise: "[Bellew's] smile faded at once. Surprise, incredulity, and — was it understanding? — passed over his features" (p. 226). Was it understanding, or was it not? Bellew's expression cannot be interpreted with certainty, and again Irene is confronted with a nothing that may mean something: Has Bellew recognized her? Has he made the connection between Felise Freeman and his wife? Again, Clare sets off a chain of suspicions, a nested order of uncertainty in which Irene is suspicious about Bellew's suspicions about Clare.

Like Irene's suspicions about Brian's relation to Clare, Bellew's suspicions about his wife remain just that: suspicions. He cannot discover any truth about Clare, instead he draws his conclusions from a sort of transitive knowledge of association that Butler likens to contagion: "if she associates with blacks, she becomes black, where the sign of blackness is contracted, as it were, through proximity, where 'race' itself is figured as a contagion transmissible through proximity." [65] As he has insisted, the purity of his own whiteness is assured by his absolute separation from blackness: "No niggers in my family. Never have been and never will be" (p. 171). But if, as Butler suggests, Clare's own blackness is acquired through association and "contagion" then Bellew himself is suddenly at risk of such a contagion, and "must destroy this spectre to avoid the kind of association that might destabilize the territorial boundaries of his own whiteness." [66] Bellew bursts in on Felise Freeman's Christmas party in a rage and confronts Clare: "So you're a nigger, a damned dirty nigger!" (p. 238). This speech falls like a blow, with all the force and violence of racial discipline. In order to assure the stability and impermeability of Bellew's own whiteness, Bellew must transform the implicit blackness that Clare has acquired through association into essential truth. In his rage, he embodies the power of racial order, the forces that maintain it, and the danger of refusing it. Hurling the epithet "nigger" at Clare, Bellew attempts to restore the certainty of racial knowledge to Clare's body, which in its passing has become the site of a nothing against which all certainty must be measured and found wanting.

In the face of Bellew's rage, Clare remains calm, even bemused: "Clare stood at the window, as composed as if everyone were not staring at her in curiosity and wonder, as if the whole structure of her life were not lying in fragments before her. . . . There was even a faint smile on her full, red lips, and in her shining eyes" (p. 239). Clare's smile in this final encounter with Bellew recalls Irene's hysterical laughter at her first meeting with the man. Both Clare's smile and Irene's laughter signal the nothingness of race, its reduction to an empty marker. The truth of race is not the apparent, natural race identities that form the foundation of social order; rather, it is the possibility that any apparent truth is *not* true, that because race is a *nothing*, it can never in fact be what it appears to be. What Gibson calls the "enigma of the thing that is what it is not, and is not what it is" threatens to unleash not only empirical uncertainty but a kind of disorder and insecurity that is for Irene unbearable: "It was that smile that maddened Irene. She ran across the room, her terror tinged with ferocity, and laid a hand on Clare's bare arm. One thought possessed her. She couldn't have Clare Kendry cast aside by Bellew. She couldn't have her free" (p. 239). The repetition of denial in this passage, "she couldn't have Clare Kendry. . . . She couldn't have her," is both the banishing of disorder and the final disavowal of desire, and in the next instant Clare disappears: "One moment Clare had been there, a vital glowing thing, like a flame of red and gold. The next she was gone" (p. 239).

Claudia Tate points out that while traditional critics have unquestioningly assumed that Irene pushes Clare out the window, "the evidence against her, no matter how convincing, is purely circumstantial." Tate sees this as an important aspect of the artistry of the novel. Larsen "avoided narrative clarity by weaving ambiguity into Irene's every thought and expression"; therefore, meaning "must be pieced together like a complicated puzzle from allusion and suggestions." [67] But can meaning be pieced together? Or must we be satisfied with indeterminate allusions and suggestions? If, in this final confrontation between Bellew, Clare, Irene, and Brian, the players are unmasked, it is crucial to note that absolutely nothing has been revealed. Knowledge is indistinguishable from suspicion, implication, connotation. There is no certainty here. The deep subjectivity of the narrative, the persistence, virtually unbroken, of Irene's consciousness, produces an impenetrable barrier between what might have happened and what Irene thinks or what the reader can know. The text insists on maintaining the mysteries at its core. There is no evidence that will prove definitively whether Clare and Brian were having an affair or if it only appeared so because Irene has projected her desire for Clare onto Brian. There is no evidence that will make certain whether Clare fell out the window or if Irene pushed her. But the text does not present these puzzles as mysteries to which there is an answer that the text refuses to disclose. Rather, the text seems to insist that there is nothing more than what we are told, that this is all knowledge can be, an unreliable, scattered filtering of events and artifacts that refuse to add up to a truth.

Clare's death forecloses not only the possibility of a narrative revelation of truth but the possibility of narrative itself. Despite the title's apparent reference to Clare—it is Clare who is passing—the novel seems to be less about Clare than about Irene; but it is equally true that the novel as narrative space does not exist without Clare. The novel opens and closes with Clare, beginning with Clare's letter to Irene and ending with Clare's death. When Clare dies, Irene loses consciousness, and the novel ends with her blackout: "She moaned and sank down, moaned again. . . . Then everything was dark" (p. 242). I would suggest that Irene's loss of consciousness is not simply tidy narrative closure; it is the necessary result of the foreclosure of desire marked by Clare's death. Irene's consciousness in this novel is not only the consciousness *of* desire, it is consciousness *as* desire. If subjectivity is an effect of desire and desire is, as Lacan suggests, "the desire of the Other," then Clare's death is not only the abolishing of the "nameless shameful impulse" of protolesbian desire but the end of desire itself and, with it, the end of the subject.

Passing is the mark of a gap where we expect true being to be. In the epistemologico-political context of Western modernity, certainty and order seem to depend on this true being as the legitimate source of stability and constancy. The figure of passing tears open the surface of orderly relations, threatening to expose what must, from the perspective of presumed certainty and order, be a terrifying emptiness at the center of race, at the center of desire, and at the center of knowledge. Clare embodies the failure of knowledge to attain certainty, the failure of identity to achieve self-sameness, the failure of desire to grasp satisfaction. Clare exposes the fault line in the edifice of identity, truth, and order. Clare's dead body is the only possible plug to stop the leakage of un-certainty, dis-satisfaction, non-identity. Clare's death exposes the violence necessary to produce and maintain the effect of a stable, fixed, authentic racial identity. The lynching scene in *The Autobiography* serves the same function as Clare's drop from the window in *Passing*; each is a violent dramatization of the force of racial discipline to demand that each subject take up her or his proper place in the racial order in accordance with, and as a means of producing, racial separation and racial hierarchy. The epistemological abyss of "the thing that is what it is not, and is not what it is" threatens disorder, a disorder that seems violent and frightening in its very unpredictability; but equally, it is only through the violence of racial discipline that this abyss is forcibly sutured by demanding that each embody, express, and experience her or his true identity.

Yet while the narrative seems to demand Clare's destruction in order to restore the apparent truth of being and seeming, it is also the case that without Clare, and the continual failure of order that she embodies, there is no desire, no subject, and no narrative. Excluding Clare does not restore satisfaction or security; rather, without the excess and disruption that is Clare, there is nothing. Clare is a risk: a danger, but also a chance. Clare cannot free herself from the demand and discipline of racial order; but perhaps Clare's body breaks open a space of freedom. Such a freedom can only be a threat to the ordered security of Irene or Bellew insofar as it marks radical unknowability, undecidability, and the absence of any rule or principle that would assure that the future will continue in the same way as the present (thus, the implicit collusion of Irene and Bellew in Clare's destruction). But if freedom is to be something more than a right or a rule, then perhaps such a freedom must be risky—dangerous, chancy, a terrible, awesome opportunity.

## 5. Community and Contagion

### *Zora Neale Hurston's*
### *Risky Practice*

It has become fairly commonplace in discussions of Zora Neale Hurston's work to refer to her as a "literary foremother" or as the "mother of a tradition." It was Alice Walker's epoch-making essay "Looking for Zora," published in *Ms.* magazine in 1975, that positioned Hurston as the lost mother found. As it unfolds in Walker's narrative, the search for a mother is the search for an origin, an identity, a home. But reading Walker, and thinking about Hurston's career, one begins to wonder, how does the very search construct its object? Can mothers be created ex post facto? Might the recovery of an origin or the naming of an ancestor have about it some element of arbitrariness, selectivity, violence?[1] These questions hint at the ambivalence I want to locate both around and in the figure of Hurston. For contemporary critics, Hurston has marked the symbolic center of a project of ancestral recovery and communal revaluation. This project of recovery, one that focuses on the racial politics of identity and community, has simultaneously been a recuperation of Hurston's reputation, challenging an earlier critical marginalization of the writer and her work. What is seldom noticed, however, is the extent to which Hurston is engaged in the reconsideration (and frequently rejection) of precisely these terms: ancestry, community, race, and identity. While many contemporary readers of Hurston have sought the security of recovery, Hurston herself is oftentimes far more interested in the risks—both dangers and opportunities—of loss.

In the previous chapter, I suggested that at the conclusion of *Passing*,

Clare's ambivalent body must be eliminated if truth and certainty are to be restored; Clare's death is a sign of the violence necessary to sustain racial division and hierarchy. Clare's death, like the lynching witnessed by the narrator of *The Autobiography*, seems to be another instance of racial discipline, that historical violence that has enslaved, tortured, exploited, impoverished, silenced, rendered invisible, and otherwise sought to debase African-Americans in order to preserve the exclusive white privileges and benefits of property, freedom and democracy. However, it is not only the white racist Bellew but also the black woman Irene who seems to demand Clare's final destruction. For both black and white, the chaos embodied in Clare disrupts the certainty of identity, interrupts the mutual recognition and obligation of community, and thus calls into question the stability of identity and community insofar as they would serve as the basis for political life. Such chaos appears as a violent threat of disorder; the necessity of Clare's death suggests that such a threat must be countered by another, far more vengeful violence that cloaks its true nature under the banner of order, discipline, and truth. It is this latter violence that concerns Hurston. For Hurston, this violence not only founds and conserves white supremacy; white supremacy is a particular instance of a more general condition of violence that Hurston diagnoses in the global instabilities of the 1940s. In the name of communities of race and nation, in both the established nations of Europe and the emerging nations of the decolonized Third World, Hurston argues, violence continues unabated. In this chapter, I will suggest that it is in an effort to end or escape this violence that Hurston repudiates not only nationalism but race consciousness, a truly risky practice for a black woman in the 1940s but perhaps no less so today. The challenge in rereading Hurston with an eye to her avowed positions on international and racial politics is, I think, to discover to what extent she was merely repeating the platitudes of liberalism and individualism common in her day or, alternatively, to what extent she was struggling to articulate a different vision of community.

This risky Hurston has been occluded by the narratives of recovery that surround her work. Hurston is in fact profoundly suspicious of recovery, origin, community, and identity, the very terms that have defined her most recent canonization. In the place of the secure stability and certainty offered by historical narrative, ancestral inheritance, or indissoluble identity, Hurston constantly and consistently chooses another path. Hurston offers us a vision of what I will call *cosmic upset*, a refusal to accept the divisions and boundaries that order the social world by determining difference and identity. Instead of identity, Hurston discovers a body and a self that cannot be bounded or contained; instead of history and ancestry that would connect a community to its past, Hurston discovers the accidental connections of wandering and chance encounters. The implications of Hurston's revisionary imagination are profound. The autonomous, independent subject no longer appears as the foundational grounds for freedom or for community. Freedom for Hurston cannot be the freedom of this subject; likewise, community cannot emerge so long as the subject is conceived as prior to and therefore separate from community. The relation of subject to other, in which the subject is always granted priority, gives way in Hurston's writing to a relation of simultaneity and togetherness, in which singular encounters rather than unity or obligation become the condition of community.

In her revision of community beyond the alternatives offered within the modern liberal tradition, Hurston offers the possibility of a transformed relation of being together in the world. In the final part of this chapter, I will try to suggest the magnitude of transformation that I think Hurston implies. My reading of Hurston will demand a new critical vocabulary to mark definitively her distance from the politics of subject, identity, and community. For Hurston, the violence of the subject's Hegelian struggle for recognition gives way to the extravagant gift of *touch*; the system of state-sanctioned vengeance and exchange understood as justice gives way to an ethical relation to the other that I will call *just-ness*; and the demands of conformity and unity that form the silent and oftentimes violent underside of community give way to the accidental and unpredictable togetherness of *contagion*.

Hurston's way is the way of accident, of chance, of fortune and luck — in every sense, a risky practice. By calling Hurston's ambivalence toward race, identity, and community a risky practice I intend to emphasize the double aspect of her vision. Hurston is cognizant, I believe, of the dangers and uncertainties of abandoning the security of home; for contemporary readers, the struggles over identity politics suggest the real hazards attendant on attempting to question the basis or function of racial identity. But Hurston is willing to gamble, to venture the risk of loss on the chance that an end to violence, to bloodshed, to hatred and mistrust, can come only from a radical revision of community, responsibility, and relation.

## Exhuming the Corpse:
## Hurston and the Recovery of Community

The rediscovery of lost ancestors and forgotten histories has been central to the widespread cultural and critical revaluation of African-American culture that has been building in the past two decades. During the same period, cultural theorists have begun working with such ideas as the "invention of ethnicity" and "imagined communities" to provide a nonessentializing account of cultural difference. For example, eschewing notions of an essential or absolute cultural identity, the new ethnic criticism (exemplified in the work of such critics as Werner Sollors, Mary Dearborn, and William Boelhower) is interested in the invention of ethnicity, the way in which ethnic and racial identities and particularities are invented in the present in response to diverse pressures and conditions so as to appear to be rooted in the past. Similarly, one can trace the invention of a lineage linking a real past with the conditions or circumstances of the present. Interestingly, Alice Walker's discovery of her literary foremother in the lost body of Zora Neale Hurston has all the elements of just such an invention. Walker writes in the introduction to Robert Hemenway's biography of Hurston: "I became aware of my need of Zora Neale Hurston's work some time before I knew her work existed." Dianne Sadoff suggests that this willful positing of a literary precursor "masks an underlying anxiety about the black woman writer's singularity in white America,"[2] suggesting both the importance and the inventedness of Walker's genealogy. By finding a reflection of herself in another whom she can identify as the same as herself, Walker is able to erect a literary genealogy in which to insert herself.

In "Looking for Zora," Walker describes her pilgrimage to Hurston's unmarked grave. On her arrival in Eatonville, Florida, she decides on a subterfuge to help in her search for Zora. She tells people she is Zora's niece. But this lie of convenience is quickly revealed as something more: "the lie comes with perfect naturalness to my lips. . . . As far as I'm concerned, she *is* my aunt—and that of all black people as well."[3] The text also suggests obliquely that claiming Zora as ancestor will impart something greater than literary validity. Walker chooses for Zora's gravestone "a tall black stone . . . as majestic as Zora herself" (p. 106). Dr. Benton, one of Zora's friends, echoes Walker in his description of Zora as "a big woman, *erect*" (p. 110). The claim to Zora as metaphoric ancestor goes beyond mere genealogy—to claim Zora is to claim the power of a big, black, beautiful, female phallus. The power of remembering, of recovering the ethnic past of the community, is for Walker both female and phallic. I would suggest that this conjunction is not as contradictory as it might seem if we view the phallus not as simply the sign of masculinity but also in its patriarchal function as the veiled sign of naming, ordering, and identifying.[4] Recovering Hurston as the lost ethnic past reinserts Walker into history, where history is the narrative and patriarchal-familial ordering of the community.

Despite Walker's powerful claim to a common ancestry, in her efforts to retrace Zora's tracks she has trouble passing as Zora's niece. The shape of her cheekbones, the size of her eyes, the nappiness of her hair give her away. "Well," she replies to an incredulous local, feigning shy dignity, "I'm illegitimate" (p. 109). The resort to a notion of illegitimacy to explain Walker's relation to Hurston, and more importantly the relation of the present to the past, is especially suggestive. Like all lineages of tradition, Walker's relation to Hurston is fictive, and her relation can be claimed and established only by projecting the present into the past. Walker cannot be a legitimate descendant, literary or otherwise, of Hurston. She only comes into relation with Hurston by inventing that relation *in the present*. In this sense, all relations of descent, all relations of influence, are illegitimate. Writers do not reach out from the past to influence the present; rather, the present reclaims the writers of the past as a source of influence. If the past is mother to the present, it is a peculiar sort of motherhood: the past necessarily remains ignorant of, and indifferent to, its literary offspring.[5]

Much is at stake in this search for literary or spiritual ancestors. As the object of Walker's search for a past, Hurston mediates between Walker's sense of artistic and cultural isolation and the possibility of a community originating in the past and extending into the present, producing a history in which Walker can locate herself and give her work context and meaning. This echoes the strategy of much of the new ethnic criticism, in which the invention of ethnicity as community counters the violence and fragmentation of modernity. Michael Fischer, for example, argues that the individual project of remembering and searching out an ethnic tradition is directed toward an ethical vision of the relation between the self and the community that aims to counter the leveling, dehistoricizing, atomizing effects of modernity. If the crisis of modernity is the loss of history, and hence the loss of community, then the solution is for the subject to become ethnic, to discover and invent ties to a past that write the self into a collective narrative.

The mute resistance of Hurston's elusive corpse, however, disrupts the harmony between self and collective that Walker seeks to establish. Walker's effort to memorialize Hurston by marking her grave simultaneously desecrates the real but unlocatable site of her burial. Walker's claims to Hurston, and the community Hurston has (imaginatively) engendered, can only ever be illegitimate. In effect, Hurston's body seems to stand in the way of the very community her body is meant to reproduce. Only by effacing the necessary absence of her actual body (the corpse, wherever it is buried) can a community be founded on the imaginative fiction of her symbolic body. Hurston's mute, invisible, and yet resistant body reveals the constitutive illegitimacy of community and the violence that illegitimacy entails. The material body itself is slippery and elusive, sliding around and escaping the boundaries of the community that would contain it.

## Racial Consciousness and the Trouble with Zora

Walker's recovery of Hurston's lost body made Hurston—or rather, Walker's invention of Hurston—imaginatively available for a new generation of readers hungry for positive, life-embracing representations of black women.[6] In the past decade or so, *Their Eyes Were Watching God* has gained a reputation and a readership that place it firmly in the canon of American classics.[7] Contemporary readers have found in Hurston what Alice Walker calls a symbol of "racial health—a sense of black people as complete, complex, *undiminished* human beings, a sense that is lacking in so much black writing and literature."[8] But Hurston's commitment to a literary celebration of black folkways and Southern black rural life in texts such as *Their Eyes Were Watching God* and *Mules and Men* seems to be undermined by her repudiation elsewhere of the very concepts of race pride, race solidarity, and race unity.

To address the question of Hurston's position on the "race issue," I want to consider in detail what many have viewed to be a problem text, Hurston's reluctant autobiography, *Dust Tracks on a Road*.[9] The most casual reader will immediately see what is wrong with Hurston's autobiography. "Negroes," she writes, are "supposed to write about the Race Problem. I was and am thoroughly sick of the subject."[10] Hurston's biographer, Robert Hemenway, summarizes the generally unsympathetic reception, at least until very recently, of Hurston's autobiography: "Arna Bontemps noted that 'Miss Hurston deals very simply with the more serious aspects

of Negro life in America—she ignores them.' Her old nemesis, Harold
Preece, was even harsher, calling the book 'the tragedy of a gifted, sensitive
mind, eaten up by an egocentrism fed on the patronizing admiration of the
dominant white world.' " [11]

Readers were shocked and dismayed that Hurston had retreated from
the grim realities of racial politics into a conservative smoke screen of individualism. Such an impression was easily borne out by her iteration of
sentiments mocking "race clichés" and celebrating individual effort and
achievement throughout *Dust Tracks*. Indeed, many critics from both Hurston's time and our own have disparaged Hurston's later writings for their
apparent callousness. However, sympathetic readers have suggested that
Hurston's individualism is in fact an effort to resist the sterility and fixity
of the roles to which she has been relegated as a black woman in early-
twentieth-century America.[12] Elizabeth Fox-Genovese, for example, suggests that Hurston "aspires, in some way, to transcend the constraints of
group identification. By insisting on being a self independent of history,
race, and gender, she comes close to insisting on being a self independent
of a body." [13]

Is Hurston's refusal of race in fact, as Fox-Genovese seems to imply, an
attempt to wrench the (universal) self out of the (particular, limited-by-
history-race-and-gender) body? In attempts to pin down Hurston's racial
politics, she seems stretched between two poles: either the independent self
or group identification; either a politics of liberal individualism or a politics
of racial collectivism. But are these two poles really so separate? Charles
Taylor suggests that both sorts of political claims—those made in the name
of the universal rights of the individual (what he calls the politics of universalism) and those made in the name of the distinctive interests of a particular group (what he calls the politics of difference)—originate in the modern
ideal of subjective authenticity. The modern notion of identity is that of an
"individualized identity, one that is particular to me, and that I discover in
myself." [14] This individualized identity carries with it the ideal of authenticity, "that of being true to myself and my own particular way of being."
Thus, liberal individualism and racial collectivism could from this perspective be seen as varying primarily in their understanding of the relation
of individual identity to group identity. The politics of universalism begins
from the premise that each individual must be equally free to realize his or
her authentic being, and therefore individuals must be treated equally. On
the other hand, the politics of difference insists that the individuals who

make up each group realize their own authentic being in a different way, and hence the recognition of these differences is necessary to make it possible for each to realize him- or herself fully. But both of these perspectives operate from within the framework of the modern view of subjectivity as inhering essentially in the depths of the individual and seek a politics and a political community that can best allow for the expression and realization of the individual's authentic identity. However, there is no absolute necessity limiting our thought to the modern view of the subject; the historical contingencies of this view ensure that alternatives are possible. Perhaps there is some other way of approaching the question of the relation between the race, individual, and community that does not begin from the premise of the autonomous, authentic subject, and therefore one that does not limit the alternatives to racial collectivism or liberal individualism.

To illuminate the tension between the contemporary politics of racialism and Hurston's own worldview, I want to consider a portion of *Dust Tracks* that was not included in the original publication—a piece of vituperative political writing that explicitly links race, nation, and global politics. It was at her editor's insistence that this particular piece, appended to the most recent edition as "Seeing the World as It Really Is," was left out. Scribbled at the bottom of the manuscript page are the words: "Suggest eliminating international opinions as irrelevant to autobiography." [15] Her editors, I would suggest, missed the point: it is precisely as it insists on the link between "international opinions" regarding the politics of nation, and individual identity as it emerges within the politics of race, that Hurston's autobiographical project creates its most interesting and challenging effects.

"Seeing the World as It Really Is" was intended to be the final chapter in Hurston's autobiography. Her editors omitted it from the original published version, probably, as Henry Louis Gates Jr. suggests, because although it was "obviously written prior to December 7, 1941," it "contains too many anti-American statements to be published after Pearl Harbor" (p. 212). Thus, it appears in the most recent edition as a supplement; both one with, and separate from, the autobiography proper. Hurston begins the chapter by being transported by time and experience to "high towers of elevation so that I might look out on the breadth of things" (p. 237). From this expansive perspective, she discovers that race is an illusion: "All clumps of people turn out to be individuals on close inspection" (p. 238). She insists that individuals, not races, have been responsible both for human achievement and for human failing. Race pride is not, therefore, a virtue;

rather, "it is a sapping vice. It has caused more suffering in the world than religious opinion and that is saying a lot" (p. 239). Hurston refuses to distinguish between race consciousness as specific to black America and race consciousness as it has operated as a force in human history: "What the world is crying for and dying for at this moment is less race consciousness. The human race would blot itself out entirely if it had any more" (p. 240).

This is a provocative claim, one that seems to demand further consideration. But Hurston does not pause to explain; rather, she quickly turns from her refusal to dwell on, or even recognize, racial injustice to a meditation on the politics of justice itself. "It is foolish," she remarks, "to expect any justice untwisted by the selfish hand" (p. 244). For Hurston, the rhetoric of justice operates as a screen for the real motor of history, self-interest: "We can give up neither our platitudes nor our profits. The platitudes sound beautiful, and the profits feel like silk" (p. 246). Actual justice, she implies, would require a transformed and transformative view of the whole rather than the partial, partisan perspectives that come from belonging to one group or another. Otherwise, justice is simply a question of where one sits: "The other man's side commits gross butcheries. One's own side wins smashing victories" (p. 247). Thus, Hurston suggests, nationalism and race pride obscure the violence perpetrated in the name of national right and racial chauvinism. Etienne Balibar has suggested that nationalism must be seen as constantly dividing: "There is always a 'good' nationalism and a 'bad' nationalism. There is the one which tends to construct a state or a community and the one which tends to subjugate, to destroy; the one which refers to right and the one which refers to might." [16] But if we take Hurston's critique of nationalism seriously, then we must see these not as two different nationalisms; rather, this equivocation is nationalism itself. For Hurston, race and nation are too easily transformed from the grounds of resistance to oppression into the justification of violence and injustice.

Racialism, as it has been defined by Anthony Appiah, is the belief that "all members of [a particular race] share certain traits and tendencies with each other that they do not share with members of any other race." [17] Whether conceived in spiritual, cultural, or political terms, racialism is based on a vision of a community that unites diverse and discrete individuals into the collective body of the race. Hurston's challenge to the concept of race is thus double-edged. On the one side, she insists that the ideology of racialism, like the ideology of nationalism, is necessarily allied with violence—against both the challenge posed by the other side and the deviance within one's own side. At the same time, in her repeated assertions that the race cannot contain all the variations of individuals, she is contesting the possibility of asserting the commonality of race as a basis for community. For Hurston, racialism is both undesirable and impossible as a basis for collective action or collective identity.

Here we come to the crux of the difficulty in understanding Hurston's vision of race and community. As we typically understand it, community provides the individual with meaning and purpose, with a sense of belonging to something larger and more powerful than the self, and with a strong foundation for resisting the oppressions of systemic and institutional prejudice that continue to structure American political and social life. Community is seen as both the practical basis and the utopian desideratum of American political and cultural discourse. In this context, especially given the racist pressures facing black Americans in the 1930s and 1940s, Hurston's repudiation of community seems at best naive. More seriously, one might conclude that Hurston's personal history of white patronage and elite education had led her to abandon her own racial community and to misidentify with the perspectives or interests of her white friends and patrons. I think that such dismissals of Hurston's racial politics are too quick and too easy. To call Hurston's racial politics naive or white-identified implies a fairly narrow conception of what racial politics ought to be. Indeed, the trouble with Hurston is that she troubles the received notions of race, identity, and community on which the politics of racial collectivism (in Hurston's day and in our own) are based. Hurston forces us to *rethink* race, identity, and community—a project far more complex than the simple disavowal of race or the abandonment of community.

The idea and ideal of community has increasingly become a rhetorical touchstone on both the right and the left in contemporary American political discourse. An increased sense of community is commonly posed as the solution to any and all social ills: crime, poverty, teen pregnancy, suicide, and so on—all these modern crises are traced, in popular thought, to the loss of community. But what exactly is this community that is continually posed as the counter to modern atomization and alienation? The ambiguities of the root word *common* point toward a constitutive equivocation at the heart of modern theories of community. The Latin source for *common* is *communis*, but the derivation of *communis* is uncertain: either it is *com* (together) + *munis* (bound, under obligation); or it is *com* (together) + *unis* (one). A typology of contemporary political theories of community might separate these two derivations as alternative ways of thinking about community.[18] On the one hand, *com-munis* points toward juridical, economic, and social relations of obligation, reciprocity, indebtedness, and exchange. It indicates community formed in relation to the external principle imposed on each member of mutual obligation. On the other hand, *com-unis* suggests a foundational commonality, community as union, communion. Thus, *com-unis* indicates community formed through the rule of commonality internal to each member.

These appear to be two competing models of community, what we might loosely call the juridical (*munis*, obligation) and the ontological (*unis*, union). But it should be noted that both alternatives are constituted in a similar way; both the juridical and the ontological models of community are formulated in terms of a rule that precedes and founds the community and to which the community must conform if it is to be community. Thus, despite the denotative distance between *munis* and *unis*, we might say that the ambiguities of an inaudibly doubled *m* sustain the mutual cohabitation of these two seemingly discrete possibilities; one might write *com(m)unity* to indicate this doubled equivocation. The "in common" that founds com(m)unity is not just a description but a rule, one that necessarily participates in both the juridical and the ontological registers. The juridical force of a social contract establishing a community as exchange and obligation is inseparable from the ontological unity of the several in one, the communion of the many in a singular body.

It is the submission of the conception of community to such a rule, alternately conceived as internal-ontological or external-juridical, that is the condition of the violence of community. The constant companion to a discourse of the ideal harmony sought in the name of community is a practice of force and violence against deviance.[19] The violence that aims to exclude or suppress deviance appears as external to the true matter of com(m)unity; but it is precisely this violence that establishes and sustains com(m)unity. But if violence is necessarily at the heart of *com-unis* and *com-munis*, then is there any community that is not predicated on such violence? I am of course not the first to ask such a question; the problem of reconciling community with freedom is perhaps *the* political problem of modernity, a problem that concerns thinkers from Rousseau to Marx. But this tradition of modern political theory seeks a community that would be consistent with the essential freedom proper to a subject; thus, the protection or realization of the freedom *of the subject* determines in advance the possibility for freedom in a social community. It is for this reason that community must appear either as *com-unis*, in which freedom is guaranteed by the communion of subjects in a common essence, or as *com-munis*, in which freedom is achieved by submitting the subject to a law she or he has made for her- or himself. The question that arises, then, is whether there can be another freedom, one that does not begin from the subject and, likewise, whether there is a way of thinking about community as something other than the community of subjects. As opposed to the freedom as autonomy that is proper to the independent, authentic subject, this alternative freedom would be a freedom as community, a freedom whose very meaning would be inseparable from community. And, in turn, such a community would not be a community of autonomous subjects and would therefore be somehow outside the logic of *com-unis* and *com-munis*.

## Cosmic Upset: Hurston and Fanon

Hurston's resistance to nationalism in "Seeing the World as It Really Is"—whether the nationalism of the oppressor or the nationalism of the oppressed—is a sign of her powerful insight that the call to national unity as a foundation of identity, order, and allegiance is fundamentally a call to the violent suppression and exclusion of any challenge to the communion of the community in its collective body. The choice between a white supremacist order and a black nationalist order is still, for Hurston, the choice between enforcing one form of order or another. It is the imperative of order itself that cloaks a drive to destroy everything "other." Hurston's adamant refusal to implicate herself in this choice of one violence or another points toward another strategy of resistance: not the opposition of one good order to another bad order but the refusal to choose any order at all.

Hurston's refusal to choose an order does not, however, mean that we must conclude that she has chosen chaos instead. Rather, I would suggest, she seeks to refuse the violence of order that follows on the determination to exclude and prevent chaos, the determination to eliminate accident, ambiguity, and disorder. "The stuff of being," Hurston writes elsewhere in *Dust Tracks*, "is matter, ever changing, ever moving, but never lost" (pp. 202–3). The opposing poles of individualism and communalism that characterize the modern understanding of politics leave no room for the "ever changing, ever moving." Thus, her refusal to live "in a space whose boundaries are race and nation" (p. 243) is not a repudiation of collective identity in

the name of a radical individualism. Rather, it is a challenge both to the
fixity and boundedness of such categories of identity as race and nation and
to the premise of the autonomous individual whose supposed authenticity
would exclude the flux of the ever changing. Hurston is seeking instead a
politics that can leave room for the "stuff of being," which has been suppressed and denied by the politics of order.

There is no justice, Hurston insists, in the struggle between races or between nations. If there is to be a possible justice, it must originate in a much
more elemental struggle: "I am not bloodthirsty and I have no yearning for
strife, but, if what they say is true, that there must be this upset, why not
make it cosmic?" (p. 253). Here, Hurston seems to return politics to the
"stuff of being" by suggesting that a meaningful transformation must be
more than a reordering of power, it must take place at a more fundamental level. Against the violence of oppression and struggle between nations
and peoples through which order is necessarily secured, Hurston evokes a
more expansive and illimitable *cosmic upset*.

The idea of cosmic upset is a complex one, and it is the nature of its
complexity that makes it what we might, without being too nostalgic, call
a *revolutionary* idea. *Kosmos* in classical Greek usage referred not to the
universe or the world but to order and harmony. Philologists argue that
it has come to mean universe or world via its original reference to order:
the underlying order of the world makes it a *kosmos*. In its more mundane
usages, the corresponding Greek verb means to order, dispose, to rule or
govern. Thus, its reference to orderly institutions such as governments and
armies is extended to the perfect order that underlies the continual flux
and change of the world. In its relation to the institutional foundations of
law and order, the harmony of *kosmos* is linked to the human institutions of
order governed by *logos* and *nomos*. If this is the full implication of *cosmic*,
then *cosmic upset* suggests a contradiction. The cosmos cannot exist in a
state of upset; if it could, it would not be cosmos. Cosmic upset cannot be
another state of the cosmos, another cosmos; rather, it must be that which
resists or upsets the very principle of cosmos itself.

Cosmic upset is the refusal to choose order, to enforce or demand order.
However, it must also be emphasized that to embrace cosmic upset is not
to choose total disorder. Cosmic upset is the force of resistance to order,
but it is not a contrary or opposing state or condition. Rather, the refusal
to positively choose order takes the risk of exposing order to the disorder it
seeks to suppress, exclude, or disavow. We might call this disorder order's

enclosed outside. To speak of an outside is not to invoke something distinct, separate, or autonomous that comes from elsewhere to disturb the order of the inside. Rather, outside in this context refers to a provisional zone of exclusion: the difference, randomness, or deviation that order must deny, repress, exclude, or destroy in order to assure its own place as order. The violence threatened by this disorder is not the systematic violence of state and law, which represses, excludes, and normalizes in the name of conformity and order. Rather, this violence of disorder counters the violence of order by interrupting its totalizing tendencies. To consider the chaos of this outside and its relation to the orders of the inside, I want to turn to Frantz Fanon's writings on colonial struggle. Fanon's writing on the violence of decolonization, I will suggest, resonates with Hurston's project of cosmic upset by driving a wedge into the oppositional frameworks that pit individual against community, assimilation against cultural difference.

In *The Wretched of the Earth*, Fanon chronicles the violent upheavals that necessarily accompany the process of decolonization in Africa. Although the struggles of decolonization may proceed in the name of an emergent nationalism, I would suggest that for Fanon decolonization is not the same thing as the nationalism of resistance. Where emergent nationalisms aim to replace colonial rule with local rule, the violence of decolonization is not precisely coincident with this objective. *Decolonization* as Fanon uses the term is not isolatable to the in-between of the struggle between colonizer and colonized, foreign and indigenous, or white and black. Rather, the violence of decolonization erupts in the midst of these oppositions, unsettling and undermining them. I read Fanon here as simultaneously philosopher and political strategist, such that the force of his revolutionary stance is directed both to the material relations of the colonial situation and to the principles of subjectivity, agency, recognition, and representation that correspond to the colonial condition. I would suggest that Fanon's revolutionary vision demands a reconstitution not only of the institutions and relations of colonial power but, perhaps more profoundly, a radical revision of the status of the subject and identity: one that opens these bounded entities to chance, risk, and accident, to the unpredictable paths of uncertainty and singularity.

For Fanon, one cannot be both *black* and *man*. This is the Manichaean structure of the colonial situation: humanist *man* is defined against the absolutely excluded colonial other.[20] Diana Fuss has clarified this relation by utilizing the psychoanalytical distinction between the symbolic "Other" (the locus of intersubjectivity) and the imaginary "other" (object of a narcissistic or specular relation). Fuss suggests that the position occupied by the black man is not that of the Other, that alterity through which white subjectivity constitutes itself; rather, the otherness of the black man is other to this Other, outside the circuit of subjectivity, inhabiting instead "the static ontological space of the timeless 'primitive.' "[21] The autonomy of the white subject who manages to be simultaneously "Self" and "Other" would seem to suggest an indifference to the presence of the black man as mere "object." But such white autonomy is in fact dependent on that very presence of blackness: "when subjectivity becomes the exclusive property of 'the master,' the colonizer can claim a sovereign right to personhood by purchasing interiority over and against the representation of the colonial other as pure exteriority."[22] It is only the determination of the black man as pure exteriority, or as Fanon puts it, as an "object in the midst of objects," that white subjectivity appears as interiorized, autonomous subjectivity and that the white subject appears as the subject simple.[23]

As a result of the disavowed dependence of white subjectivity on the presence of blackness, the black man is trapped in what Fanon calls a "vicious circle." White men rely on the presence of the black man as object to assure them of their superiority, while black men struggle to be recognized as equal, "to prove to white men, at all costs, the richness of their thought, the equal value of their intellect."[24] Such an effort must necessarily fail; the white subject cannot recognize the black man as an Other (as another subject), for the price of this recognition would be the loss of universality and autonomy, the loss, in a word, of whiteness. Thus, the possibility of rupture or revolutionary transformation cannot come from the black man as black man because the black man as such only exists within the colonial economy that has defined him as object. That is, insofar as the black man is constituted as object in relation to the white subject, he can only ever appear as object to that subject, reiterating but never upending the relation of exclusion and dependence whereby the white subject has arrogated all interiority and autonomy in the first place. A revolutionary transformation requires a more radical operation that would disrupt both subject and object. Constituted as object, the black man is "rooted at the core of a universe from which he must be extricated."[25] Hence, this "extrication" will not simply be a challenge to the meaning of blackness as blackness but will demand the collapse of the very universe in which blackness has been relegated to the status of object.

Following this instance on the vicious circle that traps the black man in the realm of the static object, Fanon suggests that the most potent threat to the racist orders of colonialism cannot come from blackness as such but must come from the existential gap between black as static object and man as interiorized subject. He calls this gap a "zone of nonbeing": "There is a zone of nonbeing, an extraordinarily sterile and arid region, an utterly naked declivity where an authentic upheaval can be born."[26] As suggested by the shift in referent from the political to the ontological register, one must conclude that, here at least, what Fanon calls "authentic upheaval" is not simply the anticolonial struggle. Rather, this authentic upheaval is directed at the "universe from which [the black man] must be extricated," an upheaval that exceeds the bounds of political struggle or institutional transformation. Its totalizing pretensions echo the enormity of Hurston's notion of cosmic upset.

As Fanon continues, it is clear that the zone of nonbeing is not the negativity of blackness in the Manichaean scheme of colonialism. Rather, this zone is outside the opposition of black and white. Therefore, the rupture toward which Fanon gestures cannot be reduced to a reformulation of black and white identities. That is, it is not a challenge from the realm of blackness to the meaning of blackness. Indeed, as Fanon points out, "in most cases, the black man lacks the advantage of being able to accomplish this descent into a real hell."[27] Rather, the outside from which authentic upheaval threatens is a zone of *nonbeing*, a place where one cannot be as either black or white, a place where there is neither subject nor object. The zone of nonbeing is conceived of as radically contradictory: it is arid and sterile but the source of a new birth; it is a real hell, but it is an advantage to be able to reach it. Within the framework of identities and institutions, we can only say that this zone is not. Or rather that it is, but its being is a nonbeing. Thus, it cannot appear, it cannot provide a ground or foundation for anything. But perhaps it can interrupt being, the being of whiteness and blackness, the being that links blackness to whiteness.

It is the rupture of a real hell of nonbeing that resurfaces in the most apocalyptic moments of *The Wretched of the Earth* as the force of decolonization. Decolonization is profoundly ambivalent in this text because Fanon seeks a cosmic revolution and at the same time comes to terms with the limitations of the postcolonial nation. It is crucial to recognize that what Fanon calls decolonization is not the same as the revolution that replaces foreign rule with native rule. The latter is an "inauthentic" upheaval, one that is merely a reordering within the order of the colonial situation. It is this reordered order that Fanon disparages as national consciousness: "National consciousness, instead of being the all-embracing crystallization of the innermost hopes of the whole people, instead of being the immediate and most obvious result of the mobilization of the people, will be in any case only an empty shell, a crude and fragile travesty of what it might have been."[28] However, simultaneous with Fanon's ongoing critique of the alternative violences of the postcolonial nation enacted in the name of national consciousness is a vision of decolonization that seeks out the possibilities of upheaval directed at the very principles that have created the colonial world.

If it is not the substitution of one (foreign, bad) rule for another (indigenous, good) one, what then is decolonization? Fanon's definition is unequivocal: "Decolonization, which sets out to change the order of the world, is a program of absolute disorder."[29] Decolonization is not a state of the world or a result of action but a program, a process, that unfolds in the presence of colonization and against it. Decolonization cannot be conceived as an achieved effect: complete disorder is unlivable. Fanon insists that the colonial world, "strewn with prohibitions, can only be called in question by absolute violence."[30] Absolute violence, like complete disorder, cannot ever be fully achieved. Thus, decolonization is not a state of being; it is, like the zone of nonbeing that Fanon locates as the source of authentic upheaval, a being that is not.

Fanon continues: "Decolonization is the meeting of two forces, opposed to each other by their very nature, which in fact owe their originality to that sort of substantification which results from and is nourished by the situation in the colonies."[31] Elsewhere Fanon calls these two forces that meet violently in the eruption of decolonization the "settler" and the "native." In this formulation, one might be led to conclude that the settler-colonizer and the native-colonized are discrete entities, absolutely opposed. But we must not forget the fact that the colonial moment brings both settler and native into being. This means that settler and native cannot be so easily separated: "For it is the settler who has brought the native into existence and who perpetuates his existence. The settler owes the fact of his very existence, that is to say, his property, to the colonial system."[32] The mutual ontological, political, and economic dependence of settler and native means that they have no separate, autonomous, absolute existence. Hence, the violent clash between these two forces occurs not so much in a space external to both but in a between that is no less a within.

The violence of decolonization is simultaneously between and within; it penetrates every mode of being that has been called into being by the colonial situation. Thus, the violence of decolonization is directed necessarily at the material conditions of the colonial circumstance, but it is also always a violence that aims at the very constitution of the being of blackness and whiteness. Thus, it is in this doubly articulated violence of decolonization that the "real hell" of nonbeing opens up. It is from this hell that "authentic upheaval" may emerge. It is important to distinguish what Fanon calls authentic upheaval from a utopian vision of the true revolution against which one measures the shortcomings of the current condition of neocolonialism. Authentic upheaval, I would argue, does not have as its objective the creation of a new order. Rather, authentic upheaval is the violence that counters the violence of the colonial order by interrupting its totalizing tendencies, exposing both subject and object to their constitutively excluded outside. Authentic upheaval is thus a violence against violence that is continuous, without a final end. This violence is the condition for the appearance and recognition of singularity as such, that otherness that cannot be recuperated into any economy of same and other-to-the-same.

Like Fanon, Hurston does not disavow violence; she acknowledges that cosmic upset may entail blood and strife. But unlike the violence tearing the world apart before her eyes in 1940 (and in the 1990s), which disguises the motivations of greed and power under the smooth platitudes of justice and democracy, Hurston's cosmic upset risks the possible violence of disorder as the only real alternative. We should not, however, mistake this turn to violence for an abandoning of ethics or responsibility. Rather, it is a recognition that the current order precludes the possibility of any ethical relation to the other insofar as it is predicated on the domination, exploitation, destruction, or repression of otherness. A truly responsible relation to otherness—a relation capable of responding to the otherness of the other rather than subsuming that otherness under the order of the same—can only occur with the wrenching open of a space for the otherness of singularity, an otherness that escapes or exceeds the opposition between (white) subject and (black) object. Cosmic upset, the disorder that violently interrupts the orderly boundaries of identity and difference, of subject and other, is then the necessary condition for ethical responsibility. And if this is the case, then such violence is also the condition for a justice that is more than the operation of power and a freedom that is not simply the right of the autonomous subject to be free of constraint. In this sense, the risk of cosmic upset is a doubled risk: violence, perhaps, but also freedom.

## The Problem of Community

If cosmic upset is the name Hurston gives to her global political vision, the risk of that upset is repeated at the level of the individual life in the intimate and personal narratives of *Dust Tracks on a Road* and *Their Eyes Were Watching God*. In these texts, Hurston continually challenges and reworks the relation between individual and community. In *Dust Tracks*, baby Zora's body is the first site of struggle between the community's demands of conformity and the slippery excess that refuses to conform. In subsequent scenes, the security and stability of continuity, affiliation, and descent come under increasing scrutiny and are gradually displaced by less predictable relations and encounters.

### IDENTITY AND BODILY EXCESS

Hurston begins her autobiography by systematically destabilizing every claim of origin or authenticity that would be established by recourse to history, fact, or tradition in the telling of her life story. She does not disguise the centrality of invention in constructing an account of her birthplace in chapter 1 of *Dust Tracks*. Although there is a historical, factual basis for this account, Hurston decorates the bare bones to produce a version of the founding of Eatonville that reads more like legend than like history. In favoring the vernacular mode of storytelling over a factual, verifiable account, Hurston has abandoned the evidentiary functions of autobiography, which would establish proof, justification, or explanation for a life. For example, the third chapter is an account of Zora's birth, entitled "I Get Born." The vernacular phrasing of "I get born" plays on the conventional "I was born" of both slave narrative and traditional autobiography.

In a fascinating analysis of the use of the black vernacular in Hurston's writing, Karla Holloway suggests that alternative syntactic structures demand attention as a special site for the production of literary effects.[33] Hurston's use of the vernacular formulation "I get born" places the event of her birth in the present tense and complicates the historicity and the continuous temporality of a life narrative. Moreover, it marks a shift in tone from the formal statement of the irrefutable fact to a vernacular invocation of a favorite family story. If the slave narrator's "I was born" aims to insist on the irrefutable facticity of the slave's life and subjectivity, Hurston's "I get born" shifts the register from the juridical individual to a self-consciously fictional subject of a tall tale. "I get born" is no longer narrative information but rather a locus of affect and intensity. Moreover, Hurston concedes that it is not even certain that the account of her birth is true. She begins the chapter with the disclaimer: "This is all hear-say. Maybe some of the details of my birth as told me might be a little inaccurate, but it is pretty well established that I really did get born" (p. 19). Hurston's humor is ir-resistible, but it is important to emphasize the ambiguities set into play by this humor. What is the standard of evidence that would provide certainty to a fact that is only "pretty well established"? Of course, Hurston's body is the proof that she was born; how does this differ from the "pretty well established" assertion that she "did get born"?

Because the facts of her birth are all hearsay, even the facts of her parent-age and ancestry take on an ambiguous status. Unlike the slave narrator who typically suffers from a shortage of legitimate parents, Zora seems to enjoy a surplus of parent figures. Her mother gives birth while her father is away; a white man appears to help her, taking the place of the midwife, cut-ting the umbilical cord and washing the baby. Mrs. Neale, a family friend, provides a name for the new daughter. An old pig persuades baby Zora that it is time to start walking. And her mother attributes Zora's penchant for wandering to "a woman who was an enemy of hers [who] had sprinkled 'travel dust' around the doorstep the day I was born" (p. 23). Zora is less the hereditary child of her mother and father than the accidental conjunc-tion of all these figures. And if Zora is the product of chance and hearsay, it is increasingly difficult to pin down an authorized history, an indisput-able narrative of origins, or an unquestionable pedigree that would assure the foundations and boundaries of an authentic community.

The death of Zora's mother is the pivotal moment in her autobiography. Hurston writes, "Mama died at sundown and changed a world. That is, the world which had been built out of her body and her heart. Even the physi-cal aspects fell apart with a suddenness that was startling" (p. 65). The lost mother is for critic Françoise Lionnet "the symbol of a veiled and occulted historical past." [34] Lionnet argues that while Zora suffers the loss of separa-tion, she also realizes the imperative of the reconstruction of the collective past: "The child who leaves Eatonville after her mother's death experiences alterity and dislocation, distances herself forever from the illusory possibility of an unexamined and unmediated participation in the network of relations which constitutes culture."[35] Thus, *Dust Tracks* is for Lionnet an effort to compensate for this constitutive loss, "a painstaking effort to be the voice of that occluded past, to fill the void of collective memory."[36] The implicit view of community behind Lionnet's interpretation is a Christian notion of (impossible) communion in the *lost* body. From this perspective, *Dust Tracks* is a narrative effort to restore wholeness by recovering the always already lost basis of community.

The problem with reading *Dust Tracks* in this way is that it is *not* a narrative of ethnic recovery. The community of Zora's childhood, Hurston suggests, has been mediated through her mother's body. The figure of the mother embodies the community as a common blood, a common origin, and a common obligation. Through the common participation in that body the individual members are submitted to a common history and a common destiny. The mother's body has built a world; the community is held together in and through that body, a collective communion in the mother's body. The mother's death thus signals a *rupture* in the relation between Zora's life narrative and the narrative of the life of the community, between autobiography and ethnography. Following her mother's death, Zora maintains an (at best) uneasy relation to any community of which she might consider herself to be a part.

For example, the first chapters of *Dust Tracks* are called "My Birthplace," "My Folks," and "I Get Born." The possessive first person locates Hurston in relation to each of these things. These chapters recount her early life in relation to her family and her community. But in subsequent chapters, this relational and chronological structure breaks down. The possessive chapter headings give way to simple nouns: "Figure and Fancy," "Backstage and the Railroad," "School Again," "Research." In these middle chapters, Hurston recounts her journeys away from her community of origin and her education into another world. In the title of chapter 12, the possessive reappears: "My People! My People!" But contrary to the immediate supposition that this is a reinvocation of the community of origin, the reader discovers that this is a parody of the lament "called forth by the observation of one class of Negro on the doings of another branch of the brother in black" (p. 157). Here, Hurston repudiates race consciousness, insisting that the race line cannot hold all the varied interests and particularities of any people. The episodic rather than continuous narrative character of *Dust Tracks* further bears out the impression that Hurston is resisting community as continuity or connection. In the later chapters, the chronological development of life events disappears altogether. The original narrative of the child Zora in relation to a community collapses under the weight of Hurston's aphoristic reflections on people she has known, places she has been, and her general philosophy of life.

Instead of writing herself into being in relation to community Hurston's life narrative revels in the singular, the discontinuous, the excessive. For this reason, Elizabeth Fox-Genovese suggests that Hurston "might have been surprised to see her multiple—and intentionally duplicitous—self-representations accepted as a progenitor of the new Afro-American female self." [37] Indeed, in *Dust Tracks on a Road* there is no single Zora to center the narrative or to provide a point of origin for future descendants. In telling her own life story, Hurston seems to delight in depicting the child Zora as the continual site of production of an excess irreducible to history, order, narrative, or community. Zora is constantly spilling out of the boundaries of self, family, and community that would fix her identity in relation to any one. In particular, Hurston insists on the uncontainability of her childhood body. Zora comes into the world on her own schedule, unexpected and unprepared for. Her mother was alone when she began labor, and Zora rushes out before the midwife arrives: "But nature, being indifferent to human arrangements, was impatient. My mother had to make it alone. She was too weak after I rushed out to do anything for herself" (p. 20). When the midwife finally arrives, she is concerned that the proper procedures for delivering the baby have not been followed and that this will have adverse effects in Zora's future life: "She complained that the cord had not been cut just right, and the belly-band had not been put on tight enough. She was mighty scared I was going to have a weak back, and that I would have trouble holding my water until I reached puberty. I did" (p. 21). Zora's trouble holding her water suggests that her body is continually escaping the confines and constrictions demanded by her family and her community. From the moment of her birth, it is Zora's body that is located as the source of her continual improprieties.

Zora's feet are especially troublesome. They seem, often of their own accord, to stubbornly resist the expectations and demands that Zora be docile and well behaved. In Hurston's account of her birth, a story of walking follows immediately on the story of her naming. In this story, naturally, the most significant parts of baby Zora's body are her feet. At first reluctant to put them to use, Zora refuses to walk. However, after an instructive encounter with an overzealous sow, she takes to walking. Or rather, her feet take to walking, and she just goes along: "With no more suggestions from the sow or anybody else, it seems that I just took to walking and kept the thing a-going. The strangest thing about it was that once I found the use of my feet, they took to wandering. I always wanted to go" (p. 22). Zora's feet seem to have a will to wander all their own, despite her mother's alarm when she "wander[s] off in the woods all alone" (p. 22).

Zora suffers at home for her inability to discipline her body to cooperate in an orderly fashion with the urinary, ambulatory, and discursive orders of her family. In particular, making up stories brings down the wrath of her grandmother. The grandmother's fury at Zora's transgression of truth is extraordinarily violent: "You hear dat young 'un stand up here and lie like dat? And you ain't doing nothing to break her of it? Grab her! Wring her coat tails over her head and wear out a handful of peach hickories on her back-side! Stomp her guts out! Ruin her! . . . Stop her! Wear her backside out. I bet if I lay my hands on her she'll stop it. I vominates a lying tongue" (p. 52). The importance attached to Zora's backside in connection with a loss of control of her front side—her mouth—points to a continuing problem of the orifice. Zora's loss of control of her urinary and oral orifices will be corrected, in the grandmother's terms, by a wearing out of her backside. Indeed, Zora's spurting orifices threaten others' loss of control. Zora's running off at the mouth causes the grandmother also to spew out of her mouth, "I vominates [vomit + abominate] a lying tongue." The grandmother must spit Zora's tongue out of her own mouth to ward off the contamination of the loss of control marked by Zora's "lying" and her incontinence. The resonance of "abomination" with the biblical sin of sodomy suggests too that Zora's bodily and discursive improprieties are equally sexual and familial improprieties, violations of the heterosexual, patriarchal order of the family and the community.[38]

Zora's body must be disciplined to remain within its bounds; the violence of discipline suggests that the threat of a body out of bounds must be enormous. Mere beating is not enough to control the threat Zora represents: "God knows, grandmother would break me or kill me, if she had her way. Killing me looked like the best one, anyway. All I was good for was to lay up and wet the bed half the time and tell lies, besides being the spitting image of dat good-for-nothing yaller bastard" (p. 53). Zora's body spills over, wandering outside its edges. Killing, destroying the body itself, is the only way to staunch the constant, uncontrollable flow issuing from Zora's body: wetting the bed, telling lies, and being the "*spitting* image" of her father. The grandmother's fury suggests that Zora's "spills," her lies and her urine, threaten the orderly array of bodies in their proper places, of authentic truths, of verifiable identities. But Zora's bodily improprieties suggest that such orders need not be venerated as the sole guarantors of life or meaning.

Throughout her work, Hurston has little regard for the ordering principles of boundary, propriety, and stable identity. In an essay that Alice Walker notes represents "Zora at her most exasperating," Hurston offers one version of a theory of identity:

> I feel like a brown bag of miscellany propped against a wall. Against a wall in company with other bags, white, red and yellow. Pour out the contents, and there is discovered a jumble of small things priceless and worthless . . . so much like the jumble in the [other] bags, could they be emptied, that all might be dumped in a single heap and the bags refilled without altering the content of any greatly.[39]

This is not a humanist universalism, a claim that if we peel off our skin we will discover that we are all the same underneath. The "jumble" that fills the bag that is Zora is very particular, despite the fact that it is not particular to *her*: "a first-water diamond, an empty spool, bits of broken glass, lengths of string, a key to a door long since crumbled away" (p. 155). No two bags of jumble are the same. But equally, there is no order in the jumble, no reason any two things in the bag are together, no reason anything should go in one bag and not the other. Zora's leaky body is the extension of the logic of the self as bag of jumble; if the *I* is just a jumble, no matter if some spill or if some other is collected to replace it. This principle is reflected in Hurston's life writing, as disorder and impropriety contest the boundaries of communal, familial, or personal identity.

### HISTORY AND ANACHRONY

Just as *Dust Tracks* disrupts the identity of the individual through the continual production of bodily excess, it also undermines the orderly and fixed relations of time and history through narrative practices of dislocation and anachrony. The centrality of anachrony to Hurston's work was initially suggested to me by Karla Holloway, who calls Hurston an "anachronism of the 1920s."[40] While we could speculate with Holloway that Hurston might have fared better among her peers in, say, the 1970s than in the 1920s, I would also insist that the term *anachrony* suggests a much more interesting aspect of Hurston's writing. It is anachrony that best describes the relations of time and linear filiation that emerge, or fail to emerge, in Hurston's texts. A close consideration of the word *anachrony* will help to explain what I mean. *Ana-* is the prefix of negation; where such contemporary usages as *anachronistic* suggest being in the wrong time, the Greek *anachronos* translates literally as "time negated." Anachrony negates the logic of chronology, the ordered and orderly progression of time. *Chronology* might also refer to the account of the progression of time, the narrative of the orderly passing of the past: in a word, history. History is an account of origins and ends, causes and effects. History locates the present in relation to a determinate and narrativizable past and establishes a relation to the future as the continuation of the historical project, as historical destiny. Anachrony upsets history. It upsets the orderly progression from cause to effect, from mother to daughter, from ancestor to identity. Hurston gives us neither memory nor history but instead a sense of being wrenched out of time, out of sequence, out of necessary relation of influence or cause and effect.

In *Dust Tracks*, wandering enacts anachrony by displacing the coherence of a continuous historical narrative that would connect the individual to the community and the destiny of the community to the destiny of the world. Unlike the directed travel of a journey, wandering has neither origin nor end. Because there is no end to wandering, wandering becomes a way of inhabiting the world. For Zora, wandering is not merely the movement of her body from place to place but the way she experiences life: "That hour began my wanderings. Not so much in geography but in time. Then not so much in time as in spirit" (p. 65). Geography, time, and spirit are linked under the sign of "wandering." Imagined in a Hegelian historiography as a coordinate system of physical and ontological identity, the conjunction of geography, time, and spirit simultaneously locates an individual and characterizes a people. However, this identificatory function is displaced by Hurston's invocation of wandering: wandering here is an explicit challenge to the idea of a determinate relation between geography, time, spirit, and a people. The play of affirmation and negation (not in geography but in time, not in time but in spirit) disconnects the apparent simultaneity of these terms that normally allows us to speak of history.

The beginning of Hurston's wandering coincides with the death of her mother, a death that "set [her] feet in strange ways" (p. 64). After the death of her mother, the young Zora "was forever shifting. I walked by my corpse. I smelt it and felt it. I smelt the corpses of those among whom I must live, though they did not. They were as much at home with theirs as death in a tomb" (p. 86). The intimate narrative proximity of the stillness of death and the mobility of wandering suggests that to refuse wandering, to cling to the security of community and history, is to approach death. It is only in wandering, in shifting about, that Zora evades the corpselike existence of those around her. Unlike the "corpses" that surround her, Zora neither anticipates a future nor depends on a past. Constantly shifting or wandering, she refuses the temporal connections of ancestry and history. The loss of the mother in *Dust Tracks* is not, then, the loss of wholeness or of identity; rather, it is the loss of the *false* security of home, ancestry, and origin and the recognition of the price by which such false securities are purchased.[41]

When considered from the point of view of wandering, Zora of *Dust Tracks* has much in common with another well-known Hurston character, Janie of *Their Eyes Were Watching God*. As Janie becomes increasingly autonomous and independent in the course of the novel, she succumbs to the force of wandering, following where whim and opportunity may lead her. For both Zora and Janie, the anachronistic relations of wandering supplant the social, biological, or juridical ties of family and community. Like the uncontrollable excesses that mark the self in *Dust Tracks* as a "bag of jumble," the relations to others enacted in wandering are also uncontrollable and unpredictable, accidental and temporary. It is this emphasis on accident, chance, and risk that suggests the most powerful continuities between the two works. *Their Eyes* shares in *Dust Tracks*'s risky practice of imagining the self and the self's relation to others without recourse to the deceptive security of identity and community.

### INCORPORATION AND RE-PRODUCTION

I have suggested that the death of Zora's mother in *Dust Tracks* is not a moment of loss that demands recovery but rather the event that exposes the demands and constraints of the community. *Their Eyes Were Watching God* takes the productive possibilities of the loss of the mother even further, rejecting absolutely the position of mother or progenitor. In place of mothers and daughters, inheritance and descent, *Their Eyes* develops around the affiliations of accident, chance, and proximity.

The story of domestic life spun out in *Their Eyes* is remarkable for the almost complete absence of mothers. Janie grows up without her own mother and herself remains childless through three marriages. As Janie's grandmother Nanny makes clear, motherhood in this horrifying world is neither celebrated nor sought out. Rather, it is allied with abuse and animality: "Ah didn't want to be used for a work-ox and a brood-sow and Ah didn't want mah daughter used dat way neither."[42] For Nanny, motherhood is the loss of self and soul. Nanny was raped by her owner; the resulting child was Janie's mother. Nanny explains her light-haired baby to the plantation mistress by saying "Ah don't know nothin' but what Ah'm told tuh do, 'cause Ah ain't nothin' but uh nigger and uh slave" (p. 17). The master's rape of Nanny and Nanny's subsequent pregnancy and motherhood reinforce her existence as "uh nigger and uh slave." To escape from the object categories of "nigger" and "slave" demands an escape from being a mother as well; motherhood in this world is inseparable from rape, enslavement, abuse, and oppression.

Janie seems to erase her own potential to become a mother by an act of will. In the only mention in the entire book of the possibility, pregnancy is figured in terms of a marital act of violence recalling the rape of the slave. Nanny asks Janie, "don't tell me you done got knocked up already." "Knocked up" is such a common colloquialism for pregnancy that we perhaps forget that it equates getting pregnant with getting beaten. Janie replies, "Ah'm all right dat way. Ah *know* tain't nothin' dere" (p. 21). Janie seems to "know" herself into infertility; even Tea Cake's sexual virility is unable to penetrate the barrier of her will not to reproduce.

The suppression and repudiation of traditional mothering in the novel is for Molly Hite a transformation of the mother-daughter relation. In *Their Eyes*, Hite argues, mothering is redefined as the production of narrative and wisdom: "In replacing Nanny's story about sexual oppression with an alternative story about sexual love . . . Janie in effect takes on the maternal function, in company of course with her listener Pheoby."[43] Hite suggests that the central plot of heterosexual romance, the story Janie tells Pheoby about her two failed marriages and her final true love, is supplanted by a union of Janie and Pheoby in a same-sex narratorial couple that produces the text as its offspring. The marginal frame, which consists of the narrative exchange between Janie and Pheoby, thus becomes central to Hite's understanding of the novel.

While I agree that we must center our attention on the frame of this novel, I would point out that there is a substantial discontinuity in the two halves of the frame. This discontinuity functions to displace the reproduc-

tion of community through ancestry, matrilineality, or filiation. In particular, between the opening and the closing of the frame there is a shift in the
relation between Janie and the community. The opening of the frame poses
an agonistic relation in which Janie appears as the community's other. In
this opening, the tension between Janie and the rest of the community appears to demand a dialectical resolution in which Janie will be restored to
the whole. While this tension does in fact dissipate in the end of the frame,
it is not an effect of restoration or resolution that reconnects Janie to the
community. Rather, the end of the frame shifts from reciprocity and exchange to self-reflexivity. I will argue, however, that this self-reflexivity is
not coextensive with the rejection of community or the turn to autonomy
and isolation. Rather, I will suggest that this self-reflexivity opens up the
possibility of an alternative conception of community.

The novel opens with Janie's return to Eatonville after her travels with
Tea Cake. The community has gathered together after a day of labor, distributed among the porches that line the road down which Janie must walk.
They sit in judgment of Janie, of the way she has violated the norms and
expectations of this community. Against the deviation that Janie embodies,
the community establishes its identity in the unanimity of judgment. Voices
mutter, but they are not the utterances of individuals; rather, through individual judgment the community unites in voice:

> They made burning statements with questions, and killing tools out of
> laughs. . . .
>   "What she doin' coming back here in dem overhalls? Can't she find no dress
> to put on? — Where's dat blue satin dress she left here in? — Where all dat money
> her husband took and died and left her? — What dat ole forty year ole 'oman
> doin' wid her hair swingin' down her back lak some young gal?" (p. 2)

Despite these vehement exclamations of disgust, the community does not
simply turn away; rather, it offers understanding and possible forgiveness in
exchange for knowing. The community's curiosity is inseparable from the
community's need to defuse the threat of Janie's difference. In their need
to know Janie's story, they seek to reincorporate her wayward body into the
body of the community, to know her and thereby possess her, to make her
one of them again. Janie's storytelling — the body of the novel — is provoked
by the community's need to reestablish its coherence and its identity.

However, while the first part of the frame promises the reconstitution
and continuity of the community through the narrative reproduction of

Janie's story, the conclusion of the frame radically displaces this promise. On hearing the story, Pheoby (who has been commissioned by the community to find out the story and bring it back to the others) does not stay with Janie or leave to join the others. Instead, Pheoby turns toward her husband: "Ah ain't satisfied wid mahself no mo' . . . Ah means tuh make Sam take me fishin wid him after this" (p. 183). Nor does Janie seek out the community; rather, she turns toward herself. As Janie finishes her story, the sound of the wind in the pine trees "made Janie think about that room upstairs— her bedroom" (p. 183). Further pleasure, this moment suggests, will be sensual rather than narratorial. For Pheoby, it will be heterosexual: no longer satisfied with herself, she will seek pleasure with her husband. In contrast, Janie's pleasure is autoerotic: she turns toward herself for satisfaction. The narrative does not expand itself into the future, does not produce any imperative to reproduce itself. Rather, it draws back inward around the figure of Janie, just as she pulls in her horizon "like a great fish-net. Pull[s] it from around the waist of the world and drape[s] it over her shoulder" (p. 184).

In this final image, it appears that the novel concludes with neither production nor reproduction. Janie sends neither child nor narrative into the world to engender future generations. Rather than reaching toward the future, Janie's narrative circles back in on the figure of her body. Her self-enclosed body interrupts the linear trajectory of filiation, of family, community, and history. The last image resonates with self-sufficiency and self-satisfaction. In the sexualized language of the frame, we might read this image as invoking a practice of nonproductive, but fully satisfying, autoeroticism. Janie does not reach out to touch others; her narrative circles around, to touch herself.

## Beyond the Subject

Is Janie's final moment of solitude a negation or repudiation of community? If her story is in fact a gift to the community as suggested by the opening portion of the frame, by the conclusion of the narrative she has absented herself from the relations of exchange through which her story will circulate. The novel does not end with the restored community as the dialectical incorporation of one in the whole. In Janie's final self-touch is the refusal to reach out, to incorporate others into her self, to share with others her knowledge or understanding. On the other hand, to read her solitude as a moment of tragic modernist isolation or a reaffirmation of radical individualism seems to violate the affirmative spirit of the novel. I think the solution to this apparent contradiction lies in a reconsideration of the relation of gift, touch, and community. Janie's touch is a selfless, extravagant gift. It is a gift that serves, not to establish obligation or reciprocity between subjects, but rather to open a space of togetherness as a relation of touch. *Their Eyes*, I will suggest, culminates with the relations of common being, law, or obligation being displaced by relations of touch, contact, and contagion.

### THE GIFT OF SELF-TOUCH

Janie's final self-touch is a gift that gives, not a dialectical resolution of particularity or difference in the universal of community but instead a sharing, a togetherness that preserves and sustains the singular. This togetherness is not the community of obligation or communion between subjects; rather, in this togetherness would be a community without rule, in which otherness, or singularity, would occur without being destroyed or incorporated through the imposition of the identity of the same.

Anthropological researches such as Marcel Mauss's *The Gift: The Form and Reason for Exchange in Archaic Societies* have argued for the fundamental importance of the gift in the formation of community. However, this social form of the gift is always conceived in terms of reciprocity, indebtedness, and exchange. But if the gift functions socially as a form of exchange, how is the gift to be distinguished from any other economic activity? As Jacques Derrida suggests in *Given Time*, the gift founders on a paradox: the gift is, by definition, the thing given that is not remunerated or reciprocated, but as soon as there is the consciousness or intention of gift there is no gift. The act of giving happens within a circuit between gift giver and recipient; thus, because both are simultaneously implicated in the gift-event, the gift necessarily is transformed into an exchange. That is, once a gift is recognized and acknowledged as a gift, it is no longer truly a gift because that recognition or acknowledgment has in fact been given in exchange for the gift. The recipient's recognition, gratitude, and obligation form as much a part of the gift-event as the endowing of the gift. It is for this reason that the gift is a form of social glue, binding potential antagonists in relations of mutual recognition and obligation.

As important as the cycle of exchange and obligation set into motion by the gift, however, is the reconstitution of the position of the subject that takes place in every gift-event. The gift, seen in this way, works not only to solidify community but also to strengthen the subject-effect, the appearance of an autonomous and independent agent as the origin of the gift. What comes back to the subject of the gift is not simply recognition or gratitude but, in that recognition, the assurance of the subject's own identity: "[The gift supposes] a subject identical to itself and conscious of its identity, indeed seeking through the gesture of the gift to constitute its own unity and, precisely, to get its own identity recognized so that it can reappropriate its identity: as its *property*."[44] Derrida emphasizes that identity comes back as property: my identity is emphatically *mine*. Thus, the return of identity in the gift is implicated in the economy of giving as fundamentally an economy of property and property relations. If the gift is meant to be that which has no relation of reciprocity, return, or exchange, then "there where there is subject and object, the gift would be excluded."[45] The subject, the self-conscious, self-identical one who gives, can engage only in the exchange of properties, not in the giving of gifts.

As opposed to the reciprocity of the gift-event that inaugurates community by establishing the subject for itself and for another subject, there is the extravagant gift, the impossible gift, the gift without exchange. Derrida insists that this gift cannot appear as a gift; for if it were to appear as such, its status as a gift would be immediately annulled. This is because the gift that is recognized as gift is immediately inserted into an economy of exchange and recognition; hence, recognition nullifies the gift. Rather, "there is gift, if there is any, only in what interrupts the system as well as the symbol, in a partition without return and without division, without being-with-self of the gift-counter-gift."[46] The gift without return interrupts the circuit of recognition between subject and other and hence suspends the priority of the autonomous subject that is constituted in the gift as exchange. A gift that does not solicit recognition, either on the part of the one who gives or on the part of the one who receives, is an "extravagant" gift that does not return in a circuit of exchange, recognition, or reciprocity.

We might view Janie's self-touch, then, not as a gesture of isolation or narcissism, but as just such an extravagant gift. If we view Janie's narrative as approaching the limit of extravagance, as being launched into the world without soliciting recognition or reciprocity, then we must consider how such a gift might transform the relations of self with other and the relations among selves. The extravagant gift, Derrida insists, creates the possibility of the common without the proper, without the return of the self-same as property. Hence, where there is extravagant gift, we can no longer speak of proper selves or autonomous, bounded subjects. If this is the effect of extravagance, then the gift without return gives us a way of conceiving of community without assuming in advance the priority of the subject. This would be a community whose possibilities would not be limited and determined in advance by the necessity to conform to and reflect the subject's individual authenticity, a community not bound by a rule or maintained by force, a community beyond the indebtedness of *com-munis* or the conformity of *com-unis*. Indeed, while the gift as exchange appears to establish community as recognition and reciprocity, the individual subject of the gift might be said to be closed off from community, insofar as this subject is conceived of as essentially individual and therefore detached and closed off from any but formal, juridical, or economic relations. In the gift without return, the interruption of the circuit of exchange establishing subject and other in their respective autonomy opens a space for a being-in-relation, a togetherness no longer limited by the boundedness of the autonomous, individual, and therefore isolated subjects of the gift as exchange.

### THE SELFISH HAND OF JUSTICE
### AND THE SELF-LESS TOUCH OF JUST-NESS

The extravagant gift without return displaces the individual, autonomous subject as origin and end of community. If Janie's self-touch is such an extravagant gift, then the self of that self-touch is no longer the self-identical, dialectically conceived self that emerges in opposition to the other. In this self-touch, self is suspended; if self is suspended, then other is as well. Hence, the reflexivity of Janie's self-touch provokes a thinking of touch as another relation to the other. There is something already in the touch that undermines the separation and identification of subject and other. The touch is a simultaneity, a sense of the in-between that is neither from me to you nor from you to me. For, at the same time, touching another is always touching myself: when I touch (another), I feel the touch, I feel myself.[47] In the touch is a relation to the other that neither attempts to create more of the same by incorporating the other into the self nor to escape the threat of otherness by destroying the otherness of the other. Touch is neither a relation of self-identity nor one of dialectical difference but a togetherness in the touch that exceeds and effaces boundedness and distinction, without producing a mystical communion.

As extravagant gift, Janie's self-touch is a touch that has abandoned the demand for a proper, bounded self. Thus, we might say that this self-touch is the touch of a *self-less* hand. In order to begin thinking about what Janie's

self(less)-touch might imply, I want to return briefly to Hurston's meditation on justice in "Seeing the World as It Really Is." As I have already
noted, Hurston insists that "it is foolish to expect any justice untwisted by
the selfish hand" (p. 244). Not coincidentally, justice appears here as a particular kind of touch. The self-ish hand that twists justice strikes a powerful
counterpoint to the self-less hand of Janie's extravagant self-touch.

In "Seeing the World as It Really Is," Hurston is clear that true justice
is not the justice of laws and courts, not a justice that weighs injury against
cost and reconciles conflict through a calculus of exchange. Hurston insists that what passes as a system of justice in the twentieth century is a
relation to the other based, in principle, on right and recompense and, in
reality, on power and greed. This justice is not a gift but an exchange, an
exchange that reasserts and reestablishes the boundedness of the subject
and the separation of the other. As Hurston suggests, in the practice or act
of justice, the self touches (i.e., negates, incorporates, destroys) the other
self-ishly. That is, the self touches the other in order to sustain the self.
This is why justice is the play of power and greed; its aim is not the amelio-
ration of the condition of the other but the preservation and augmentation
of the self. For Hurston, true justice must be outside the realm of exploitation and profit or of recompense and exchange: a justice "untwisted by
the selfish hand." Modernity envisions the possibility of a justice unselfish
because it would be totally objective and nonbiased. This is not Hurston's
justice; Hurston recognizes that for the modern subject there can be no
position of objectivity, of disinterest. If true justice is a justice beyond the
work of a "selfish hand," Hurston's alternative vision of justice will be one
that abandons the self and therefore demands nothing of the other: not recognition or exchange or conformity.

It is the possibility of an alternative to the fatal logic of justice as recompense that is at stake in the thinking of the extravagant gift, the gift without
return. True justice is necessarily extravagant. As Diane Elam suggests:

> Justice does not involve paying one's debts. Believing that one's debts can be
> paid is a fundamentally irresponsible belief: the desire to wash one's hands of
> responsibility to others. Rather, justice involves recognition of the debts that
> cannot be paid, the debts that set a limit to one's autonomy. To recognize such
> debts as unpayable is not to write them off, either—it is to commit oneself to an
> endless work of reparation without the final solace of redemption.[48]

The extravagance of Janie's self-less touch touches on this justice, displacing the justice of the selfish touch that destroys in the name of law and

right with the responsibility of the gift without redemption, recognition, or return. This responsibility is not a choice, such that one might choose whether to take responsibility; nor is it the cancellation of an indebtedness, as the obligation to give back what one has received or taken. Rather, this responsibility is outside the circuit of exchange and obligation, of measurable debts that can be canceled. This responsibility is a position of *responding*, not of paying or returning.

Envisioning justice in terms of the self-less touch transforms justice from the juridical determination of right and recompense to the responsibility of a community engendered in the togetherness of the touch, an alternative justice that might be termed *just-ness*. This neologism is meant to bring to light a ghostly doubled meaning that haunts the idea of justice. In English, the single word stem *just* takes the place of two Latin words, the noun *iustus* and the preposition *iuxta*. *Iustus* is the just of what we typically call justice, the lawful practice of right. *Iuxta*, on the other hand, means close by, near, meeting or touching, as in *juxtapose* or *adjust*. By just-ness, I mean to signal the possibility of thinking justice in terms of *iuxta* rather than *iustus*. Just-ness gestures toward a justice that abandons the fatality of vengeance, a justice removed from the logic of the law that demands the right to recompense, an eye for an eye. Instead, just-ness marks a relation of meeting or touching; this is a relation to the other as other that does not demand that the other become the same or disappear. This touching is both the condition and circumstance of responsibility; in touching the other, there is always also response.

The contact or relation I am calling just-ness is a touch that cannot be incorporated into the circuit of identity whereby the subject establishes itself in relation to an object. Just-ness happens in the realm of the self-less touch, a touch without subject or object. Thus, just-ness is a touch, but it is not the directed touch that conserves the distinction and autonomy of subject and other, the reciprocal exchange of recognition enacted in "*I* touch *you*." Rather, it is the touch of the in-between, a touching-together that is also a togetherness without proper distinctions, without reconstituting the propriety of the subject. This together-touching is community, but it is a community without rule, a community whose only being is in the touch of the together-touching.

Hurston, I want to suggest, has not abandoned community; rather, she is searching for the possibility of community beyond the boundaries of self and other, and beyond the selfish, violent, destructive hand of justice. This is the community of the together-touching, a community that appears in *Their Eyes* in the form of contagion. While contagion may not immediately seem relevant to a rethinking of justice, community, or self, we should not lose sight of the literal meaning of *contagion*, derived from the Latin prefix *con-*, meaning "together," and the verb *tangere*, meaning "to touch." The together-touching of contagion is a different way of conceiving of or experiencing community; and while contagion carries disturbing prospects of its own, for Hurston the apparent safety of the alternatives of *com-munis* or *com-unis* couches an even more frightening violence.

Thus, it is as contagion that Hurston explores the difficult and risky possibilities of another justice, one that refuses the orders of the subject as well as the reorderings of both vengeance and recompense. The trajectories of contagion in *Their Eyes* disrupt the boundedness and exclusion of subject and object, marking the possibility of a togetherness that is based on neither the proper nor the in-common. The contagion that transforms the world of *Their Eyes* offers the possibility of rethinking justice in terms of just-ness, as a togetherness that cannot be aligned with the orders of identity, race, and nation and that evades the attendant forms of violence that sustain and preserve such orders.

## COSMIC UPSET AND CONTAGION

An apocalyptic hurricane and the flooding that follows mark the dramatic climax of *Their Eyes Were Watching God*. In the most spectacular and memorable passages of the novel, Hurston stages the collapse of the distinctions of proper subjects, of rigorous and exclusive identities and rigid differences. The violence of this hurricane resonates with the violence of another of Hurston's figures of radical transformation, one that we have already considered in detail: cosmic upset. As a figure for cosmic upset, the hurricane sets in motion the collapse of distinctions and orders, a collapse of the cosmos that has controlled the world of Janie and Tea Cake. The cosmic upset of the hurricane opens up a space for contagion, for risky connections, for chance encounters and transformed identities. In Hurston's working through of the force and effects of the hurricane, we can get a glimpse of the sorts of transformations — of self, other, and community — that Hurston might have envisioned as a counter to the deadly work of selfish justice.

Contagion begins with the flooding of the muck where Tea Cake and Janie have made their home. The muck has been created by the damming up of the lake, bounding and containing the fluidity and indifferent power of the water. When the hurricane hits, fierce winds transform the lake into a horrifying beast. It bursts through its retaining wall and comes rushing toward the cabins: "The monstropolous beast had left his bed. The two hundred miles an hour wind had loosed his chains. He seized hold of his dikes and ran forward until he met the quarters; uprooted them like grass and rushed on. . . . The sea was walking the earth with a heavy heel" (p. 153). In spilling its boundaries, the lake sets in motion a series of contagions whereby other boundaries are breached, fracturing the apparent stability of discrete entities and identities.

The hurricane works a transformation on everything it touches. Hurston's colorful portrayal of the hurricane as a "monstropolous beast" might be taken for the voice of the folk tale; but let us for a moment take this folk tale at its word and imagine that the hurricane does transform the lake into an animate being. Proper boundaries of animate and inanimate break down in the chaos of the flood. Wild animals, snakes, and men huddle together: "Common danger made common friends. Nothing sought a conquest over the other" (p. 156). The flood waters seethe with creatures, "things living and dead. Things that didn't belong in the water" (p. 156). Janie falls into the water and is saved from drowning by an approaching cow. She grabs hold of the cow and becomes attached in an assemblage of animal life, a flotilla of terror:

> Janie achieved the tail of the cow and lifted her head up along the cow's rump, as far as she could above water. The cow sunk a little with the added load and thrashed a moment in terror. Thought she was being pulled down by a gator. Then she continued on. The dog stood up and growled like a lion, stiff-standing hackles, stiff muscles, teeth uncovered as he lashed up his fury for the charge. Tea Cake split the water like an otter, opening his knife as he dived. (p. 157)

The scene is populated by a menagerie, each one melting into another. Janie feels like a gator as she clings to the cow; the dog becomes lion; Tea Cake becomes otter. The interpenetration of dog, cow, Janie, and Tea Cake is literalized when the dog lunges and bites Tea Cake, and Tea Cake in turn slashes the dog with his knife.

The struggle between Tea Cake and the dog syntactically enacts the violent breaching of boundaries that is being depicted:

> Tea Cake rose out of the water at the cow's rump and seized the dog by the neck. But he was a powerful dog and Tea Cake was over-tired. So he didn't kill the dog with one stroke as he had intended. But the dog couldn't free himself either. They fought and somehow he managed to bite Tea Cake high up on his

cheek-bone once. Then Tea Cake finished him and sent him to the bottom to
stay there. (p. 157)

In this struggle, Tea Cake and the dog change places syntactically several
times over. Each is alternately the subject of the sentence. Twice the named
subject of the previous sentence is displaced by the unnamed "he" in the
next, such that the reader is momentarily disoriented as to the subject of
the action. This effect is particularly evident in the shift from the first to
the second sentence in the preceding passage, where Tea Cake appears to
be the one about whom the narrator states, "he was a powerful dog." In the
structure of this passage, as in the dog's bite and the slash of the knife, the
boundaries between Tea Cake and the dog are blurred.

The breaching of boundaries set in motion by the hurricane spills over
into the realm of racial identity. When Tea Cake and Janie finally reach dry
land, Tea Cake is conscripted into the army of grave diggers who will clean
up the mess left in the hurricane's wake. In its trail, the hurricane has left
a racial difference without a difference. The white guards stop the men who
are engaged in the nasty work of disposing of the dead bodies: "Hey, dere,
y'all! Don't dump dem bodies in de hole lak dat! Examine every last one of
'em and find out if they's white or black" (p. 162). One of the men responds,
"Whut difference do it make 'bout de color? . . . Nobody can't tell nothin'
'bout some uh dese bodies, de shape dey's in. Can't tell whether dey's
white or black" (p. 163). The repetition of "can't tell" places the predicates
"nothin' " and "whether dey's white or black" in apposition. Whether the
bodies are white or black *is* in this formula a "nothing." The flood has set
into motion an uncontrollable overspilling of boundaries, disrupting the
system of discernibility that ensures racial order. Neither black nor white
are immune to its effects; black and white bodies drown indifferently and
are collected into a community of the dead to which race cannot apply.

Although the hurricane has subsided, Tea Cake carries within his body
the continuing effects of its contagions. From the bite of the dog, he has contracted rabies, a lethal contagion that signals the end of his self. The effect
of the rabies is to populate Tea Cake's body with others, to expose his body
as a battlefield on which these others will struggle. The touch of the dog has
injected his body with an alien substance that has the power to transform
Tea Cake into the one by whom he was infected. As Tea Cake's condition
worsens, rabies becomes the contagion of personality: Tea Cake slowly becomes the mad dog who bites Janie. Tea Cake's illness sets into motion a
complexity of intermingling involving Tea Cake, the water he struggles to

drink, the floodwaters, the dead bodies of others, a demon at his throat, and a mad dog with "hatred in his eyes." His descent into madness is not simply the loss of reason or of control; madness is figured as the opening up of the self to the presence of all these others, the failure to sustain the rigid boundaries that keep Tea Cake separate from the dog or the lake separate from the land. This contagion is terrifying and dangerous and deadly, but it is also transformative, tearing open the fabric of life to its constitutive outside in order — to return to Hurston's image of the bags of jumble — to insist that those bags of stuff we call identity can be torn open, emptied, refilled.

Overwhelmed by madness, Tea Cake becomes increasingly irrational and violent: "The fiend in him must kill and Janie was the only thing living he saw" (p. 175). He pulls a gun on Janie; she shoots him a split second before he pulls the trigger on his pistol, killing him and causing his shot to just miss her head. The trajectory of contagion set into motion by the hurricane continues as Tea Cake bites Janie in his last moment: "Janie saw the look on his face and leaped forward as he crashed forward in her arms. She was trying to hover him as he closed his teeth in the flesh of her forearm" (p. 175). Tea Cake's dying embrace is oddly erotic in its violence. In this moment, their bodies are peculiarly joined; Janie is forced to "pr[y] the dead Tea Cake's teeth from her arm." It is as if those teeth have embedded in her arm permanently, transgressing the boundedness of Janie's body and threatening her own death, even as her flesh incorporates a part of Tea Cake.

Nevertheless, the two are not joined into one. The connection of Tea Cake's dead body with Janie's living one prevents us from seeing this embrace as a moment of transcendent union. Rather, Tea Cake's bite marks the accidental contact of contagion that transforms both their bodies without incorporating them into a higher unity. This dying embrace displaces the heterosexual embrace of reproduction that would position Janie as origin or ancestor, as mother to the future. The offspring of this union will not be the familial, legitimate offspring who might preserve the ancestral line of Tea Cake and Janie in the future. Rather, Tea Cake's bite repeats the bite of the dog, joining Janie into the trajectory of contagion and the collapse of boundaries. The results of this embrace are unpredictable, accidental; the bite marks the touch as the touch of chance, of fortune (good or bad).

The common usage of the word *contagion* links it to sickness and disease, but I want to provisionally suspend these negative connotations in order to explore further the implications of the literal meaning, "together-touching." Not only bad things, but also good things, may be transmitted by the action of contagion: we think of the virus, the infection, but also of the laughter, the mood. Contagion—whether good or bad—is accidental, it follows from touching. At the moment of contagion there is no intention to infect the other, to give the other something of the self. In this sense, contagion is a giving without subject or object; contagion happens between and joins together, but it is not the same trajectory as the gift-counter-gift, which begins with the subject giving and ends with the subject receiving. Contagion happens by accident, by proximity, by touch. One cannot foresee the trajectories contagion may take; one cannot predict the mutations that may be produced in its wake. Indeed, one cannot always distinguish the direction of contagion: the sudden simultaneity of an epidemic may preclude the question of who infected whom. Hence, the together-touching of contagion is not from one (subject) to another (subject) but wells up in the between and the within, between one and another and within each.

The risk of contagion is the risk of the touch, the risk attendant on being exposed to the touch, the risk of a touch that may come as a blow, as a caress, as a wound, as a kiss. The risk is not the touch itself but the exposure to the possibility of touch, the opening onto the possibility of contagion as together-touching. Contagion as together-touching is neither the contract between subjects that binds a community of disparate individuals together in mutual obligation nor is it the in-common of subjects that guarantees community as a unity of essence. The *you* and *me* of contagion are neither joined by essential identity nor separated by agonistic difference. *We* are rather singular and touching, together in our singularity. We cannot choose contagion; contagion is what happens to us. Equally, *we* are what happens in contagion. Perhaps we might imagine contagion as the gift that does not appear, the gift that gives *us* as together-touching.

Thus, contagion is not another law of identity and difference but the lawlessness that the law always struggles to contain or exclude. Contagion does not recognize the boundaries of community that delineate same and other. Contagion does not speak the language of identity and difference; rather, it marks the risk of proximity, of accident, of connections that may or may not be made, of commonalities that may or may not matter. Contagion may seem to some to be a wholly negative model of being together; it offers no security, no assurance, no soothing sense of history and continuity. Contagion appears to be too closely aligned with death; both the end of the autonomous, individual subject who is displaced by the touch and, at the

limit, the physical death that marks the body overwhelmed by an infesta-
tion that exceeds its tolerance. A politics of contagion would seem to be a
politics of death: the loss of subjectivity, of meaning, of purpose. But it is
not certain that death is wholly on the side of contagion. Jean-Luc Nancy
argues just the opposite, that it is the work of community that is the work
of death:

> Immanence, communal fusion, contains no other logic than that of the suicide
> of the community that is governed by it. Thus the logic of Nazi Germany was
> not only that of the extermination of the other, of the subhuman deemed ex-
> terior to the communion of blood and soil, but also, effectively, the logic of
> sacrifice aimed at all those in the "Aryan" community who did not satisfy the
> criteria of *pure* immanence, so much so that—it being obviously impossible to
> set a limit on such criteria—the suicide of the German nation itself might have
> represented a plausible extrapolation of the process.[49]

Each act of exclusion of the other, Nancy suggests, reveals the presence of
another other to be excluded, on and on without limit. This chilling diagnosis of the logic of fascism asks that we see the systematic violence of
Nazi Germany not as an evil aberration in the history of human society but
as perhaps the most extreme example of an attempt to realize community
through the operation of a rule of identity and commonality. For Nancy,
this is the work of community, although it may not always appear in such
a stark form. Community demands the paring away of deviations, of differences; at the limit, Nancy insists, the modern ideal of community based on
identity itself tends toward auto-destruction.

   The real danger for Hurston lies in the seductiveness of such a community, its (unrealizable) promise of harmony and unity and the violence that
is couched in the guise of security and commonality. If it is indeed Hurston's aim to abandon the politics of identity and difference in favor of the
risks of contagion, it is not at all surprising that the philosopher Spinoza is
invoked at the conclusion of *Dust Tracks* as the muse of her labors: "When
I get old, and my joints and bones tell me about it, I can sit around and
write for myself, if for nobody else, and read slowly and carefully the mys-
ticism of the East, and re-read Spinoza with love and care" (p. 209). Hurston's invocation of Spinoza, the philosopher of spontaneity and singularity,
highlights the importance of her repudiation of a more properly Hegelian
vision of history and identity, of a dialectic of universal and particular that
seeks to incorporate or sublate or destroy the particularity of the particu-

lar in the name of order. Hurston offers an instance of what Antonio Negri calls "Spinozian thought," a thought that "proposes a physics of society: in other words, a mechanics of individual pressures and a dynamics of associative relationships, which characteristically are never closed in the absolute but, rather, proceed by ontological dislocations."[50] Hurston's Spinozian thought refuses a politics of totality, the absolute, or the same. Instead, she struggles to open life up to the "ontological dislocations" of accident, contact, proximity, and chance.

Hurston's work is a practice of risky connections that calls into question the possibility of justice or freedom within a community bounded by either racial identity or the individual authenticity of the subject. We might call this a practice of contagion; and if it is a risky practice, we should not forget that it is also a productive and transformative practice as well. It may be true that Hurston's willful denial of any political or practical relevance for race is, in the context of 1940s America, wishful thinking, if not downright delusional. Perhaps, as Priscilla Wald has suggested, "the exigencies of American politics mitigated the possibilities that Hurston envisioned in her poetics."[51] But Hurston could not deny her vision that violence in the name of race and nation is both preceded by and implicated in the violence of exclusion and abstraction that enables racial identity and national identity. There is in Hurston's fantasy of a cosmic transformation the sense of a possibility that is radically other than a reordering or redistribution in the name of justice. Hurston does not aim to reconstruct a common history in order to salvage identity and community in the face of opposition and domination. Instead, she opens a space for provisional relations of togetherness around the chance encounters of wandering and contagion. Hurston offers us a vision of the future as cosmic upset, a future open to the provisionalities and possibilities of risk, accident, ambivalence, and uncertainty.

In the current political climate of revanchist white supremacy in the name of color blindness and individual rights, increased racial consciousness on the part of those whose group histories have been denied and effaced seems critical to launching an effective resistance. And while Hurston tended to be critical of the race consciousness of African-Americans, at the same time the most forceful aspect of her charge was directed against the violent abuse of power in the name of race or nation—a power much more in the hands of the dominant than the dominated. Thus, insofar as it is the white race that has sought, and continues in the name of color blindness or merit to seek, the domination and exclusion of others from the national (and human) community, it is the violent exclusions and purgings of *whiteness* that are challenged and resisted by the workings of contagion. It is the maintenance of *white* privilege in the current political climate that has provoked the most violent and repressive measures aimed at enforcing boundaries and denying the contact and responsibility of contagion. But while Hurston's critique is certainly directed against the exclusive power of whiteness, it also reveals the danger of capitulating to the pluralist vision of discrete and bounded communities whereby other racially defined communities might counter the exclusive force of whiteness with demands for recognition or inclusion. Community as contagion cannot be a racially defined community; indeed, it cannot be defined in any way in advance by boundaries or qualities that would make up the limits of inclusion. For Hurston, a pluralist politics of identity and difference, even in the name of racial justice, can only further entrench the conditions of injustice, of "justice twisted by the selfish hand."

Nevertheless, Hurston's turning to what might be called a politics of contagion does not provide us with a program of action. We cannot choose contagion; contagion is what happens to and *as* us. What is needed, perhaps, is an openness to this contagion, a willingness to recognize and respond to contagion rather than attempting to restore purity and autonomy. This openness to contagion is an ethical posture, a way of being in the world. But this is not the ethics of the modern subject, the ethics that takes as its supreme object the realization of the inner being, the authentic self of the subject. Rather, it is an ethics that begins from together-touching, from the condition that we exist only in our togetherness and that therefore our first responsibility is to and in terms of that togetherness. In this vision of community as contagion, Hurston calls into question our faith in security, in cleansing, in the power of boundaries to achieve and assure the community and the freedom that everyone desires. The lure of community in the name of identity demands the disavowal or repression of contagion. But Hurston insists that we recognize that contagion is not a dangerous elsewhere; it is right here, it is us. Contagion erupts constantly and uncontrollably in the midst of the orders and identities of community. How do we respond? It is, in fact, always and precisely a question of response, of responsibility, of responding to the other otherness that erupts in contagion. This is the only possibility of responsibility or of justice: to respond and be responsible to rather than seeking to destroy, control, or contain the other otherness, the singular, that which is unknown, unpredictable, uncertain, uncontrollable. This is the justice of just-ness, the gift of community as together-touching that demands not more security, more gates and fences to keep out the contaminating other, but rather an embrace of singularity, an abandoning of the self, an opening of the "bag of jumble" to both the risks and the rewards of contagion.

# 6. Speculations

## *Hybridity and Singularity*

The liberal idea of politics as envisioned in twentieth-century America centers on the mediation and resolution of competing interests and claims within an ideally neutral political arena. The state, in this view, is the mechanism through which these competing voices resolve themselves into a realization of the common good. Thus, differences in identity or interest precede the entry into the political arena and are reflected in, but not formed by, the workings of politics. This is what is most commonly understood by identity politics, whereby diverse social groups, defined in terms of socially salient identities, seek representation of their interests and recognition of their demands in the public and political sphere. Literature enters into the realm of identity politics as an organ of representation. This has been, as Michael Awkward argues, the predominant presumption of the African-American literary critical tradition. Awkward suggests that in this traditional view, black expressive art is called on to "right/write the race" by representing accurately, and affirmatively, the reality of black experience.[1]

This reading tradition is informed by the positivist assumption that literary representation is or ought to be a transparent reflection of the real social world, a "mirror of nature," rather than itself participating in a complex politics of representation. Such assumptions of course have not been applied to all literature at all times; throughout most of this century, works regarded as canonical have been evaluated and read according to various aesthetic criteria, while noncanonical works, particularly those marked in some way by race, ethnicity, or gender, have generally been aesthetically devalued and evaluated and read according to a sociological standard of authenticity or representativeness. John Guillory has argued that the contemporary canon wars have been played out according to such a logic of representation, such that "the movement to open the canon to noncanonical authors submits the syllabus to a kind of demographic oversight. Canonical and noncanonical authors are supposed to *stand for* particular social groups, dominant or subordinate." [2] While it is only recently that some have argued that *canonical* texts represent the interests, perspectives, and values of *particular* social groups (especially the white, male, heterosexual, Protestant, political and social elite, a.k.a. the infamous "dead white males"), such an approach to literatures written from the political margins has a long history. As Gates notes, this was the primary understanding of the importance of early African-American writings, particularly slave narrative, because "the very *face* of the race . . . was contingent upon the recording of the black *voice*." [3] In this reading, the aim of the textual voice is to create an image, a representation of the race. And this representation is political insofar as it competes with and contests the negative representations, the negative "faces," produced by Anglo-European racist discourse.

But what are these faces, these representations of the identity of the black race or, for that matter, the white race? Deleuze and Guattari's "facialization machines" suggest an alternative approach to such faces that does not posit them as existing prior to or outside of the representational and political practices in which they appear and are contested. [4] The facialization machine is a metaphor for a process without subject, an unlocalizable assemblage of automatic and autonomous mechanisms whereby singularity, multiplicity, polyvocality, and indeterminacy are channeled and translated into regularized "faces" or social identities. Such social identities are important to the order of the modern state insofar as they organize singularity into conformity, or "the face," and deviance, or "the other." The machine metaphor emphasizes that this process takes place beyond will or volition, outside the realm of individual choice. It is not we as independent subjects who construct the facialization machine as a means of extending our power; rather, the facialization machine constitutes us as seemingly independent subjects who bear such socially significant identities as race and gender. This is not to assign some kind of prior agency or existence to the facialization machine but rather to suggest that the facialization machine names a *process*, what Judith Butler describes as the "reiteration by which both 'subjects' and 'acts' come to appear at all. There is no power that acts, but only a reiterated acting that is power in its persistence and instability."[5]

The facialization process is not simply the origin of the subject; rather, the apparent autonomy and identity of the subject is continually and iteratively constituted and confirmed by the workings of the facialization machine. Further, as the facialization metaphor suggests, this subject is always constituted and determined as an embodied subject, a subject identified and characterized by the contours of the body. But this facialization process is not simply the symbolization of the body, the translation of a natural body into a socially marked, and thereby socially meaningful, body. The matter of the body (the female body, the black body) is not a neutral, autonomous site or a surface but, as Butler puts it, "a process of materialization that stabilizes over time to produce the effect of boundary, fixity, and surface we call matter."[6] "Matter," the reality effect of embodied social identities, is created through time as "a sedimented effect of a reiterative or ritual practice."[7] The facialization machine joins body, subject, and social identity, producing the natural-seeming effect of essentially embodied racial identities through the ongoing production of visibility, of knowledge, and of the subject.

If the racialized subject is constituted by the various historical processes and discourses metaphorized as the facialization machine (including some I have discussed in this book, such as the determination of the subject as property, the emergence of difference as division, or the translation of visibility into embodiment), then identity politics, insofar as it is predicated on the prior assumption of the racialized subject, will always be limited in advance by its inability to take into account the contingency of such notions as the subject and difference. If the subject is not the ontological grounding of the political, but rather a politically achieved effect, then an alternative politics might begin from the question of the constitution of the subject. This demands an account of politics as taking place not only at the level of the representations of the face (as in identity politics) but equally in the production of face and body themselves. The political struggle for equality, freedom, and justice cannot simply address the representation of identity, either the representation of interests in the political arena or the representation of experience in the cultural arena. Rather, what must be questioned and contested is the constitution of this realm of the political as the mediation of difference in terms of identities.

Power is not simply the power of one group over another group, the direct power of domination across lines of difference; rather, power is first the power of subjectification, the power to transform singularity into identity and to assign, regulate, distribute, and control identities. Such power is not localizable; it plays across multiple sites, including the realms of knowledge, electoral politics, the body, law, medicine, popular culture, and so on. This power has no singular source or subject but rather circulates as the condition of appearance of the subject. From this perspective, we might gain an alternative view of political struggle. As opposed to what we commonly perceive as political struggle, the struggle between competing identities within the terms laid out by the state or a struggle for control or conquest of the state, we might consider the extent to which politics happens as the struggle between, on the one side, the ordering operations of subjectification and identity-formation and, on the other, what might be termed *singularities*, that which appears from the perspective of identity as disorder, excess, non-identity, inassimilable difference.[8] From the point of view of a struggle between identity and singularity, one might conclude that identity politics is precisely a-political, insofar as it reinstitutes the priority of representable identities. Where a politics of identity contributes to the iterative process of subjectification and facialization, a politics of singularity (if there can be such a thing) would interrupt such a process, expose it to its own boundaries and exclusions, undermine its logic and its coherence.

A politics that begins from singularity, rather than from individuals or identities, would necessarily advance an alternative vision of justice, one much closer to what I have been calling just-ness. As I suggested in Chapter 3, the justice that begins from the right of the subject, a justice of commensurability, account, and calculation, is but another name for the violent destructiveness of vengeance and retribution. This justice is always, as Hurston points out, a justice "twisted by the selfish hand." But if there is a thinking of community that is open to the contingencies of singularity, then perhaps another justice may happen, not between or in negotiation with individuals, but rather in the spacing, the together-touching, of singularities. Singularities must not be confused with the singular; singularities are always only in relation, as the originary simultaneity of community. In contrast, the individual subject strongly conceived as autonomous and independent would be in its autonomy isolated, cut off from all relation. Social justice cannot be individual justice, cannot, that is, be a justice that begins from the autonomy and priority of the individual. If there is to be social justice, it must be the justice of the community beyond *com-unis* and *com-munis*, the just-ness of together-touching, which begins from the simultaneous togetherness and singularity of those who make up, and who exist as, the (unbounded, illimitable) community. Beginning from the community, rather than from the individual, there is no place for the refusal of responsibility in the name of the innocent bystander. Rather than justice as a matter of the individual's right, justice begins from the condition of simultaneous and inescapable responsibility.

This is a difficult responsibility because it is always a matter of responding to the unknown and the unknowable. Justice cannot be based on a right determined in advance but must proceed from the condition of not knowing, of confronting the limits of certainty and control. This uncertainty or undecidability is not, as many have charged, the end of politics; quite the contrary, it is from undecidability that politics must proceed. If justice is decided in advance, there is no politics, only administration. At the same time, undecidability does not absolve anyone from the responsibility to decide. To be responsible, one must always make a decision, a decision that always is confronted with the impossibility of prediction or certainty. Undecidability means that one must decide because there is no rule or principle to follow that would allow one to avoid decision. Responsibility becomes possible only when decision is truly possible; and there can be no decision when justice and freedom are a matter of rule and principle to be applied unthinkingly, without decision. Responsibility requires the recognition of singularity, the unique, the unrepeatable, the unknowable, the irreducible otherness of the other.

If singularity is the condition of another way of thinking about justice and responsibility, it should not be surprising that it might also lead to another way of thinking about freedom. In Chapter 2, I suggested that while the fugitive could not be mistaken for a figure of freedom, the recognition of the condition of fugitivity opened up a space for thinking about freedom as other than the freedom of the subject, that is, other than the freedom subordinated to the autonomy of the subject and conceived as property or right. Taken to its limit, the ideal of the autonomous subject demands a being without relation, because any relation would impinge on the originary autonomy of such a subject. But a freedom without relation would be empty, meaningless. Freedom cannot be realized by detaching the self from every relation or limitation; rather, if there is freedom it can only come within relation. Thus, if we return to the questions of community raised in Chapter 5, it appears that community as *com-unis* or *com-munis* necessarily forecloses the possibility of such a freedom by positing the priority of the autonomous subject as the element of community. Community as *com-unis* or *com-munis* is the negation of all relation, either by submitting members of the community to the demand of a communion in the same (where all is the same, there is no relation) or else by regulating community in the rules and laws of mutual obligation, thereby insisting on the originary separation and absence of relation between those making up the community (where there is no relation, community must be legislated). But if freedom is really free, it cannot operate according to a rule or be contained as the right of the subject. The freedom of freedom would mean that it would always surprise us, that in its freedom it would always exceed any rule, prediction, principle, or expectation. This freedom, which is both always in relation and unknowable in advance, is perhaps the freedom of community as contagion, the chance relations of together-touching in which *we* are as we are exposed to the other and to our own freedom.

There is a risk here of slipping into a careless celebration of fragmentation, singularity, and dispersal, of asserting that the condition of postmodernity is the becoming-singular of the subject such that politics becomes nothing more than the passive contemplation of a heterogeneity that seems already to have swept across the globe. This is the outcome when one too quickly assumes that all it takes is a substitution of a (good) multiplicity or heterogeneity in the place of a (bad) essentialized identity, implying that we can simply choose one or the other. Such a substitution is predicated on the standards of freedom and choice established by liberal individualism: "I as an individual am free to choose what and who I will be." I would not dispute the claim that, when it is a question of rights already defined within the terms of the state, the freedom to choose one's way is definitely a right worth defending. However, in focusing on the appeal of liberal rights–based choice, one risks losing sight of the fact that, just as one does not choose to become an essentially determined subject, one cannot choose to *not* be such a subject (despite the paradoxical fact that, as I have argued throughout this book, this essentialized subject does not and cannot exist). As Gayatri Spivak puts it, "the subject must identify itself with its self-perceived intention. The fact that it must do so is not a description of what it is. That is the difference between decentered and centered. There is no way the subject can be anything but centered. . . . There is no such thing as the decentered subject." [9] The one who chooses, in the liberal framework,

only exists as and in terms defined by the autonomous, essential, interiorized subject, even as the boundaries of this subject are constantly traversed
or exceeded. Insofar as it continues to be based on a rhetoric of choice, the
appeal to heterogeneity as liberation from the oppressions of essentialism
rings a little hollow, sounding an eerie echo to the pluralist appeal for tolerance, "free to be you and me," now repackaged in the fancy garb of a
commodified postmodernism. The critique of the essential subject loses its
edge just as soon as thought is displaced by the slogan, worthy of a Madison Avenue campaign: "Choose fragmentation!"

It is for this reason that the responsibility to singularity cannot be conceived as simply an individual responsibility, a responsibility originating
or ending in the individual. If this were the case, then community and
justice would once more be subordinated to the demands of individual autonomy, authenticity, and choice. Singularity is not the individual; singularity is always plural, emerging within the mutually constituting relation
of togetherness. Thus, responsibility to singularity must likewise also be
plural, originating and ending in the relation that gives *us* rather than in
*my* relation to *you*. A politics that begins from singularity will not, then, be
a politics of individual rights or freedoms. Rather, such a politics, it seems
to me, might happen in relation to the conditions of togetherness, of exposure and responsibility.

For example, it might be argued that the most dangerous word in American politics today is *security*. In the name of security, boundaries of all
kinds are being drawn with increasing force. Such actions aim toward the
production of bounded, secure enclaves of homogeneity that shore up the
image of the bounded, secure individual. As I argued in the first chapter,
such spatial practices are inextricably also racial and racializing practices.
I have in mind, for example, the interiorization and privatization of previously public spaces, such as shopping malls and enclosed corporate atri-
ums; the "cleaning up" of public parks and streets to remove the homeless
and other undesirables from view; the increasing divisions of a multitiered
public transportation system (taxis, buses, subways, etc.) that allows those
with the means to escape the crush of the masses; the withdrawal of the
largely white middle classes to the suburbs and the transformation of the
suburbs into privately owned, policed, and governed gated communities;
and, finally, at the national level, the shoring up of the nation's borders
against the incursions of an alien menace.[10]

As David Goldberg remarks, "spatial control is not simply a reaction to

natural divisions and social pathologies in the urban [and nonurban] population but is constitutive of them." [11] Each of these efforts at isolation and
boundedness repeats at another location the same gesture of exclusion; and
if the racial politics of such exclusion are not self-evident, we witness them
bursting to the surface in the hysteria of anti-immigrant sentiment. These
developments are aimed, whether implicitly or explicitly, at the realization
of the fantasy of social purification, the escape from contingency, the elimi-
nation of occasions for the risky, contagious encounter. Such acts of exclusion are absolutely necessary to sustain the effect of the autonomous individual. But if we see such individualizing practices as these redistributions
of space as simultaneously social products and socially productive, then the
position of the individual can no longer operate as the ultimate foundation
for politics. One might imagine alternative configurations of transportation, parks, or housing that would begin, not from the homogeneity of the
individual as separate and autonomous, but from the heterogeneity of us
in our togetherness. Thus, one way of imagining a politics of singularity
rather than of the individual might be in the reconfiguring of social space,
disturbing the secure boundedness of the individual by increasing the occasions for exposure and for the chancy encounters of contact and contagion.

Finally, it is time to return to the question raised at the beginning of this
book, namely, how we might account for the tension between the workings
of the color line (and racial identity) and the irreducible presence of hybridity in some other way than simply substituting the one for the other.
The demands of fixity, knowability, identity, and authenticity given form
in the figure of the color line are constantly exceeded by something else, by
a force we might call hybridity. But the hybridity that has emerged in the
course of this book is not another substance, however socially constructed,
that would displace the essentially conceived notion of blackness. The individual is not hybrid; rather, hybridity constantly traverses the boundaries
of the individual. Hence, hybridity appears for the racially constituted subject as that which cannot appear.

The hybridity that does not become another hyphenated or qualified
identity would be hybridity as singularity, hybridity as the uncontainable,
the unknowable, the unforeseeable. This hybridity cannot be positioned
as a goal or an end; it is therefore not subject to the teleological narrative of the beyond that would rescue us from error. Thus, to surrender to
the insecurities of this hybridity will always be risky. This might be the
hybridity Homi Bhabha calls "the perplexity of the living as it interrupts

the representation of the fullness of life." [12] Where the various forms of power and authority metaphorized as the "facialization machine" pretend to be capable of representing the "fullness of life" in an adequately conceived and cataloged array of pregiven identities and essences, hybridity as singularity simultaneously evades and interrupts this representation. This notion of hybridity is indeed perplexing insofar as it is not subject to the standards of representability or knowability that would allow us to determine with certainty its form and contours, its *thereness*. But perhaps it is precisely this perplexity that demands our attention, not as a puzzle to be solved, but as a condition to learn to inhabit.

What I am calling perplexity might seem to imply political disengagement, a sort of paralysis in the face of the impossibility of certainty or absolute decision. But this need not be the case. Perhaps the introduction of perplexity into the various struggles by which we enact politics may also be political, insofar as perplexity demands the suspension of the standards of right and authority by which any particular interest or position becomes unassailable, self-evident, or commonsensical. In the face of perplexity or hybridity, "we cannot be sure that we have judged justly or committed the right political act. . . . There are no assurances, and for that reason we are more not less responsible." [13] Without absolute assurance of the right or the just, we are faced with the continual, and necessarily political, demand of responsibility not just for one time or for one decision but at each instant, in each relation. This means more political engagement, not less, more challenging, more questioning, more struggling to expose and counter the violence disguised and justified in the name of self-evidence, nature, justice, or common sense.

# Reference Matter

# Notes

Complete authors' names, titles, and publication data for sources cited in short form in the notes are given in the Bibliography, pp. 241–58.

## Chapter 1

1. "Race and Racism," 1.
2. Ibid., emphasis added.
3. Ibid., 31.
4. Ibid., 17.
5. For a good representative sampling of the "state of the art," see the essays collected in Goldberg, *Multiculturalism*.
6. Rosello, *Practices of Hybridity*, 4.
7. This is not to suggest an absolute unanimity. bell hooks, for example, has been consistently skeptical of the flight from essentialism, suggesting that the postmodern critique of identity and the subject devalues such politically achieved effects just at the moment when African-Americans are finding their voice as political subjects. See her "Postmodern Blackness."
8. de Lauretis, "Essence of the Triangle," 3.
9. Dr. Josiah C. Nott was the most well-known proponent of this view. As George Fredrickson points out, "his 'research' consisted primarily of what he thought he had found out about Negroes in the course of practicing medicine in Mobile" (p. 79).
10. Young, *Colonial Desire*, 25.
11. Appiah, "Uncompleted Argument," 35.
12. Omi and Winant, *Racial Formation*.
13. Butler, "Contingent Foundations," 42.

14. Du Bois, *Souls*, 3.

15. See especially Winant, *Racial Conditions*, 59–62.

16. Edsall and Edsall, "Race"; quoted in Winant, *Racial Conditions*, 74–75.

17. C. Harris, "Whiteness," 1767.

18. Goldberg, *Racist Culture*, 185.

19. For example, the definition in *Webster's New World Dictionary* (1980) confirms the equation of races with places as the basic common sense of geography, which is "the *descriptive* science dealing with the surface of the earth, its division into continents and countries, and the climate, plants, animals, natural resources, inhabitants, and industries of the various divisions" (emphasis added). That climate, plants, and inhabitants should each be given equal and interchangeable place in such a practice of description implies a certain organic interrelation, one hardly removed from Herder's notion of race.

20. Soja, *Postmodern Geographies*, 123.

21. Of course, the meaning of mountain ranges and oceans is equally constructed (one thinks of the political investments in the determination of the seemingly natural forms of the continents). But the apparently irrefutable empirical "thereness" of a mountain or an ocean becomes a powerful metaphor for a more amorphous and nebulous division of human beings, once "inhabitants" are placed on the same descriptive plane as mountains and oceans.

22. *Brown v Board of Education*, 347 U.S. 483 (1954). See page 494, quoting the Kansas District Court's finding in the same case (although the lower court had ruled against the plaintiff).

23. Thomas, Dissenting opinion.

24. Ibid.

25. Orfield, *Must We Bus?* 69.

26. Winant, *Racial Conditions*, 63.

27. Ibid., 74.

28. C. Harris, "Whiteness."

29. Soja, *Postmodern Geographies*, 6.

30. See, for example, Guillaumin, "Idea of Race," and Omi and Winant, *Racial Formation*.

31. See, for example, Holt, "Marking," and Wiegman, *American Anatomies*.

32. Butler, "Lana's 'Imitation,'" 10.

33. Benjamin, "Critique of Violence," 284.

34. Derrida, "Force of Law," 38.

35. Spivak, *Post-Colonial Critic*, 51.

36. Rosello, *Practices of Hybridity*, 5.

## Chapter 2

1. Nancy, *Experience*, 2.

2. Ibid., 7.

3. The arguments made against and in favor of slavery in the course of these debates are recorded in Thomas Dew, *Review of the Debate in the Virginia Legislature*

*of 1831 and 1832* (1832). George Fredrickson calls Dew's work "the most thorough and comprehensive justification of the institution that the South had yet produced" (*Black Image*, p. 44).

4. Wiecek, *Sources*.

5. Fredrickson, *Black Image*, 30. The national group grew out of the New England Anti-Slavery Society, which had been founded in 1831. William Shade reports that by 1835, "there were 225 auxiliaries of the American Anti-Slavery Society, a number that grew to 1,346 in the next three years; and by 1840 there were 1,650 such organizations with a total of between 130,000 and 170,000 members" ("Antislavery," p. 138).

6. Starling, *Slave Narrative*, 19.

7. Baker, Introduction, 19–20.

8. Starling, *Slave Narrative*, 36.

9. Gates, for example, asks, "Since the status of the slave narrative as history and literature seems self-evident to us now, how could the narratives have been 'lost' to us for such a dark period?" (*Classic Slave Narratives*, p. x). Insofar as Gates never really answers this question, it seems to be a rhetorical gesture that further reinforces the "self-evidence" of the current valuation.

10. "MLA Survey," 12. The other three authors most frequently named were Harriet Beecher Stowe, Margaret Fuller, and Rebecca Harding Davis.

11. Ulrich B. Phillips, *American Negro Slavery* (1918), quoted in Davis and Gates, *Slave's Narrative*, xxxii.

12. Starling, *Slave Narrative*, xxix.

13. Davis and Gates, *Slave's Narrative*, xxxiv.

14. Although there were early pioneers, the first real wave of historians of U.S. slavery using slave testimony came in the 1940s, following the massive collection of interviews with former slaves carried out by the Federal Writers' Project. Early studies sought to counter the widely accepted plantation perspective on the South by reconstructing the antebellum period from the slave's perspective, using slave narrative as evidence against the official (white) documentary record; E. Franklin Frazier's *The Negro Family in the United States* (1939) and Herbert Aptheker's *American Negro Slave Revolts* (1943) are still widely read. The trend toward histories of slavery from the slave's perspective exploded in the 1970s; the most well known of the recent work includes John Blassingame's *The Slave Community: Plantation Life in the Antebellum South* (1972); Eugene Genovese's *Roll, Jordan, Roll: The World the Slaves Made* (1974); and Herbert Gutman's *The Black Family in Slavery and Freedom, 1750–1925* (1976).

15. Andrews, "Toward a Poetics," 82.

16. For examples of slave narrative anthologies published in the wake of the Civil Rights movement, see Chapman, *Steal Away* (1971); Nichols, *Black Men in Chains* (1972); Pease and Pease, *Slave Narratives* (1969).

17. Awkward, *Negotiating Difference*, 26. Awkward seeks to defuse the power

of recourse to the "authority of experience" to exclude certain forms of critical activity (in particular the use of "theory") or the work of certain (usually white) critics. He argues that the singular political focus of traditional African-American criticism has "denied afrocentric reading its full complexity" due to a "lack of a full commitment to energetic analysis of the art, thematic diversity, and ideological heterogeneity of Black expressive texts" (p. 26). I would agree with Awkward that certain textual complexities, possibilities, and implications, which may carry a powerful political charge, may have passed unnoticed due in large part to the explicit political commitments of much African-American criticism; it is one of the projects of this book to illuminate what I see as some possible alternatives.

18. Olney, *Metaphors of Self*, 44. See Wesling, "Writing as Power," for an interesting discussion of slave narrative as a "reproach" to the canonical (that is, confessional and psychologizing) reading of the autobiographical self. See also Ryan's critique ("Self-Evidence") of the dominant understanding of autobiography as self-evidence, in both the testimonial and epistemological senses.

19. Gates, "From Wheatley to Douglass," 52.

20. Ibid., 52, 57.

21. Sundquist, *Frederick Douglass*, 11.

22. Baker, "Autobiographical Acts," 245.

23. Wesling, "Writing as Power," 462.

24. Deborah McDowell, for example, has suggested ("In the First Place") that Douglass's priority has resulted in the continuing undervaluation of female-authored narratives.

25. Gates, *Classic Slave Narratives*, x.

26. Davis and Gates, *Slave's Narrative*, xxvi–xxvii.

27. See especially "Subaltern Studies," 205.

28. Ibid., 207–15.

29. See for example Stone, "Identity and Art"; Niemtzow, "Problematic of Self"; Sundquist, Introduction to *Frederick Douglass*; Baker, "Autobiographical Acts"; Gates, "Binary Oppositions"; Fishkin and Peterson, " 'We Hold These Truths' "; Olney, "The Founding Fathers" and " 'I was born.' "

30. Baker, "Autobiographical Acts," 245. In my discussions of Douglass and, later in this chapter, Hegel, Locke, and Rousseau, I have not sought to generalize or distort their arguments by adding the feminine pronoun where they use exclusively the masculine. While I do not think that the exclusive use of the masculine pronoun *automatically* excludes the feminine, I certainly do not think that every use automatically *includes* it either. In my discussions later in this chapter of Douglass's marriage and Jacobs's relation to contract, many questions regarding the specificity of the gender of the slave and the "free man" will be raised explicitly. But there are many more questions to be asked about the status of the masculine pronoun in each of the texts under consideration, questions that I have skirted or

ignored in order to pursue a different line of inquiry. By preserving the specificity of a particular writer's language, I seek both to be true to the form of the text and to leave open the questions raised by the exclusive use of the masculine pronoun.

31. Gates, "Binary Oppositions," 90. Douglass quotation from Douglass, *Narrative*, 107. Subsequent citations for this work in this chapter appear in the text.

32. Andrews, "Toward a Poetics," 82. In a similar vein, Sacvan Bercovitch ("Problem of Ideology") gestures toward an ambivalent relation between Douglass and American free enterprise ideology, suggesting that Douglass manipulates the terms of that ideology ("the rhetoric of equal opportunity, contract society, upward mobility, free trade, and the sanctity of private property" [p. 648]) to justify his flight to freedom, while at the same time being manipulated and energized by those same terms.

33. Gilroy, *Black Atlantic*, 60. See also Ziolkowski, "Antithesis," for another consideration of the appearance of the Hegelian narrative in Douglass. For Hegel, see Hegel, *Phenomenology*. Subsequent citations to this text in this chapter appear in the text.

34. Gilroy, *Black Atlantic*, 63. One important difference between my reading of the Hegelian narrative of mastery and Gilroy's is that Gilroy emphasizes the struggle itself, from which the master emerges victorious, as an allegory for the emergence of modern sociality from the "natal core" of slavery. However, it is important to remember that the master's victory is illusory in that it is for Hegel the slave who finally "wins" by becoming a consciousness in and for itself through labor. If Hegel's allegory of master and slave represents, as Gilroy suggests, "the master's view of modern civilization" (p. 63), then it must be noted that the master's position is also politically anxious and existentially hopeless.

35. See Hegel's remarks on Africa in the introduction to his *Philosophy of History*, 91–99. Hegel concludes his remarks with a statement that perfectly encapsulates the European view of Africa's relation to history: "At this point we leave Africa, not to mention it again. For it is no historical part of the World; it has no movement or development to exhibit. . . . What we properly understand by Africa, is the Unhistorical, Undeveloped Spirit, still involved in the conditions of mere nature, and which had to be presented here only as on the threshold of the World's History" (p. 99).

36. Gates, "Binary Oppositions," 91, emphasis added.

37. McDowell, "In the First Place," 203.

38. Baker, *Blues*, 48.

39. C. Kaplan, "Narrative Contracts," 109.

40. Sánchez-Eppler, "Bodily Bonds," 31.

41. Shklar, *American Citizenship*, 16.

42. Roediger, *Wages*, 36.

43. John Adams, quoted in Roediger, *Wages*, 28.

44. Rousseau, "Social Contract." Although the framework I am using here to discuss freedom and the state is derived from Rousseau, the basic terms are shared by those modern political theorists who envision the modern state as the coincidence of "subject" and "citizen." Especially relevant is Hegel, *Philosophy of Right*.

45. This reading is reinforced by Rousseau's discussion of sociality in the "Discourse on the Origin of Inequality," in which society originates in the relation of dependence, which is for Rousseau the necessary precondition of servitude. Slavery seems almost to follow necessarily from society: "since the bonds of servitude are formed merely from the mutual dependence of men and the reciprocal needs that unite them, it is impossible to enslave a man without having first put him in the position of being incapable of doing without another. This [is] a situation that did not exist in the state of nature" [i.e., it is a situation unique to the condition of sociality] (p. 59).

46. C. Harris, "Whiteness," 1724.

47. Jordan, *White over Black*, 80.

48. Stampp, *Peculiar Institution*, 194.

49. Article 4, Section 2: "No person held to service or labor in one state, under the laws thereof, escaping into another, shall, in consequence of any law or regulation therein, be discharged from such service or labor, but shall be delivered up on claim of the party to whom such service or labor may be due."

50. Northup, *Twelve Years*.

51. *New England Anti-Slavery Almanac*, quoted in Davis and Gates, *Slave's Narrative*, ii.

52. Stampp, *Peculiar Institution*, 192–93; Genovese, *Roll, Jordan, Roll*, 28–37.

53. J. G. deRoulhac Hamilton, ed., *The Papers of Thomas Ruffin*, vol. 4, 255–57; quoted in Genovese, *Roll, Jordan, Roll*, 35, emphasis added. See also Storing, "Slavery," 49–50. Both Genovese and Storing argue that Ruffin reached this conclusion against his humanitarian impulses but in accordance with what he considered to be the legal imperatives of the case. As Genovese remarks, "never has the logic of slavery been followed so faithfully by a humane and responsible man" (p. 35). See *State v Mann*, 13 N.C. 263 (1829).

54. Spillers, "Mama's Baby," 78.

55. Spillers suggests that the denial of kinship relations to the slave was one important aspect of ensuring the status of slave-as-property: "the enslaved must not be permitted to perceive that he or she has any human rights that matter. Certainly if 'kinship' were possible, the property relations would be undermined, since the offspring would then 'belong' to a mother and a father" ("Mama's Baby," p. 75).

56. Martin does not mention this episode in his intellectual biography of Douglass; Foner mentions it briefly but does not grant it much significance (pp. 71–73). Starling offers the most complete account of these events, and it is her description on which I base my discussion here.

57. Editorial from the *Boston Chronotype*, January 15, 1847, 6; quoted in Starling, *Slave Narrative*, 42.

58. Judy, "Nigga Authenticity," 225.

59. Macpherson, *Possessive Individualism*. See Wald, "Terms of Assimilation," for a further discussion of the importance of self-ownership to the emergence of the American conception of citizenship in the nineteenth century and in relation to the exclusion of slaves and members of indigenous tribes who "constitute two ways of not owning the self" (p. 86). Guillaumin also emphasizes the links between citizenship, self-ownership, and race in her "Idea of Race."

60. Locke is widely regarded as the source for the rights of "life, liberty, and the pursuit of happiness" that characterize the aims of the American Declaration of Independence. Significantly, however, Locke's rights are slightly different: life, liberty, and *estate*. For a discussion of the relation of American political principles to the natural law tradition, see Becker, *Declaration of Independence*, and Boyd, *Declaration of Independence*.

61. Locke, *Two Treatises*, 329.

62. Guillaumin, "Idea of Race," 49.

63. Wald, "Terms of Assimilation," 80.

64. Ibid., 79.

65. I would distinguish Hegel's discussion of property in *Philosophy of Right* from a similar discussion in *Phenomenology of Spirit*; in the latter, one appropriates the external world through work or transformation, such that the object as it is produced becomes the external embodiment of my will. In *Philosophy of Right*, the labor of work or transformation has been suppressed, and the claim itself is sufficient to establish property.

66. Judy, "Nigga Authenticity," 225.

67. Stepto, *Behind the Veil*, 25.

68. Douglass, *Life and Times*, 196.

69. Van Deburg, *Slavery and Race*, 86; Aptheker, *Slave Revolts*.

70. *New York Emancipator* (1839), quoted in Starling, *Slave Narrative*, 30.

71. One might also conclude that these images appealed because the representation of bondage, violence, or suffering might simultaneously fascinate and repulse. Karen Sánchez-Eppler's reading of sentimental abolitionist narrative supports this interpretation. Sánchez-Eppler suggests that antislavery sentiment was not the only reason for the popularity of fictional or artistic depictions of slavery in such abolitionist publications as the Boston Female Anti-Slavery Society's gift book titled, *Liberty Bell*: "the horrific events narrated in these tales attract precisely to the extent that the buyers of these representations of slavery are fascinated by the abuses they ostensibly oppose. For despite their clear abolitionist stance such stories are fueled by the allure of bondage, an appeal which suggests that the valuation of depictions of slavery may rest upon the same psychic grounds as slave-

holding itself" ("Bodily Bonds," p. 35). Commentators have frequently suggested that the lurid and graphic accounts of bodily violation in slave narrative might be viewed as a species of nineteenth-century pornography.

72. Ransom, *Conflict*, 62.

73. Ibid., 70.

74. Even slaves able to earn or acquire enough money were often bitterly disappointed when masters took their money and refused to honor the agreement. As Stampp notes, a slave "could not be a party to a contract. No promise of freedom, oral or written, was binding upon his master" (*Peculiar Institution*, p. 197). Because legally both the slave's labor and the slave's money belonged to the master, the courts would not recognize as binding any arrangement exchanging the one for the other.

75. See Ransom, *Conflict*, for an extended analysis of the relation of the demand for slaves to the price of slaves in the open market.

76. Butler, "Contingent Foundations," 46.

77. Ibid.

78. Bibb's narrative has merited little sustained commentary; Robert Stepto uses it to exemplify the "first stage" of slave narrative that seeks authentication through materials appended rather than integrated into the primary narrative (*Behind the Veil*, pp. 6–10); Charles Nichols employs Bibb's narrative alongside several others to draw parallels between picaresque fiction and the tradition of black autobiography ("Slave Narrators," pp. 283–86); Melvin Dixon reads Bibb's narrative as characteristic of those "slave autobiographies in which the protagonist confronts and is confronted by the challenge of survival and deliverance from the wilderness" ("Singing Swords," p. 312). Subsequent citations for Bibb in this chapter appear in the text.

79. Baker, *Blues*, 36.

80. Ibid., 35; Equiano, *Narrative*.

81. Genovese, *Roll, Jordan, Roll*, 650; Stampp, *Peculiar Institution*, 109.

82. Olney, " 'I was born,' " 164.

83. Stepto, *Behind the Veil*, 10.

84. Nichols, "Slave Narrators," 284.

85. This argument is made most strongly by C. Harris, "Whiteness." See also Wald, "Terms of Assimilation."

86. Ellen Weinauer reads the Crafts' narrative, *Running a Thousand Miles for Freedom*, as a passing story, suggesting that Ellen Craft's cross-dressing inverts the material relationships of both slavery and marriage, such that "Ellen becomes master, owner rather than owned, controlling subject rather than passive object," thereby disrupting the stability and naturalness of these categories ("Respectable-Looking Gentleman," p. 49). In relation to my arguments about property and the subject in this chapter, Weinauer's account is especially interesting in its conclusion that William Craft, who authors the narrative, can assert his own identity only

by restoring Ellen discursively to the position of passive, feminine wife at the end of the narrative, thereby shoring up his own emergent subjectivity as a free, self-possessed, and possessing (masculine) individual. Craft, like Douglass, "relies on some of the very categories that his own text seeks to complicate and from which he would free both himself and his wife," revealing "the tenacity of (white and male) legal norms in the production of subjectivity in antebellum America" (p. 39).

87. Olney, " 'I was born,' " 159.

88. While the basic facts of Brown's escape from slavery are the same in both versions of his narrative, the following reading is based on the text of the second edition (1852), in which the account of escape is significantly expanded upon.

89. Brown, Narrative (1852), 51. Subsequent citations for Brown in this chapter appear in the text.

90. The name of the company that shipped Brown's box was "Adam's Express."

91. For a fascinating discussion of the implications of the modern postal system for thinking about the subject and that original, confessional expression of the truth of the subject known as literature, see Siegert, Relais. Siegert offers a much more extended and detailed theorization of the relation between the mail and the subject than I can develop here.

92. Siegert, Relais, no page.

93. Fox-Genovese, "My Statue, My Self"; V. Smith, "Loopholes of Retreat"; Yellin, Introduction.

94. V. Smith, "Loopholes of Retreat," 230.

95. See, for example, Andrews, To Tell a Free Story; Baker, Blues; Burnham, "Loopholes"; V. Smith, "Loopholes of Retreat"; Yellin, Introduction.

96. C. Kaplan, "Narrative Contracts," 103.

97. Douglass, Narrative, 150.

98. Jacobs, Incidents, 201. Subsequent citations for Jacobs in this chapter appear in the text.

99. Reply to Henry C. Wright published in The Liberator, January 29, 1847; quoted in Starling, Slave Narrative, 45.

100. C. Kaplan, "Narrative Contracts," 115.

101. See especially Burnham, "Loopholes"; V. Smith, "Loopholes of Retreat."

102. Burnham, "Loopholes," 59.

103. C. Kaplan, "Narrative Contracts," 116.

104. Elam, Feminism and Deconstruction, 59.

105. Butler, "Contingent Foundations," 47.

106. Nancy, Experience, 3.

## Chapter 3

1. Judy, "Nigga Authenticity," 223.

2. Fiscus, Affirmative Action, 8.

3. C. Harris, "Whiteness," 1782.

4. Chesnutt, letter to Walter Hines Page, 1899; quoted in Sundquist, *Wake*, 422.

5. Tourgée, letter to President William McKinley, November 23, 1898, quoted in Caccavari, "Reconstruction," 238.

6. H. Chesnutt, *Chesnutt*, 176.

7. Quoted in Wideman, "Chesnutt," 131.

8. See, for example, Sundquist, *Wake*; Bruce, *Black American Writing*; Gleason, "Voices at the Nadir"; Wideman, "Chesnutt"; Reilly, "Dilemma"; Delmar, "Moral Dilemma."

9. There are some significant exceptions: Joyce Pettis addresses this subplot as "a coherent, functioning structure [that] acts as a correlative to the main plot, illustrating in concise and dramatic terms the tragedies of tradition as well as the bonds of kinship that are deplored and ignored in the South" (Pettis, "Chesnutt's Use of History," p. 40). Eric Sundquist suggests the figures of rape and miscegenation link this genealogical plot as the familial counterpart to the political plot of the riot; Olivia's "hysteria" when confronted with the evidence of her father's miscegenational desire is "the female counterpart to the male hysteria of racial violence that governs the novel's political plot" (Sundquist, *Wake*, p. 407). Thus, for both Pettis and Sundquist, the plot of the sisters is implicitly secondary and derivative, reflecting and refracting the sexual and familial aspects of the racial violence given public form in the conspiracy and riot. I will argue for the inversion of priority between political plot and familial plot; it is in and through the relation between Olivia and Janet, not the riot, that the question of racial justice is most profoundly addressed.

10. See Gillman, *Dark Twins*; Sundquist, "Mark Twain."

11. The Rhodes-Burgess Compromise is the name given by historians to a compromise version of Civil War history worked out independently by James Rhodes and John Burgess at the turn of the century that reconciled Southern and Northern accounts of the causes and outcomes of the war. See James Ford Rhodes, *History of the United States from the Compromise of 1850* (1893–1906); *The Civil War and the Constitution, 1859–1965*, 2 vols. (1901); and John William Burgess, *Reconstruction and the Constitution, 1866–1876* (1902). See Van Deburg, *Slavery and Race*, for a history of histories of the Civil War.

12. Michaels, "Souls," 188.

13. Ibid.

14. See A. Kaplan, "Black and Blue," for a fascinating reading of white representations of the battle as occluding the presence of Cuban soldiers and Spanish enemy and transforming heroic African-American soldiers into helpless and passive bodies in order to write the war as a reaffirmation of the nation in terms of white masculine dominion over black bodies.

15. Sundquist, "Mark Twain," 104.

16. Woodward, *Jim Crow*, 12.

17. Williamson, *Rage*, 25.

18. Gotanda, "Critique," 34.

19. C. Harris, "Whiteness," 1718.

20. Roediger, *Wages of Whiteness*, especially chap. 4, "White Slaves, Wage Slaves and Free White Labor."

21. See especially Mangum, *Legal Status*.

22. Williamson, *Rage*, 176.

23. C. Harris, "Whiteness," 1742.

24. *Plessy v Ferguson*, 163 U.S. 537 (1896), 543.

25. Michaels, "Souls," 189.

26. *Plessy*, 540, 547.

27. The *Brown* decision reversing *Plessy* refers to "the 'separate but equal' doctrine adopted in *Plessy v Ferguson*" (pp. 483, 488, 491). See *Brown v Board of Education*, 347 U.S. 483 (1954).

28. Ibid., 495.

29. Sundquist, *Wake*, 453.

30. On the settled expectations of whiteness, see C. Harris, "Whiteness," 1768.

31. Sundquist, *Wake*, 446.

32. Ibid., 275.

33. As Williamson has pointed out, colored servants were the major exception to separate car laws; "Obviously, the whites made the rules, and they could alter them at will to suit their convenience" (*Rage*, p. 176). All citations for Chesnutt, *Marrow*, in this chapter appear in the text.

34. *Plessy*, 551.

35. H. Chesnutt, *Chesnutt*, 158–59.

36. Prather, *We Have Taken*, 106.

37. This brief account is based on Leon Prather's study of the Wilmington riot, *We Have Taken a City: Wilmington Racial Massacre and Coup of 1898*. Prather's account is preferable to those that ignore the conscious strategies employed in the planning and execution of what amounted to a coup d'état, insofar as such narrow and politically naive accounts attribute the violence only to something like "that unnamed hysteria that swept through the white communities in the black belts of the South in the 1890s" (Williamson, *Rage*, p. 133).

38. Chesnutt, letter to Houghton Mifflin and Company, 1901; quoted in Gleason, "Voices at the Nadir," 40 n. 18.

39. Tourgée, "Brief."

40. *Plessy*, 549. See also Lofgren, *Plessy Case*, for a detailed discussion of the question of reputation in the arguments and briefs on the case.

41. Douglas, "White Reputation," 2.

42. C. Harris, "Whiteness," 1746.

43. Ibid., 1745.

44. *Dred Scott v Sanders*, 19 Howard 393 (1857), 404, 405.

45. Fehrenbacher, *Dred Scott*, 343.

46. Quoted in Sundquist, *Wake*, 242.

47. Sundquist, "Mark Twain," 111.

48. In *White by Definition*, Virginia Domínguez provides a historical overview of Louisiana law regulating interracial marriage and inheritance. Domínguez shows how throughout the nineteenth and twentieth centuries the courts have sought "to regulate consanguinity by regulating marriage . . . [and thus] to restrict the flow of property across category lines," suggesting what amounts to an "unstated conspiracy" to "limit non-white access to property held by whites" (pp. 57, 89).

49. Sedgwick, *Between Men*, 91–92.

50. This is also the condition Fanon diagnoses in *Black Skin, White Masks*.

51. *Oxford English Dictionary*, 1st ed., s.v. "apple."

52. Sundquist, *Wake*, 275.

53. Ibid., 260.

54. Ibid., 433.

55. Lott, *Love and Theft*, 59.

56. Rousseau, "Social Contract," 150.

57. Carby, "Ideologies of Black Folk," 125–26.

58. As Andrews points out, other contemporary African-American novelists did imagine possible alternatives to the bleak circumstances of Southern segregation and racial violence. For example, J. McHenry Jones's *Hearts of Gold* (1896) concludes with an escape to the North to evade racial exploitation, while Sutton Griggs's *Imperium in Imperio* (1899) imagines racial struggle through a secret army of resistance. Interestingly, Chesnutt's earliest plans for the novel ended with Miller leaving Wellington and going north—a form of resolution that the final version explicitly refuses (Andrews, *Literary Career*, p. 188).

59. Ferguson, "Chesnutt's Genuine Blacks," 109, 111.

60. Chesnutt, "Future American," 99.

61. Ferguson, "Chesnutt's Genuine Blacks," 116.

### Chapter 4

1. Quoted in Gibson, *Politics*, 126.

2. Gibson, *Politics*, 126.

3. Chesnutt, *House*, 113.

4. Andrews, Foreword, xii.

5. Myrdal, *American Dilemma*, 683.

6. Bayliss, "Novels," 25.

7. Wirth and Goldhamer, "Hybrid."

8. Conyers, "Negro Passing," 23.

9. Ibid., 317.

10. Wirth and Goldhamer, "Hybrid," 306.

11. Carol Eymann and Joy Laten, "Black or White?" unpublished manuscript, University of the Pacific, Stockton, Calif.; cited in Conyers, "Negro Passing," 34.

12. Conyers, "Negro Passing," 37, emphasis added.

13. Piper, "Passing," 14.

14. Goldberg, *Racist Culture*, 149.

15. Foucault, "Prison Talk," 52.

16. See Domínguez for a fascinating account of the potential conflicts between laws defining racial identity and subjective accounts of racial identity, as revealed in legal challenges to individuals' racial designations adjudicated in the Louisiana courts. Most famous of these, perhaps, is the Phipps case. In 1982, Susie Guillory Phipps lost her suit against the Louisiana Bureau of Vital Records to change her racial classification from black to white. A 1970 state law defined anyone with at least 1/32 "Negro blood" to be black. Under this law, Phipps's one slave ancestor made her legally black, even though she had been living all her 46 years as a white woman. Phipps lost the case when the court upheld the constitutionality of the state law quantifying racial identity. However, following Phipps's suit, the law was repealed. See Trillin, "American Chronicles," for an extended discussion.

17. Wiegman, *Anatomies*, 22.

18. See especially Gossett, *Race*.

19. See especially Stepan, *Idea of Race*, and Gossett, *Race*.

20. See especially Guillaumin, "Race and Nature," and Wiegman, *Anatomies*.

21. Wiegman, *Anatomies*, 30.

22. Saks, "Miscegenation Law," 40.

23. Ibid., 58.

24. Wiegman, *Anatomies*, 22.

25. This dichotomous division is peculiar to the United States. Other multiracial cultures have developed more complex systems of naming and definition that differentiate more strenuously between individuals having different portions of different racial ancestry. For a comparativist and historicizing account of the development of racial definitions in the United States, see Davis, *Who Is Black?*

26. Williamson, *New People*, 98.

27. Jones, *Diva*, 50–51.

28. Johnson, *The Autobiography*, xl.

29. Awkward, *Negotiating Difference*, 181.

30. Gusdorf, "Conditions and Limits," 35.

31. Ibid., 43.

32. A further complication in the relation between prior subject and autobiography as representation of the subject is raised by the imitative relation between the fictional *The Autobiography of an Ex-Coloured Man* and Johnson's own autobiography written six years later, *Along This Way*. The novel was taken for "true" autobiography until the *real* "true" autobiography appeared; but the latter repeats phrases and entire episodes originally appearing in the former. Johnson's life experience may of course have been a source for some of the episodes or characters in *The Autobiography*; this would seem to grant logical priority to Johnson's actual autobiography. But the temporal priority of *The Autobiography* suggests a recipro-

cal relation between the "true-life" autobiography and "fictional" autobiography. I discuss the relation of these two texts and their significance for the theme of passing at greater length in my article "(Passing for) Black Passing for White."

33. There is one exception, so glaring that it seems to prove the rule of namelessness. John Brown is the name given a Southern African-American preacher whom the narrator observes while collecting raw material in the South.

34. Lacan, *The Ego*, 169; quoted in Butler, *Bodies*, 153.

35. While one might connect the namelessness of Johnson's characters with the rejection of slave names, as in Malcolm X, or with a commentary on the effacement of African-American experience, as in Ralph Ellison's *Invisible Man*, it seems to me that neither of these interpretations would fully account for Johnson's decision to leave nameless both black and white characters.

36. Winant, *Racial Conditions*, 16–17.

37. Collier, "Endless Journey." I am drawing on Collier's reading of the novel as a story "built upon a framework of two journeys: a physical and a psychological one" (p. 365). However, my approach to the figure of travel or movement aims to go beyond Collier's interpretation of *The Autobiography* as an exploration of the "dilemma of the light-skinned Negro" (p. 373). All citations for Johnson, *The Autobiography*, in this chapter appear in the text.

38. B. Johnson, "Fanon and Lacan."

39. For an extended analysis of the "drama of the pass" as a triangular structure, see Robinson, "It Takes One to Know One." Robinson discusses the basic triangular structure repeated in passing scenarios, in which "three participants — the passer, the dupe, and a representative of the in-group — enact a complex narrative scenario in which a successful pass is performed in the presence of a literate member of the in-group" (p. 723). The upshot of this triangular encounter, Robinson argues, is to expose the gap between the dupe's mimetic reading of the pass, in which appearing is taken for being, and the in-group's recognition of the performative aspect of the passer's appearance, which does not accurately represent the "being" of the passer. Although Robinson views this drama as politically significant insofar as it enacts the in-group's appropriation of hegemonic interpretive power, I think it is important to note the (acknowledged) limits of this analysis, in particular the conclusion that passing necessarily invokes and reinforces an essentializing view of identity. Both the in-group and the dupe, in Robinson's reading, assume there is a real identity beneath the appearance; the dupe sees the appearance as true, while the in-group sees the appearance as false. However, for the in-group, there is still the possibility of an appearance that would be true, were the passer to remove the disguise. It is for this reason that, within the spectatorial triangle that Robinson specifies, passing depends on and repeats the epistemology of race based on the mutual translation of appearing and being.

40. Letter of Aug. 12, 1912. M. Jackson, "Letters," 189.

41. Such undecidability accounts for the widely divergent interpretations that have been offered of this novel. Joseph Skerrett characterizes readers as being divided into two distinct camps: "One group . . . feels that Johnson's narrator and his opinions are more or less direct reflections of their author. The other group . . . argues that Johnson's treatment of his narrator is essentially ironic" ("Irony," p. 540). If critics have disagreed over the question of whether the novel is sincere or ironic, it is interesting to note that the problem of irony essentially repeats the problem of passing. On one hand, the recognition of irony, like the recognition of passing, depends on suspending one's faith in the truth of appearances. On the other, both passing and irony retain their ambivalence because there can be no absolute guarantee of the truth behind appearances.

42. Stepto, *Behind the Veil*, 95–128.

43. MacKethan, "*Black Boy*," 140.

44. See also Bone, *Negro Novel*; Davis, "Nella Larsen"; Gayle, *Black Novel*; Ramsey, "Black Identity."

45. Barth, *Ethnic Groups*, 14.

46. In light of the current interest in the rhetoric of purity and miscegenation, it is interesting to note that the word *miscegenation* first appeared in an 1864 pamphlet called *Miscegenation: The Theory of the Blending of the Races, Applied to the American White Man and Negro*. This pamphlet called for the merging of the races. The anonymous authors (David Croly and George Wakeman) argued, in opposition to the beliefs of perhaps every white American, that the Anglo-Saxon race was weak and dissipated and needed to be revived by mixing with the Negro race. In 1934, Sidney Kaplan exposed the pamphlet as a hoax, part of the anti-abolitionist Democrats' efforts to undermine President Lincoln's bid for reelection by linking Lincoln's antislavery positions with what amounted to, from the point of view of white Americans, a call for racial pollution. See Kaplan, "Miscegenation"; Young, *Colonial Desire*, 144–48. In addition to the political complexities of the term *miscegenation*, we should also note the subtle shift in its meaning, from the product of race mixing to the act itself.

47. For a more extensive consideration of miscegenation as sexual and racial taboo, see Busia, "Miscegenation"; Gilman, *Difference and Pathology*; Sollors, "Never Was Born."

48. In this light, I would suggest that the sexual ambiguity of Faulkner's passing figures, particularly Joe Christmas in *Light in August* and Charles Bon in *Absalom, Absalom!* is inseparable from these figures' racial ambiguity.

49. Saks, "Miscegenation Law," 63–67.

50. See Peter Brooks in particular for a consideration of "the connection between the desire *of* narrative, the dynamic of its plot, and the desire *for* narrative, the dynamic of its narrating" ("Narrative Desire," p. 321). Following Freud's *Beyond the Pleasure Principle*, Brooks suggests that, like the subject for whom the

total realization of desire is the death of the self, narrative also continually moves forward, always striving to mean something other than what it is able to say: "Narrative is hence condemned to *saying* other than what it *would mean*, spinning out its movement toward a meaning that would be the end of its movement" (p. 322).

51. Skerrett, "Irony," 542.

52. Stephen Ross ("Audience and Irony") has argued that Johnson is making use of the conventions of sentimental fiction to direct an "ironic condemnation" at the white stereotypes and values that render impossible the sentimental conclusion, "love reigns supreme," for a man fragmented by race.

53. Clarke, "Race, Homosocial Desire."

54. Ibid., 93.

55. The divergence in the treatment of lynching in these two examples is also instructive. Although both *Birth of a Nation* and *The Marrow of Tradition* emphasize the role of the charge of sexual violation in fanning the flames of lynch mob sentiments, *Birth* perpetuates the Southern defense of lynching by representing the black man as a "sexual brute," while *Marrow* is a critical intervention in the popular discourse of lynching, one that seeks to expose the political manipulation of public fears in order to perpetuate white control over the black population.

56. Carby, "On the Threshold," 308.

57. Sartre, *Being and Nothingness*, 116.

58. Larsen, *Passing*, 206. All citations for Larsen in this chapter appear in the text.

59. Butler, *Bodies*, 171.

60. Michel Foucault links laughter with the disordering chaos of the breakdown of structures of identity: "This book first arose out of a passage in Borges, out of the laughter that shattered, as I read the passage, all the familiar landmarks of my thought . . . breaking up all the ordered surfaces . . . and continuing long afterwards to disturb and threaten with collapse our age-old distinction between the Same and the Other" (*Order of Things*, p. xv).

61. McDowell, *"Quicksand" and "Passing."* All citations for McDowell in this chapter appear in the text.

62. Butler, *Bodies*, 174. Subsequent citations for Butler in this chapter appear in the text.

63. Throughout her reading of the novel, Butler (*Bodies*) never really questions the view of passing as concealing. This becomes the occasion for what I think is a misrepresentation of the circumstances surrounding the end of Larsen's writing career. Butler notes: "Tragically, the logic of 'passing' and 'exposure' came to afflict and, indeed, to end Nella Larsen's own authorial career, for when she published a short story, 'Sanctuary,' in 1930, she was accused of plagiarism, that is, exposed as 'passing' as the true originator of the work. Her response to this condemning exposure was to recede into an anonymity from which she did not emerge" (*Bodies*,

p. 185). By calling the accusation of plagiarism a "condemning exposure," Butler implies that Larsen really did plagiarize someone else's work. But this conclusion is not wholly consistent with the facts surrounding the case. Readers had complained to the editor of *Forum* that "Sanctuary" bore a too close resemblance to a story published in *Century* eight years earlier. Larsen was given the opportunity to defend herself in print, and the circumstances she related of the origins of the story make it difficult to assert that she had copied the original work of another or that the author of the *Century* story was in fact the true originator: "The story is one that was told to me by an old Negro woman. . . . For some fifteen years, I believed this story absolutely and entertained a kind of admiring pity for the old woman. But lately, in talking it over with Negroes, I find that the tale is so old and so well known that it is almost folklore. . . . Anyone could have written it up at any time" (Nella Larsen, letter to the editor, *Forum* supplement 4, 83 [April 1930]: 41–42). If we accept Larsen's version of the story's inception, then it seems there was no single, original version of this story, no unique author to whom it could be unequivocally assigned (however, see Wall, *Women*, p. 134) for a more skeptical interpretation of Larsen's defense). It is only by insisting that there really was a true author somewhere, against which Larsen's falsity could be absolutely determined, that one could conclude Larsen was a false author passing for true. Having said that, I would nevertheless read this story about Larsen as a passing story, but only after first rejecting the commonsense understanding of passing as deception or concealment of some hidden truth; in Larsen's authorial passing, as in the case of the narrator of *The Autobiography*, passing exposes not the deception of the one who passes but rather the impossibility of any original or true alternative.

64. McDowell, Introduction, xxvii.    65. Butler, *Bodies*, 171.
66. Ibid., 184.    67. Tate, "Larsen's *Passing*," 145.

## Chapter 5

1. My consideration of ancestry and recovery in the following pages is in part the flowering of a seed originally planted by Michelle Wallace's essay, "Who Owns Zora Neale Hurston?"

2. Sadoff, "Black Matrilineage," 7.

3. Walker, "Looking for Zora," 102. All subsequent citations for this essay in this chapter appear in the text.

4. See Lacan, "Signification of the Phallus."

5. The tension between the demand for ancestry and the fictiveness of descent is especially evident in the work of critics who have sought to illuminate the a priori presumption of a literary affiliation between Hurston and Walker. For example, in Henry Louis Gates Jr.'s influential essay "Color Me Zora," the critic confesses that "I have always found it difficult to identify this bond [between *The Color Purple* and

*Their Eyes Were Watching God*] textually, by which I mean that I have not found Hurston's literal presence in Walker's text" (p. 150).

6. Mary Helen Washington has made the strongest claim for Walker's instrumental role in the recovery of Hurston. In the foreword to *Their Eyes Were Watching God*, Washington argues that the publication of "Looking for Zora" directly precipitated the current Hurston renascence.

7. Michael Awkward catalogs the dimensions of Hurston's recovery in the introductory essay to the recent volume of collected Hurston criticism, *New Essays on "Their Eyes Were Watching God,"* especially pp. 4–5.

8. Quoted in Gates, Afterword, 262.

9. Hurston had hoped to begin a new novel in the winter of 1941. Instead, her publisher "urged her to think about an autobiography; when she objected that her career was hardly over, he proposed that it be the first volume of a multivolume work" (Hemenway, *Hurston*, p. 275). Hurston resisted personal disclosure; she once remarked of her autobiography, "I did not want to write it at all, because it is too hard to reveal one's inner self" (Hemenway, *Hurston*, p. 278).

10. Hurston, *Dust Tracks*, 151. All subsequent citations for *Dust Tracks* in this chapter appear in the text.

11. Hemenway, *Hurston*, 289. Hemenway's sources are as follows: Arna Bontemps, "From Eatonville, Florida to Harlem," *New York Herald Tribune*, Nov. 22, 1942; Harold Preece, "Dust Tracks on a Road," *Tomorrow*, Feb. 1943.

12. See especially Headon, "Beginning to See"; Lionnet, "Autoethnography"; Fox-Genovese, "My Statue, My Self."

13. Fox-Genovese, "My Statue, My Self," 196.

14. Taylor, "Politics of Recognition," 77.

15. Hemenway, *Hurston*, 288. All citations for "Seeing the World as It Really Is" in this chapter appear in the text.

16. Balibar, *Race, Nation, Class*, 47.

17. Appiah, "Racisms," 4.

18. For a fuller discussion of specific contemporary political theorists in relation to these poles of opposition, see Connolly, *Politics and Ambiguity*, and Corlett, *Community Without Unity*.

19. See Connolly, *Politics and Ambiguity*. Connolly offers a Foucauldian critique of the "politics of normalization" shared by individualism and communalism that aims to bring the individual into harmony with the community through various forms of discipline.

20. I will follow Fanon throughout this discussion in my use of the term "black man." But if, as Fanon insists, the "black man" does not exist as a human subject, then the black woman suffers the double debilitation of not only being excluded from the realm of the human but of disappearing from the realm of the nameable altogether. For a detailed consideration of the significance of Fanon's studied

ignorance of the circumstance of the black woman, see Fuss, "Interior Colonies," Chow, "Politics of Admittance," Bergner, "Masked Woman."

21. Fuss, "Interior Colonies," 21.

22. Ibid., 23.

23. Fanon, *Black Skin*, 109.

24. Fanon, *Wretched*, 10.

25. Fanon, *Black Skin*, 8.

26. Ibid.

27. Ibid.

28. Fanon, *Wretched*, 148.

29. Ibid., 36.

30. Ibid., 37.

31. Ibid., 36.

32. Ibid.

33. Holloway, *Character*; see especially the technical discussion of Hurston's linguistic structures in chap. 5, "The Word, Thus Adorned, Bodies Forth Itself."

34. Lionnet, "Autoethnography," 401.

35. Ibid., 404.

36. Ibid., 410.

37. Fox-Genovese, "My Statue, My Self," 176.

38. *Abomination* is the biblical term most often used to indicate homosexual activity, as Michael Moon originally suggested to me in reference to this passage.

39. Hurston, "How It Feels," 155.

40. Holloway, *Character*, 16.

41. For a more explicitly self-conscious reflection on the doubled risk of leaving home, see Minnie Bruce Pratt's autobiographical essay, "Identity: Skin, Blood, Heart." As Biddy Martin and Chandra Talpade Mohanty remark, "While Pratt is aware that stable notions of self and identity are based on exclusion and secured by terror, she is also aware of the risk and terror inherent in breaking through the walls of home" ("Feminist Politics," p. 197)—a risk that Pratt nonetheless insists must be taken.

42. Hurston, *Their Eyes*, 15. All subsequent citations for *Their Eyes* in this chapter appear in the text.

43. Hite, "Romance," 448.

44. Derrida, *Given Time*, 11.

45. Ibid., 24.

46. Ibid., 13.

47. This reading of the touch is based on Jean-Luc Nancy's notion of *se toucher toi* as proposed in "Corpus" and *Corpus*, 35–36. See also Derrida, "*Le toucher*," 137.

48. Elam, *Feminism and Deconstruction*, 111.

49. Nancy, "Inoperative Community," 12.

50. Negri, *Savage Anomaly*, 109. On Spinoza as a philosopher of singularity, see also Hardt, *Deleuze*.

51. Wald, "Becoming 'Colored,'" 97.

## Chapter 6

1. Awkward, *Negotiating Difference*, especially chap. 1, "Race, Gender, and the Politics of Reading."

2. Guillory, *Cultural Capital*, 7. By "canon wars," I mean to indicate the debates that occurred primarily in English departments in the 1980s about how the curriculum should respond to demands for greater representativeness, diversity, and inclusion. These debates spilled over into the public sphere, producing lively editorializing on the pages of the *New York Times* and other popular nonacademic newspapers and magazines, and culminated in an enormous conservative backlash in the early 1990s.

3. Davis and Gates, *Slave's Narrative*, xxvi.

4. Deleuze and Guattari, *Thousand Plateaus*, 167–91.

5. Butler, *Bodies*, 9.

6. Ibid.

7. Ibid., 10.

8. See Agamben, *Coming Community*, for a further discussion of politics as the struggle between identity and singularity.

9. Spivak, *Post-Colonial Critic*, 146.

10. See M. Davis, *City of Quartz*, and Zukin, *Cultures of Cities*, for analyses of the political and social implications of the redistribution of public space in Los Angeles and New York, respectively; see Egan, "Many Seek Security," for an account of the recent rise in private communities. On the matter of the U.S.-Mexican border, I cannot resist passing along the following anecdote: In early 1994, "the U.S. Border Patrol announced they are considering constructing two 10-foot tall walls across the U.S.-Mexican border, in the centers of two small Arizona towns, Douglas and Naco; walls made from the sturdy, surplus steel matting the U.S. Air Force rolls down for temporary landing strips" (Simon, "Border Fence"). The construction of this wall was not only to prevent the entry of illegal aliens but specifically to stem an alleged crime wave in Douglas and Naco, which residents claimed was the work of Mexican bandits who would pop through holes in the existing chain-link fence, burglarize and terrorize the town, and pop back through to evade arrest. This steel matting was in fact manufactured for use in the Gulf War; its reuse along the home front of the Mexican border emphasizes the extent to which questions of borders, security, purity, and safety are inextricably linked in contemporary public discourse. The phantasmic images of the "Hitleresque Saddam" and the "Mexican bandit" pose equal threats to the sanctity of the American home and the security of American property.

11. Goldberg, *Racist Culture*, 197.

12. Bhabha, "DissemiNation," 314.

13. Elam, *Feminism and Deconstruction*, 119–20.

# Bibliography

Aaron, Daniel. "The Inky Curse: Miscegenation in the White American Literary Imagination." *Social Science Information* 22 (1983): 169–90.

Agamben, Giorgio. *The Coming Community*. Translated by Michael Hardt. Minneapolis: University of Minnesota Press, 1993.

Altschuler, Glenn C. *Race, Ethnicity, and Class in American Social Thought, 1865–1919*. Arlington Heights, Ill.: Harlan Davidson, 1982.

Anderson, Benedict. *Imagined Communities: Reflections on the Origin and Spread of Nationalism*. New York: Verso, 1983.

Andrews, William L. Foreword to *The House Behind the Cedars*, by Charles W. Chesnutt. Athens: University of Georgia Press, 1988.

———. *The Literary Career of Charles W. Chesnutt*. Baton Rouge: Louisiana State University Press, 1980.

———. "Miscegenation in the Late Nineteenth Century Novel." *Southern Humanities Review* 13 (1979): 13–24.

———. *To Tell a Free Story: The First Century of Afro-American Autobiography, 1760–1865*. Urbana: University of Illinois Press, 1986.

———. "Toward a Poetics of Afro-American Autobiography." In *Afro-American Literary Study in the 1990s*, edited by Houston A. Baker Jr. and Patricia Redmond, 78–90. Chicago: University of Chicago Press, 1989.

"An Ex-Colored Man." *New York Times*, May 27, 1912, 319.

Appiah, Kwame Anthony. *In My Father's House: Africa in the Philosophy of Culture*. New York: Oxford University Press, 1992.

———. "Racisms." In *Anatomy of Racism*, edited by David Theo Goldberg, 3–17. Minneapolis: University of Minnesota Press, 1990.

————. "The Uncompleted Argument: Du Bois and the Illusion of Race." In *"Race," Writing, and Difference*, edited by Henry Louis Gates Jr., 21–37. Chicago: University of Chicago Press, 1986.

Aptheker, Herbert. *American Negro Slave Revolts*. New York: Columbia University Press, 1943.

Awkward, Michael. *Negotiating Difference: Race, Gender, and the Politics of Positionality*. Chicago: University of Chicago Press, 1995.

————. ed. *New Essays on "Their Eyes Were Watching God."* New York: Cambridge University Press, 1990.

Baker, Houston A., Jr. "Autobiographical Acts and the Voice of the Southern Slave." In *The Slave's Narrative*, edited by Charles H. Davis and Henry Louis Gates Jr., 242–61. New York: Oxford University Press, 1985.

————. *Blues, Ideology, and Afro-American Literature: A Vernacular Theory*. Chicago: University of Chicago Press, 1984.

————. Introduction to *Narrative of the Life of Frederick Douglass, an American Slave, Written by Himself*. New York: Penguin Classics, 1986.

————. *The Journey Back: Issues in Black Literature and Criticism*. Chicago: University of Chicago Press, 1980.

Balibar, Etienne. "Citizen Subject." In *Who Comes After the Subject?* edited by Eduardo Cadava and Jean-Luc Nancy, 33–57. New York: Routledge, 1991.

Balibar, Etienne, and Immanuel Wallerstein. *Race, Nation, Class: Ambiguous Identities*. New York: Verso, 1991.

Barth, Fredrik, ed. *Ethnic Groups and Boundaries: The Social Organization of Culture Difference*. Boston: Little, Brown, 1969.

Bayliss, John F. "Novels of Black Americans Passing as Whites." Ph.D. diss., Indiana University, 1976.

Becker, Carl L. *The Declaration of Independence: A Study in the History of Political Ideas*. New York: Harcourt, Brace, 1922.

Benjamin, Walter. "Critique of Violence." In *Reflections: Essays, Aphorisms, Autobiographical Writings*, translated by Edmund Jephcott, 277–300. New York: Schocken, 1986.

Bennington, Geoffrey. "Postal Politics and the Institution of the Nation." In *Nation and Narration*, edited by Homi K. Bhabha, 121–37. New York: Routledge, 1990.

Benstock, Shari. "Authorizing the Autobiographical." In *The Private Self: Theory and Practice of Women's Autobiographical Writings*, edited by Shari Benstock, 10–33. Chapel Hill: University of North Carolina Press, 1988.

Bercovitch, Sacvan. "The Problem of Ideology in American Literary History." *Critical Inquiry* 12, no. 4 (1986): 631–53.

Bergner, Gwen. "Who Is That Masked Woman? or, the Role of Gender in Fanon's *Black Skin, White Masks*." *PMLA* 110 (1995): 75–88.

Berlant, Lauren. "National Brands/National Body: *Imitation of Life*." In *Compara-*

*tive American Identities: Race, Sex, and Nationality in the Modern Text*, edited by Hortense J. Spillers, 110–40. New York: Routledge, 1991.

Bhabha, Homi K. "DissemiNation." In *Nation and Narration*, edited by Homi K. Bhabha, 291–322. New York: Routledge, 1990.

———. "Interrogating Identity: The Postcolonial Prerogative." In *Anatomy of Racism*, edited by David Theo Goldberg, 183–209. Minneapolis: University of Minnesota Press, 1990.

———. *The Location of Culture*. New York: Routledge, 1994.

Bibb, Henry. *Narrative of the Life and Adventures of Henry Bibb, an American Slave, Written by Himself*. New York, 1849. Reprinted in *Puttin' on Ole Massa: The Slave Narratives of Henry Bibb, William Wells Brown, and Solomon Northup*, edited by Gilbert Osofsky. New York: Harper and Row, 1969.

Blassingame, John W. *The Slave Community: Plantation Life in the Antebellum South*. New York: Oxford University Press, 1972.

Boelhower, William. *Through a Glass Darkly: Ethnic Semiosis in American Literature*. New York: Oxford University Press, 1987.

Bone, Robert. *The Negro Novel in America*. New Haven: Yale University Press, 1958.

Bontemps, Arna, ed. *Great Slave Narratives*. Boston: Beacon, 1969.

Boyd, Julian P. *The Declaration of Independence: The Evolution of the Text as Shown in Facsimiles of Various Drafts by its Author, Thomas Jefferson*. Princeton: Princeton University Press, 1945.

Brody, Jennifer DeVere. "Clare Kendry's 'True' Colors: Race and Class Conflict in Nella Larsen's *Passing*." *Callaloo* 15, no. 4 (1992): 1053–65.

Brooks, Peter. "Narrative Desire." *Style* 18, no. 3 (1984): 312–27.

Brown, Henry Box. *The Narrative of Henry Box Brown, Who Escaped from Slavery Enclosed in a Box Three Feet Long, Two Feet Wide, and Two-and-a Half Feet High, Written from a Statement of Facts Made by Himself. With Remarks upon the Remedy for Slavery. By Charles Stearns*. Boston: Brown and Stearns, 1849.

———. *Narrative of the Life of Henry Box Brown, Written by Himself*. 2d ed. Boston: Samuel Webb, 1852.

Brown, Sterling. "Negro Character as Seen by White Authors." *Journal of Negro Education* 11 (1933): 179–203.

———. *The Negro in American Fiction*. New York: Atheneum, 1969.

Brown, William Wells. *Narrative of William W. Brown, an American Slave, Written by Himself*. London: C. Gilpin, 1849.

Bruce, Dickson D., Jr. *Black American Writing from the Nadir: The Evolution of a Literary Tradition, 1877–1915*. Baton Rouge: Louisiana State University Press, 1989.

Burnham, Michelle. "Loopholes of Resistance: Harriet Jacobs' Slave Narrative and the Critique of Agency in Foucault." *Arizona Quarterly* 49, no. 2 (1993): 53–73.

Busia, Abena P. A. "Miscegenation as Metonymy: Sexuality and Power in the Colonial Novel." *Ethnic and Racial Studies* 9 (1986): 360–72.

Butler, Judith. *Bodies that Matter: On the Discursive Limits of "Sex."* New York: Routledge, 1993.

———. "Contingent Foundations." In *Feminist Contentions: A Philosophical Exchange*, by Seyla Benhabib, Judith Butler, Drucilla Cornell, and Nancy Fraser, 35–58. New York: Routledge, 1995.

———. *Gender Trouble: Feminism and the Subversion of Identity.* New York: Routledge, 1990.

———. "Lana's 'Imitation': Melodramatic Repetition and the Gender Performative." *Genders* 9 (Nov. 1990): 1–18.

Caccavari, Peter. "Reconstruction of Race and Culture: Albion Tourgée, Thomas Dixon, and Charles Chesnutt." Ph.D. diss., Rutgers University, 1993.

Carby, Hazel V. "Ideologies of Black Folk: The Historical Novel of Slavery." In *Slavery and the Literary Imagination*, edited by Deborah E. McDowell and Arnold Rampersad, 125–43. Baltimore: Johns Hopkins University Press, 1989.

———. " 'On the Threshold of Woman's Era': Lynching, Empire, and Sexuality in Black Feminist Theory." In *"Race," Writing, and Difference*, edited by Henry Louis Gates Jr., 301–16. Chicago: University of Chicago Press, 1986.

———. "The Quicksands of Representation: Rethinking Black Cultural Politics." In *Reading Black, Reading Feminist: A Critical Anthology*, edited by Henry Louis Gates Jr., 76–90. New York: Meridian, 1990.

Chapman, Abraham, ed. *Steal Away: Stories of the Runaway Slaves.* New York: Praeger, 1971.

Chesnutt, Charles W. "The Future American. An Essay in Three Parts." *Boston Evening Transcript* August 18, 1900, August 25, 1900, September 1, 1900. Reprint, *MELUS* 15, no. 3 (1988): 96–107.

———. *The House Behind the Cedars.* 1900. Reprint, New York: Penguin, 1993.

———. *The Marrow of Tradition.* 1901. Reprint, Ann Arbor: University of Michigan Press, 1969.

Chesnutt, Helen M. *Charles Waddell Chesnutt, Pioneer of the Color Line.* Chapel Hill: University of North Carolina Press, 1952.

Chow, Rey. "The Politics of Admittance." Paper presented at Rutgers University, March 1, 1995.

Clarke, Cheryl. "Race, Homosocial Desire, and 'Mammon' in *The Autobiography of an Ex-Coloured Man.*" In *Professions of Desire: Lesbian and Gay Studies in Literature*, edited by George Haggerty and Bonnie Zimmerman, 84–97. New York: Modern Language Association, 1995.

Collier, Eugenia. "The Endless Journey of an Ex-Coloured Man." *Phylon* 32 (winter 1971): 365–73.

Connolly, William E. *Politics and Ambiguity.* Madison: University of Wisconsin Press, 1987.

Conyers, James Ernest. "Selected Aspects of the Phenomenon of Negro Passing." Ph.D. diss., Washington State University, 1962.

Corlett, William. *Community Without Unity: A Politics of Derridian Extravagance.* Durham, N.C.: Duke University Press, 1989.

Cox, James M. *Recovering Literature's Lost Ground: Essays in American Autobiography.* Baton Rouge: Louisiana State University Press, 1989.

Craft, William. *Running a Thousand Miles for Freedom; or, The Escape of William and Ellen Craft from Slavery.* London: W. Tweedie, 1860.

Croly, David Goodman, and George Wakeman. *Miscegenation: The Theory of the Blending of the Races, Applied to the American White Man and Negro.* New York: H. Dexter, Hamilton, 1864.

Davis, Arthur P. *From the Dark Tower: Afro-American Writers 1900–1960.* Washington, D.C.: Howard University Press, 1974.

Davis, Charles T., and Henry Louis Gates Jr., eds. *The Slave's Narrative.* New York: Oxford University Press, 1985.

Davis, F. James. *Who Is Black? One Nation's Definition.* University Park: Pennsylvania State University Press, 1991.

Davis, Mike. *City of Quartz: Excavating the Future in Los Angeles.* New York: Vintage, 1992.

Davis, Thadious M. "Nella Larsen." *Dictionary of Literary Biography: Afro-American Writers from the Harlem Renaissance to 1940,* Volume 51, edited by Trudier Harris, 182–92. Detroit: Gale Research, 1987.

Dearborn, Mary V. *Pocahontas's Daughters: Gender and Ethnicity in American Culture.* New York: Oxford University Press, 1986.

de Lauretis, Teresa. "The Essence of the Triangle or, Taking the Risk of Essentialism Seriously: Feminist Theory in Italy, the U.S., and Britain." *differences* 1, no. 2 (1989): 3–37.

Deleuze, Gilles, and Félix Guattari. *A Thousand Plateaus: Capitalism and Schizophrenia.* Translated by Brian Massumi. Minneapolis: University of Minnesota Press, 1987.

Delmar, Jay P. "The Moral Dilemma in Chesnutt's *Marrow of Tradition.*" *American Literary Realism* 14, no. 2 (1981): 269–72.

Derrida, Jacques. "Force of Law: The 'Mystical Foundation of Authority.' " Translated by Mary Quaintance. In *Deconstruction and the Possibility of Justice,* edited by Drucilla Cornell, Michel Rosenfeld, and David Gray Carlson, 3–67. New York: Routledge, 1992.

———. *Given Time: I. Counterfeit Money.* Translated by Peggy Kamuf. Chicago: University of Chicago Press, 1992.

———. "*Le toucher*: Touch/to touch him." Translated by Peggy Kamuf. *Paragraph* 16, no. 2 (1993): 122–57.

———. "Violence and Metaphysics: An Essay on the Thought of Emmanuel Levinas." In *Writing and Difference,* translated by Alan Bass, 79–154. Chicago: University of Chicago Press, 1978.

Dixon, Melvin. "Singing Swords: The Literary Legacy of Slavery." In *The Slave's*

*Narrative*, edited by Charles H. Davis and Henry Louis Gates Jr., 298–317. New York: Oxford University Press, 1985.

Domínguez, Virginia R. *White by Definition: Social Classification in Creole Louisiana*. New Brunswick, N.J.: Rutgers University Press, 1986.

Douglas, Allen. " 'The Most Valuable Sort of Property': White Reputation, Defamation Law and Racial Sentiment in the South After the Civil War." Unpublished manuscript, Department of History, Rutgers University, New Brunswick, N.J., 1994.

Douglass, Frederick. *Life and Times of Frederick Douglass, Written by Himself*. 1881. Reprint, Secaucus, N.J.: Citadel, 1983.

————. *Narrative of the Life of Frederick Douglass, an American Slave, Written by Himself*. 1845. Reprint, New York: Penguin Classics, 1986.

Draper, Theodore. *The Rediscovery of Black Nationalism*. New York: Viking, 1970.

Du Bois, W. E. B. *W. E. B. Du Bois Speaks: Speeches and Addresses, 1890–1919*. Edited by Philip S. Foner. New York: Pathfinders, 1970.

————. *The Souls of Black Folk*. 1903. Reprint, New York: Vintage, 1990.

Edsall, Thomas Byrne, and Mary D. Edsall. "Race." *Atlantic*, May 1991, 53–86.

Egan, Timothy. "Many Seek Security in Private Communities." *New York Times*, September 3, 1995, national edition, 1A.

Elam, Diane. *Feminism and Deconstruction: Ms. en Abyme*. New York: Routledge, 1994.

Equiano, Olaudah. *The Interesting Narrative of the Life of Olaudah Equiano, or Gustavus Vassa, the African*. 1789. Reprint, Coral Gables, Fla.: Mnemosyne, 1989.

Fanon, Frantz. *Black Skin, White Masks*. Translated by Charles Lam Markmann. New York: Grove Weidenfeld, 1967.

————. *The Wretched of the Earth*. Translated by Constance Farrington. New York: Grove Weidenfeld, 1963.

Faulkner, William. *Go Down, Moses*. 1942. Reprint, New York: Vintage, 1990.

Fee, Elizabeth. "Nineteenth Century Craniology: The Study of the Female Skull." *Bulletin of the History of Medicine* 53 (1979): 415–33.

Fehrenbacher, Don E. *The Dred Scott Case: Its Significance in American Law and Politics*. New York: Oxford University Press, 1978.

Ferguson, Sally Ann H. "Chesnutt's Genuine Blacks and Future Americans." *MELUS* 15, no. 3 (1988): 109–19.

Fischer, Michael M. J. "Ethnicity and the Post-Modern Arts of Memory." In *Writing Culture: The Poetics and Politics of Ethnography*, edited by James Clifford and George E. Marcus, 194–233. Berkeley: University of California Press, 1986.

Fiscus, Ronald J. *The Constitutional Logic of Affirmative Action*. Durham, N.C.: Duke University Press, 1992.

Fishkin, Shelley Fisher, and Carla L. Peterson, " 'We Hold These Truths to Be Self-Evident': The Rhetoric of Frederick Douglass's Journalism." In *Frederick*

*Douglass: New Literary and Historical Essays*, edited by Eric J. Sundquist, 189–204. New York: Cambridge University Press, 1990.

*Five Slave Narratives: A Compendium.* New York: Arno Press and the New York Times, 1968.

Fleming, Robert E. "Irony as a Key to Johnson's *The Autobiography of an Ex-Coloured Man.*" *American Literature* 43 (March 1971): 83–96.

Foner, Philip S. *Frederick Douglass.* New York: Citadel, 1964.

Foster, Frances Smith. *Witnessing Slavery: The Development of Ante-Bellum Slave Narratives.* Westport, Conn.: Greenwood, 1979.

Foucault, Michel. *Discipline and Punish: The Birth of the Prison.* Translated by Alan Sheridan. New York: Vintage, 1979.

————. "The Discourse on Language." Translated by Rupert Swyer. In *The Archaeology of Knowledge*, translated by Alan Sheridan, 215–38. New York: Pantheon, 1972.

————. *The Order of Things: An Archaeology of the Human Sciences* (a translation of *Les Mots et les Choses*). New York: Vintage, 1973.

————. "Prison Talk." In *Power/Knowledge: Selected Interviews and Other Writings, 1972–1977*, edited by Colin Gordon, 37–54. New York: Pantheon, 1980.

Fox-Genovese, Elizabeth. "My Statue, My Self: Autobiographical Writings of Afro-American Women." In *Reading Black, Reading Feminist: A Critical Anthology*, edited by Henry Louis Gates Jr., 176–203. New York: Meridian, 1990.

Frazier, E. Franklin. *The Negro Family in the United States.* Chicago: University of Chicago Press, 1939.

Fredrickson, George M. *The Black Image in the White Mind: The Debate on Afro-American Character and Destiny, 1817–1914.* New York: Harper and Row, 1971.

Friedman, Susan Stanford. "Women's Autobiographical Selves: Theory and Practice." In *The Private Self: Theory and Practice of Women's Autobiographical Writings*, edited by Shari Benstock, 34–62. Chapel Hill: University of North Carolina Press, 1988.

Fuss, Diana. *Essentially Speaking: Feminism, Nature and Difference.* New York: Routledge, 1989.

————. "Interior Colonies: Frantz Fanon and the Politics of Identification." *diacritics* 24, nos. 2–3 (1994): 20–42.

Garrett, Marvin P. "Early Recollections and Structural Irony in *The Autobiography of an Ex-Coloured Man.*" *Critique: Studies in Modern Fiction* 13 (December 1971): 5–14.

Gates, Henry Louis, Jr. Afterword to *Dust Tracks on a Road*, by Zora Neale Hurston. New York: HarperCollins, 1991.

————. "Binary Oppositions in Chapter One of *Narrative of the Life of Frederick Douglass, an American Slave, Written by Himself.*" In *Critical Essays on Frederick Douglass*, edited by William L. Andrews, 79–93. Boston: G. K. Hall, 1991.

————. "Color Me Zora: Alice Walker's (Re)Writing of the Speakerly Text." In *Intertextuality and Contemporary American Fiction*, edited by Patrick O'Donnell and Robert Con Davis, 144–70. Baltimore: Johns Hopkins University Press, 1989.

————. "From Wheatley to Douglass: The Politics of Displacement." In *Frederick Douglass: New Literary and Historical Essays*, edited by Eric J. Sundquist, 47–65. New York: Cambridge University Press, 1990.

————, ed. *The Classic Slave Narratives*. New York: Mentor, 1987.

————, ed. *"Race," Writing, and Difference*. Chicago: University of Chicago Press, 1986.

Gayle, Addison, Jr. *The Way of the New World: The Black Novel in America*. Garden City, N.Y.: Anchor, 1976.

Gellner, Ernest. *Nations and Nationalism*. New York: Oxford University Press, 1983.

Genovese, Eugene D. *Roll, Jordan, Roll: The World the Slaves Made*. New York: Pantheon, 1974.

Gibson, Donald B. Introduction to *The House Behind the Cedars*, by Charles W. Chesnutt. New York: Penguin, 1993.

————. *The Politics of Literary Expression: A Study of Major Black Writers*. Westport, Conn.: Greenwood, 1981.

Giles, James R., and Thomas P. Lally. "Allegory in Chesnutt's *The Marrow of Tradition*." *Journal of General Education* 35, no. 4 (1984): 259–69.

Gillman, Susan. *Dark Twins: Imposture and Identity in Mark Twain's America*. Chicago: University of Chicago Press, 1989.

Gilman, Sander L. *Difference and Pathology: Stereotypes of Sexuality, Race, and Madness*. Ithaca, N.Y.: Cornell University Press, 1985.

Gilroy, Paul. *The Black Atlantic: Modernity and Double Consciousness*. Cambridge, Mass.: Harvard University Press, 1993.

————. *"There Ain't No Black in the Union Jack": The Cultural Politics of Race and Nation*. Chicago: University of Chicago Press, 1991.

Gleason, William. "Voices at the Nadir: Charles Chesnutt and David Bryant Fulton." *American Literary Realism* 24, no. 3 (1992): 22–41.

Goldberg, David Theo. *Racist Culture: Philosophy and the Politics of Meaning*. Cambridge, Mass.: Blackwell, 1995.

————, ed. *Multiculturalism: A Critical Reader*. Boston: Blackwell, 1994.

Gordon, Avery, and Christopher Newfield. "White Philosophy." *Critical Inquiry* 20, no. 4 (1994): 737–57.

Gossett, Thomas F. *Race: The History of an Idea in America*. Dallas: Southern Methodist University Press, 1963.

Gotanda, Neil. "A Critique of 'Our Constitution Is Colorblind.'" *Stanford Law Review* 44 (1991): 1–68.

Guillaumin, Colette. "The Idea of Race and Its Elevation to Autonomous, Scientific and Legal Status." In *Sociological Theories: Race and Colonialism*, 37–67. Paris: UNESCO, 1980.

———. "Race and Nature: The System of Marks. The Idea of a Natural Group and Social Relationships." Translated by Mary Jo Lakeland. *Feminist Issues* 8, no. 2 (1988): 25–43.

Guillory, John. *Cultural Capital: The Problem of Literary Canon Formation*. Chicago: University of Chicago Press, 1993.

Gusdorf, Georges. "Conditions and Limits of Autobiography." Translated by James Olney. In *Autobiography: Essays Theoretical and Critical*, edited by James Olney, 28–48. Princeton: Princeton University Press, 1980.

Gutman, Herbert. *The Black Family in Slavery and Freedom, 1750–1925*. New York: Pantheon, 1976.

Hall, Stuart. "New Ethnicities." In *Black Film, British Cinema*, ICA Document No. 7. London: Institute of Contemporary Arts, 1988.

———. "Race, Articulation, and Societies Structured in Dominance." In *Sociological Theories: Race and Colonialism*, 305–45. Paris: UNESCO, 1980.

Hardt, Michael. *Deleuze: An Apprenticeship in Philosophy*. Minneapolis: University of Minnesota Press, 1993.

Harris, Cheryl I. "Whiteness as Property." *Harvard Law Review* 106, no. 8 (1993): 1710–91.

Harris, Trudier. *Exorcising Blackness: Historical and Literary Lynching and Burning Rituals*. Bloomington: Indiana University Press, 1984.

Headon, David. " 'Beginning to See Things Really': The Politics of Zora Neale Hurston." In *Zora in Florida*, edited by Steve Glassman and Kathryn Lee Seidel, 28–37. Orlando: University of Central Florida Press, 1991.

Hegel, G. W. F. *Phenomenology of Spirit*. Translated by Arnold V. Miller. New York: Oxford University Press, 1977.

———. *Philosophy of History*. Translated by John Sibree. New York: Dover, 1956.

———. *Hegel's Philosophy of Right*. Translated by Thomas M. Knox. New York: Oxford University Press, 1967.

Hemenway, Robert E. *Zora Neale Hurston: A Literary Biography*. Chicago: University of Illinois Press, 1977.

Henson, Josiah. *"Truth Is Stranger than Fiction": An Autobiography of the Rev. Josiah Henson (Mrs. Harriet Beecher Stowe's "Uncle Tom"), from 1789 to 1879*. Written by Samuel A. Eliot. Boston: 1879.

Hite, Molly, "Romance, Marginality, and Matrilineage: *The Color Purple* and *Their Eyes Were Watching God*." In *Reading Black, Reading Feminist: A Critical Anthology*, edited by Henry Louis Gates Jr., 431–53. New York: Meridian, 1990.

Hobsbawm, Eric, and Terence Ranger, eds. *The Invention of Tradition*. New York: Cambridge University Press, 1983.

Holloway, Karla F. C. *The Character of the Word: The Texts of Zora Neale Hurston*. Westport, Conn.: Greenwood, 1987.

Holmes, Thomas Alan. "Race as Metaphor: 'Passing' in Twentieth Century African American Fiction." Ph.D. diss., University of Alabama, 1990.

Holt, Thomas C. "Marking: Race, Race-Making, and the Writing of History." *American Historical Review* 100, no. 1 (1995): 1–20.

hooks, bell. "Essentialism and Experience." *American Literary History* 3, no. 1 (1991): 172–83.

———. "Postmodern Blackness." In *Yearning: Race, Gender, and Cultural Politics*, 23–31. Boston: South End, 1990.

Horsman, Reginald. *Race and Manifest Destiny: The Origins of American Anglo-Saxonism*. Cambridge, Mass.: Harvard University Press, 1981.

Hurston, Zora Neale. *Dust Tracks on a Road*. New York: HarperCollins, 1991.

———. "How It Feels to Be Colored Me." In *I Love Myself When I Am Laughing: A Zora Neale Hurston Reader*, edited by Alice Walker, 152–55. Old Westbury, N.Y.: Feminist Press, 1979.

———. *Mules and Men*. New York: HarperCollins, 1990.

———. "Seeing the World as It Really Is." In *Dust Tracks on a Road*. New York: HarperCollins, 1991.

———. *Their Eyes Were Watching God*. New York: HarperCollins, 1990.

Jackson, Miles, ed. "Letters to a Friend: Correspondence from James Weldon Johnson to George A. Towns." *Phylon* 29 (1968): 183–98.

Jacobs, Harriet A. *Incidents in the Life of a Slave Girl, Written by Herself*. Edited by Jean Fagan Yellin. Cambridge, Mass.: Harvard University Press, 1987. (Originally published 1861.)

Johnson, Barbara. "Fanon and Lacan." Paper presented at the University of North Carolina, Chapel Hill, March 1991.

Johnson, James Weldon. *Along This Way: The Autobiography of James Weldon Johnson*. New York: Viking, 1933.

———. *The Autobiography of an Ex-Coloured Man*, with an introduction by Carl Van Vechten. New York: Knopf, 1927; reprinted, with an additional introduction by Henry Louis Gates Jr., New York: Vintage, 1989. (Originally published 1912.)

Jones, Lisa. *Bulletproof Diva: Tales of Race, Sex, and Hair*. New York: Doubleday, 1994.

Jordan, Winthrop. *White over Black: American Attitudes Toward the Negro, 1550–1812*. New York: W. W. Norton, 1977.

Judy, Ronald A. T. "On the Question of Nigga Authenticity." *boundary 2* 21, no. 3 (1994): 211–30.

Kaplan, Amy. "Black and Blue on San Juan Hill." In *Cultures of United States Imperialism*, edited by Amy Kaplan and Donald E. Pease, 219–36. Durham, N.C.: Duke University Press, 1993.

Kaplan, Carla. "Narrative Contracts and Emancipatory Readers: *Incidents in the Life of a Slave Girl.*" *Yale Journal of Criticism* 6, no. 1 (1993): 93–119.

Kaplan, Sidney. "The Miscegenation Issue in the Election of 1864." *Journal of Negro History* 34 (1934): 274–343.

Kawash, Samira. "*The Autobiography of an Ex-Coloured Man*: (Passing for) Black Passing for White." In *"Passing" and the Fictions of Identity*, edited by Elaine K. Ginsburg. Durham, N.C.: Duke University Press, 1996.

Lacan, Jacques. *The Ego in Freud's Theory and in the Technique of Psychoanalysis, 1954–1955.* Translated by Sylvana Tomaselli and John Forrester. Vol. 2 of *The Seminar of Jacques Lacan*, edited by Jacques-Alain Miller. New York: Cambridge University Press, 1988.

———. "The Mirror Stage as Formative of the Function of the I." In *Ecrits, a Selection*, translated by Alan Sheridan, 1–7. New York: W. W. Norton, 1977.

———. "The Signification of the Phallus." In *Ecrits, a Selection*, translated by Alan Sheridan, 281–90. New York: W. W. Norton, 1977.

Larsen, Nella. *"Quicksand" and "Passing."* 1928, 1929. Reprint, with an introduction by Deborah E. McDowell. New Brunswick, N.J.: Rutgers University Press, 1986.

Levy, Eugene. *James Weldon Johnson: Black Leader, Black Voice.* Chicago: University of Chicago Press, 1973.

Lionnet, Françoise. *Autobiographical Voices: Race, Gender, Self-Portraiture.* Ithaca, N.Y.: Cornell University Press, 1989.

———. "Autoethnography: The An-Archic Style of *Dust Tracks on a Road.*" In *Reading Black, Reading Feminist: A Critical Anthology*, edited by Henry Louis Gates Jr., 382–414. New York: Meridian, 1990.

Lloyd, David. "Race Under Representation." *Oxford Literary Review* 13, no. 1–2 (1991): 62–94.

Locke, Alain, ed. *The New Negro: An Interpretation.* 1925. Reprint, New York: Arno, 1968.

Locke, John. *Two Treatises of Government.* 1698. Reprint, edited by Peter Laslett, New York: Mentor, 1963.

Lofgren, Charles A. *The Plessy Case: A Legal-Historical Interpretation.* New York: Oxford University Press, 1987.

Lott, Eric. *Love and Theft: Blackface Minstrelsy and the American Working Class.* New York: Oxford University Press, 1993.

McDowell, Deborah E. "In the First Place: Making Frederick Douglass and the Afro-American Narrative Tradition." In *Critical Essays on Frederick Douglass*, edited by William L. Andrews, 192–214. Boston: G. K. Hall, 1991.

———. Introduction to *"Quicksand" and "Passing,"* by Nella Larsen. New Brunswick, N.J.: Rutgers University Press, 1986.

McKay, Nellie. "'Crayon Enlargements of Life': Zora Neale Hurston's *Their Eyes*

*Were Watching God* as Autobiography." In *New Essays on "Their Eyes Were Watching God*," edited by Michael Awkward, 51–70. New York: Cambridge University Press, 1990.

MacKethan, Lucinda H. "*Black Boy* and *Ex-Coloured Man*: Version and Inversion of the Slave Narrator's Quest for Voice." *CLA Journal* 32 (December 1988): 123–47.

Macpherson, Crawford B. *The Political Theory of Possessive Individualism: Hobbes to Locke*. New York: Oxford University Press, 1962.

Mangum, Charles S., Jr. *The Legal Status of the Negro*. Chapel Hill: University of North Carolina Press, 1940.

Martin, Biddy, and Chandra Talpade Mohanty. "Feminist Politics: What's Home Got to Do with It?" In *Feminist Studies, Critical Studies*, edited by Teresa de Lauretis, 191–212. Madison: University of Wisconsin Press, 1986.

Martin, Waldo E., Jr. *The Mind of Frederick Douglass*. Chapel Hill: University of North Carolina Press, 1984.

Massumi, Brian. *A User's Guide to Capitalism and Schizophrenia: Deviations from Deleuze and Guattari*. Cambridge, Mass.: MIT Press, 1992.

Mauss, Marcel. *The Gift: The Form and Reason for Exchange in Archaic Societies*. Translated by W. D. Halls. New York: Routledge, 1990.

Michaels, Walter Benn. "The Souls of White Folk." In *Literature and the Body: Essays on Populations and Persons*, edited by Elaine Scarry, 185–209. Baltimore: Johns Hopkins University Press, 1988.

"MLA Survey Casts Light on Canon Debate." *MLA Newsletter* (winter 1991): 12–14.

Moses, Wilson Jeremiah. *The Golden Age of Black Nationalism, 1850–1925*. Hamden, Conn.: Archon, 1978.

Myrdal, Gunnar. *An American Dilemma: The Negro Problem and Modern Democracy*. With the assistance of Richard Sterner and Arnold Rose. 1944. Twentieth-anniversary ed., New York: Harper and Row, 1962.

Nancy, Jean-Luc. "Corpus." Translated by Claudette Sartilot. In *The Birth to Presence*, 189–207. Stanford, Calif.: Stanford University Press, 1993.

————. *Corpus*. Paris: Editions A. M. Métailié, 1992.

————. *The Experience of Freedom*. Translated by Bridget McDonald. Stanford, Calif.: Stanford University Press, 1993.

————. "The Inoperative Community." In *The Inoperative Community*, edited by Peter Connor, translated by Peter Connor, Lisa Garbus, Michael Holland, and Simona Sawhney, 1–42. Minneapolis: University of Minnesota Press, 1991.

Negri, Antonio. *The Savage Anomaly: The Power of Spinoza's Metaphysics and Politics*. Translated by Michael Hardt. Minneapolis: University of Minnesota Press, 1991.

Nichols, Charles H. *Black Men in Chains: Narratives by Escaped Slaves*. New York: Lawrence Hill, 1972.

————. *Many Thousand Gone: The Ex-Slaves' Account of Their Bondage and Freedom*. Bloomington: Indiana University Press, 1963.

————. "The Slave Narrators and the Picaresque Mode: Archetypes for Modern Black Personae." In *The Slave's Narrative*, edited by Charles H. Davis and Henry Louis Gates Jr., 283–97. New York: Oxford University Press, 1985.

Niemtzow, Annette. "The Problematic of Self in Autobiography: The Example of the Slave Narrative." In *The Art of the Slave Narrative: Original Essays in Criticism and Theory*, edited by John Sekora and Darwin T. Turner. Macomb: Western Illinois University Press, 1982.

Northup, Solomon. *Twelve Years a Slave; Narrative of Solomon Northup, a Citizen of New York, Kidnapped in Washington City in 1841, and Rescued in 1853, from a Cotton Plantation near the Red River, in Louisiana*. Auburn, Buffalo, and London: Derby and Miller, 1853.

Olney, James. "Autobiography and the Cultural Moment: A Thematic, Historical, and Bibliographical Introduction." In *Autobiography: Essays Theoretical and Critical*, edited by James Olney, 3–27. Princeton: Princeton University Press, 1980.

————. "The Autobiography of America." *American Literary History* 3, no. 2 (1991): 376–95.

————. "The Founding Fathers—Frederick Douglass and Booker T. Washington." In *Slavery and the Literary Imagination*, edited by Deborah E. McDowell and Arnold Rampersad, 1–24. Baltimore: Johns Hopkins University Press, 1989.

————. " 'I was born': Slave Narratives, Their Status as Autobiography and as Literature." In *The Slave's Narrative*, edited by Charles H. Davis and Henry Louis Gates Jr., 148–74. New York: Oxford University Press, 1985.

————. *Metaphors of Self: The Meaning of Autobiography*. Princeton: Princeton University Press, 1964.

Omi, Michael, and Howard Winant. *Racial Formation in the United States: From the 1960s to the 1980s*. New York: Routledge and Kegan Paul, 1986.

Orfield, Gary. *Must We Bus? Segregated Schools and National Policy*. Washington, D.C.: Brookings Institution, 1978.

Parker, Andrew, Mary Russo, Doris Sommer, and Patricia Yaeger, eds. *Nationalisms and Sexualities*. New York: Routledge, 1992.

Pease, Jane H., and William H. Pease, eds. *Four Fugitive Slave Narratives*. Reading, Mass.: Addison-Wesley, 1969.

Pettis, Joyce. "The Literary Imagination and the Historic Event: Chesnutt's Use of History in *The Marrow of Tradition*." *South Atlantic Review* 55, no. 4 (1990): 37–48.

Piper, Adrian. "Passing for White, Passing for Black." *Transition* 58 (1993): 4–32.

Prather, H. Leon, Sr. *We Have Taken a City: Wilmington Racial Massacre and Coup of 1898*. Madison, N.J.: Fairleigh Dickinson University Press, 1984.

Pratt, Minnie Bruce. "Identity: Skin, Blood, Heart." In *Yours in Struggle: Three Feminist Perspectives on Anti-Semitism and Racism*, by Elly Bulkin, Minnie Bruce Pratt, and Barbara Smith, 9–64. Brooklyn, N.Y.: Long Haul Press, 1984.

"Race and Racism: A Symposium." *Social Text* 42 (spring 1995): 1–52.

Ramsey, Priscilla. "A Study of Black Identity in 'Passing' Novels of the Nineteenth and Early Twentieth Centuries." *Studies in Black Literature* 7, no. 1 (winter 1976): 1–7.

Ransom, Roger L. *Conflict and Compromise: The Political Economy of Slavery, Emancipation, and the American Civil War*. New York: Cambridge University Press, 1990.

Reilly, John M. "The Dilemma in Chesnutt's *The Marrow of Tradition*." *Phylon* 32 (March 1971): 31–38.

Ring, Betty J. " 'Painting by Numbers': Figuring Frederick Douglass." In *The Discourse of Slavery: Aphra Behn to Toni Morrison*, edited by Carl Plasa and Betty J. Ring, 118–43. New York: Routledge, 1994.

Robinson, Amy. "It Takes One to Know One: Passing and Communities of Common Interest." *Critical Inquiry* 20, no. 4 (1994): 715–36.

Roediger, David R. *The Wages of Whiteness: Race and the Making of the American Working Class*. New York: Verso, 1991.

Rogers, James Harrison. "Charles Waddell Chesnutt: The Artist as Polemicist." Ph.D. diss., University of Iowa, 1978.

Rosello, Mireille. Introduction to "Practices of Hybridity," special issue. *Paragraph* 18, no. 1 (1995): 1–12.

Ross, Stephen M. "Audience and Irony in Johnson's *The Autobiography of an Ex-Coloured Man*." *CLA Journal* 18 (December 1974): 198–210.

Rousseau, Jean-Jacques. "Discourse on the Origin of Inequality." In *The Basic Political Writings*, translated by Donald A. Cress, 25–82. Indianapolis: Hackett, 1987.

———. "On the Social Contract." In *The Basic Political Writings*, translated by Donald A. Cress, 141–227. Indianapolis: Hackett, 1987.

Ryan, Michael. "Self-Evidence." *diacritics* 10 (June 1980): 2–16.

Sadoff, Dianne F. "Black Matrilineage: The Case of Alice Walker and Zora Neale Hurston." *Signs* 11, no. 1 (1985): 4–26.

Saks, Eva. "Representing Miscegenation Law." *Raritan* 8, no. 2 (1988): 39–69.

Sánchez-Eppler, Karen. "Bodily Bonds: The Intersecting Rhetorics of Feminism and Abolition." *Representations* 24 (fall 1988): 28–59.

Sartre, Jean-Paul. *Being and Nothingness*. Translated by Hazel E. Barnes. New York: Washington Square, 1966.

Sedgwick, Eve Kosofsky. *Between Men: English Literature and Male Homosocial Desire*. New York: Columbia University Press, 1985.

Shade, William G. "Antislavery." In *Dictionary of American History*, vol. 1, 134–39. Rev. ed., New York: Charles Scribner's, 1976.

Shklar, Judith. *American Citizenship: The Quest for Inclusion*. Cambridge, Mass.: Harvard University Press, 1991.

Siegert, Bernhard. *Relais: Literature as an Epoch of the Postal Service*. Translated by Kevin Repp. Stanford, Calif.: Stanford University Press, forthcoming.

Simon, Scott. "Proposed Border Fence Meets with Opposition and Support." National Public Radio, *Weekend Edition*, February 5, 1994. NEXIS [database online]. 1057–17.

Singh, Amritjit. *The Novels of the Harlem Renaissance: Twelve Black Writers 1923–1933*. University Park: Pennsylvania State University Press, 1976.

*Six Women's Slave Narratives*. Schomburg Library of Nineteenth-Century Black Women Writers. New York: Oxford University Press, 1988.

Skerrett, Joseph T., Jr. "Irony and Symbolic Action in James Weldon Johnson's *The Autobiography of an Ex-Coloured Man*." *American Quarterly* 32 (winter 1980): 540–58.

Smith, Barbara Herrnstein. *Contingencies of Value: Alternative Perspectives for Critical Theory*. Cambridge, Mass.: Harvard University Press, 1988.

Smith, Sidonie. *Where I'm Bound: Patterns of Slavery and Freedom in Black American Autobiography*. Westport, Conn.: Greenwood, 1978.

Smith, Valerie. "'Loopholes of Retreat': Architecture and Ideology in Harriet Jacobs's *Incidents in the Life of a Slave Girl*." In *Reading Black, Reading Feminist: A Critical Anthology*, edited by Henry Louis Gates Jr., 212–26. New York: Meridian, 1990.

———. *Self-Discovery and Authority in Afro-American Narrative*. Cambridge, Mass.: Harvard University Press, 1987.

Soja, Edward W. *Postmodern Geographies: The Reassertion of Space in Critical Social Theory*. New York: Verso, 1989.

Sollors, Werner. *Beyond Ethnicity: Consent and Descent in American Culture*. New York: Oxford University Press, 1986.

———. "Never Was Born: The Mulatto, an American Tragedy?" *Massachusetts Review* 27 (1986): 293–316.

———, ed. *The Invention of Ethnicity*. New York: Oxford University Press, 1989.

Spillers, Hortense J. "Mama's Baby, Papa's Maybe: An American Grammar Book." *diacritics* 17, no. 2 (1987): 65–81.

Spivak, Gayatri Chakravorty. *The Post-Colonial Critic: Interviews, Strategies, Dialogues*, edited by Sarah Harasym. New York: Routledge, 1990.

———. "Subaltern Studies: Deconstructing Historiography." In *In Other Worlds: Essays in Cultural Politics*, 197–221. New York: Routledge, 1988.

Stampp, Kenneth M. *The Peculiar Institution: Slavery in the Antebellum South*. New York: Knopf, 1956.

Starling, Marion Wilson. *The Slave Narrative: Its Place in American History*. 2d ed., Washington, D.C.: Howard University Press, 1988.

Stepan, Nancy. "Biology and Degeneration: Races and Proper Places." In *Degeneration: The Dark Side of Progress*, edited by J. Edward Chamberlin and Sander L. Gilman, 97–120. New York: Columbia University Press, 1985.

————. *The Idea of Race in Science: Great Britain 1800–1960*. Hamden, Conn.: Archon, 1982.

Stepto, Robert B. *From Behind the Veil: A Study of Afro-American Narrative*. Urbana: University of Illinois Press, 1979.

Stone, Albert E. "Identity and Art in Frederick Douglass's *Narrative*." In *Critical Essays on Frederick Douglass*, edited by William L. Andrews, 62–78. Boston: G. K. Hall, 1991.

Storing, Herbert J. "Slavery and the Moral Foundations of the American Republic." In *Slavery and Its Consequences: The Constitution, Equality, and Race*, edited by Robert A. Goldwin and Art Kaufman, 45–63. Washington, D.C.: American Enterprise Institute for Public Policy Research, 1988.

Sundquist, Eric J. "Mark Twain and Homer Plessy." *Representations* 24 (fall 1988): 102–28.

————. *To Wake the Nations: Race in the Making of American Literature*. Cambridge, Mass.: Harvard University Press, 1993.

————, ed. *Frederick Douglass: New Literary and Historical Essays*. New York: Cambridge University Press, 1990.

Tate, Claudia. "Nella Larsen's *Passing*: A Problem of Interpretation." *Black American Literature Forum* 14, no. 4 (1980): 142–46.

Taylor, Charles. "The Politics of Recognition." In *Multiculturalism: A Critical Reader*, edited by David Theo Goldberg, 75–106. Boston: Blackwell, 1994. (Originally published separately as *Multiculturalism and "The Politics of Recognition."* Princeton: Princeton University Press, 1992.)

Thomas, Clarence. Dissenting opinion. *Missouri v Jenkins*, 115 Sup. Ct. 2038, 132 L. Ed. 2d 63 (1995). Available from the Supreme Court site of Legal Information Institute, Cornell Law School, URL http://www.law.cornell.edu/supct/; INTERNET.

Thornton, Hortense. "Sexism as Quagmire: Nella Larsen's *Quicksand*." *CLA Journal* 16 (March 1973): 285–91.

Tourgée, Albion. "Brief for Plaintiff in Error, Plessy v Ferguson." *File Copies of Briefs 1895* VIII, no. 210. U.S. Supreme Court Library, Washington D.C.

Trillin, Calvin. "American Chronicles: Black or White." *New Yorker*, April 14, 1986, 62–78.

Van Deburg, William L. *Slavery and Race in American Popular Culture*. Madison: University of Wisconsin Press, 1984.

Wald, Priscilla. "Becoming 'Colored': The Self-Authorized Language of Difference in Zora Neale Hurston." *American Literary History* 2, no. 1 (1990): 79–100.

————. "Terms of Assimilation: Legislating Subjectivity in the Emerging Nation." *boundary* 2 19, no. 3 (1992): 77–104.

Walker, Alice. Introduction to *Zora Neale Hurston: A Literary Biography*, by Robert E. Hemenway. Chicago: University of Illinois Press, 1977.

————. "Looking for Zora." In *In Search of Our Mother's Gardens*, 93–118. New York: Harcourt Brace Jovanovich, 1983.

Wall, Cheryl A. "Mules and Men and Women: Zora Neale Hurston's Strategies of Narration and Visions of Female Empowerment." *Black American Literature Forum* 23, no. 4 (1989): 661–80.

————. "Passing for What? Aspects of Identity in Nella Larsen's Novels." *Black American Literature Forum* 20, nos. 1, 2 (1986): 97–111.

————. *Women of the Harlem Renaissance*. Bloomington: Indiana University Press, 1995.

Wallace, Michelle. "Who Owns Zora Neale Hurston? Critics Carve Up the Legend." In *Invisibility Blues: From Pop to Theory*, 172–86. New York: Verso, 1990.

Washington, Mary Helen. Foreword to *Their Eyes Were Watching God*, by Zora Neale Hurston. New York: HarperCollins, 1990.

Weinauer, Ellen M. "'A Most Respectable-Looking Gentleman': Passing, Possession, and Transgression in *Running a Thousand Miles for Freedom*." In *"Passing" and the Fictions of Identity*, edited by Elaine K. Ginsburg. Durham, N.C.: Duke University Press, 1996.

Wells, Ida B. *On Lynchings: Southern Horrors, A Red Record, Mob Rule in New Orleans*. New York: Arno, 1969.

Wesling, Donald. "Writing as Power in the Slave Narrative of the Early Republic." *Michigan Quarterly Review* 26, no. 3 (1987): 459–72.

Wideman, John. "Charles Chesnutt: *The Marrow of Tradition*." *American Scholar* 42 (1972): 124–34.

Wiecek, William M. *The Sources of Antislavery Constitutionalism in America, 1760–1848*. Ithaca, N.Y.: Cornell University Press, 1977.

Wiegman, Robyn. *American Anatomies: Theorizing Race and Gender*. Durham, N.C.: Duke University Press, 1995.

Williamson, Joel. *New People: Miscegenation and Mulattoes in the United States*. New York: Free Press, 1980.

————. *A Rage for Order: Black/White Relations in the American South Since Emancipation*. New York: Oxford University Press, 1986.

Winant, Howard. *Racial Conditions: Politics, Theory, Comparisons*. Minneapolis: University of Minnesota Press, 1994.

Wirth, Louis, and Herbert Goldhamer. "The Hybrid and the Problem of Miscegenation." In *Characteristics of the American Negro*, edited by Otto Klineberg. New York: Harper and Brothers, 1944.

Woodward, C. Vann. *The Strange Career of Jim Crow*. 2d rev. ed. New York: Oxford University Press, 1966.

Yellin, Jean Fagan. Introduction to *Incidents in the Life of a Slave Girl, Written by Herself*, by Harriet A. Jacobs. Cambridge, Mass.: Harvard University Press, 1987.

————. "Text and Contexts of Harriet Jacobs' *Incidents in the Life of a Slave Girl: Written by Herself.*" In *The Slave's Narrative*, edited by Charles H. Davis and Henry Louis Gates Jr., 262–82. New York: Oxford University Press, 1985.

Youman, Mary Mabel. "Nella Larsen's *Passing*: A Study in Irony." *CLA Journal* 18, no. 2 (1974): 235–41.

Young, Robert J. C. *Colonial Desire: Hybridity in Theory, Culture and Race.* New York: Routledge, 1995.

————. *White Mythologies: Writing History and the West.* New York: Routledge, 1990.

Ziolkowski, Thad. "Antithesis: The Dialectic of Violence and Literacy in Frederick Douglass's *Narrative* of 1845." In *Critical Essays on Frederick Douglass*, edited by William L. Andrews, 148–65. Boston: G. K. Hall, 1991.

Zukin, Sharon. *The Cultures of Cities.* Cambridge, Mass.: Blackwell, 1995.

# Index

In this index "f" after a number indicates a separate reference on the next page, and "ff" indicates separate references on the next two pages. A continuous discussion over two or more pages is indicated by a span of page numbers. *Passim* is used for a cluster of references in close but not consecutive sequence.

Library of Congress Cataloging-in-Publication Data

Kawash, Samira.
Dislocating the color line : identity, hybridity, and singularity in African-American narrative /
Samira Kawash.
p.   cm. — (Mestizo spaces = Espaces métissés)
Includes bibliographical references (p.    ) and index.
ISBN 0-8047-2774-0 (cloth : alk. paper). — ISBN 0-8047-2775-9 (pbk. : alk. paper)
1. American literature—Afro-American authors—History and criticism.    2. Chesnutt, Charles
Waddell, 1858–1932—Criticism and interpretation.    3. Hurston, Zora Neale—Criticism and
interpretation.    4. Racially mixed people in literature.    5. Afro-Americans in literature.
6. Group identity in literature.    7. Individuality in literature.    8. Afro-Americans—Color.
9. Slaves in literature.    10. Race in literature.    I. Title.    II. Series: Mestizo spaces.
PS153.N5K38   1997
810.9'896073—dc20                                                                      96-25759
                                                                                            CIP

⊗ This book is printed on acid-free, recycled paper.

Original printing 1997
Last figure below indicates year of this printing
06   05   04   03   02   01   00   99   98   97